Democratic Socialism

Democratic Socialism

A Global Survey

Donald F. Busky

PRAEGER Westport, Connecticut
London

Library of Congress Cataloging-in-Publication Data

Busky, Donald F., 1951–
  Democratic socialism : a global survey / Donald F. Busky.
    p. cm.
  Includes bibliographical references and index.
  ISBN 0-275-96886-3 (alk. paper)
  1. Socialism. 2. Democracy. I. Title.
HX73.B875   2000
335.5—dc21   99-059849

British Library Cataloguing in Publication Data is available.

Copyright © 2000 by Donald F. Busky

All rights reserved. No portion of this book may be reproduced, by any process or technique, without the express written consent of the publisher.

Library of Congress Catalog Card Number: 99-059849
ISBN: 0-275-96886-3

First published in 2000

Praeger Publishers, 88 Post Road West, Westport, CT 06881
An imprint of Greenwood Publishing Group, Inc.
www.praeger.com

Printed in the United States of America

The paper used in this book complies with the
Permanent Paper Standard issued by the National
Information Standards Organization (Z39.48-1984).

10 9 8 7 6 5 4 3 2 1

Dedicated to all those who struggle for democracy and socialism.

Contents

	Preface	ix
	Introduction	xi
1	Defining Democratic Socialism	1
2	Democratic Socialism in Continental Europe	17
3	Democratic Socialism in Great Britain and Ireland	75
4	Democratic Socialism in North America	143
5	Democratic Socialism in Central America, the Caribbean, and South America	179
6	Democratic Socialism in Asia, Australia, Africa, and the Middle East	201
	Bibliography	215
	Index	223

Preface

This is the thirtieth anniversary of my involvement in radical politics. In 1969, I participated in my first demonstration in Washington, D.C. as a senior from Philadelphia's Central High School against the Vietnam War. It was not long afterward that I arrived at Temple University and joined the Students for a Democratic Society and continued my fight against racism and war. This is the twenty-first anniversary of my joining the Socialist Party, USA, and, on August 28, 1978, of my election as local chairperson of the Socialist Party of Greater Philadelphia. Additionally, this is the eleventh anniversary of the founding of the Socialist Party of Pennsylvania and my election as state chairperson. Finally, this is the eleventh anniversary of my doctorate in political science from Temple University. All of these events led to my writing of this book.

I would like to sincerely thank my beloved father, Robert Busky, an avid reader, who taught me the basics of politics; my professors Aryeh Botwinick, Robert J. Osborn, and Conrad Weiler, Jr., of the Department of Political Science of Temple University; my college friend Dr. Paul Halpern, a physicist, for many helpful discussions over the years; my many comrades in the Socialist Party, USA, among them Robert W. Tucker and former Socialist mayor of Milwaukee Frank P. Zeidler for the rare and valuable books they have given me that went into the research for this work; and Merle Sue Marcus, who I think was happier than anyone for me when she heard the news about this book being published. Last but not least, I would like to thank Dr. James T. Sabin, Director of Academic Research and Development for the Greenwood Publishing Group, Inc., and copy editor Judy Cardanha for their generous and kind help in publishing this work.

Perseverantia Vincit is the motto of my three-time alma mater Temple University, where I received my bachelor's, master's, and doctoral degrees in political science. It is Latin for "Perseverance conquers." I have discovered for myself the truth in these words, after trying for eleven years to become a published author and enduring many disappointments along the way. Perseverance conquers, indeed.

Donald F. Busky
Philadelphia, Pennsylvania
August 1999

Introduction

There is an alternative to the inequalities of capitalism and communism. There is an alternative to a class-divided society, to rich and poor, to owners and slaves of varying degrees, and to the desperation of unemployment, hunger, and homelessness. There is an alternative to corporate greed and exploitation and to the alienation of workers from their labor and the products of their work. There is an alternative to the lack of democracy; to conservatism, authoritarianism, fascism, the injustice of dictatorship and oligarchy, the repression of freedoms of all kinds; and to totalitarianism of either the right or the left. There is an alternative to racism, sexism, and all other forms of bigotry, discrimination, and oppression of minorities. There is an alternative to massive spending on arms, conventional and nuclear war, and imperialist domination and exploitation of other peoples and lands. Finally, there is an alternative to a pollution-poisoned world and ecological destruction. That alternative is *democratic socialism.*

Democratic socialism is the movement of people to end their own exploitation and the destruction of the environment. It takes power out of the hands of elites who run political and economic systems solely for their own benefit at the direct expense to everyone and everything else. Democratic socialism did not emerge full-blown; rather it continues to develop as human society matures, much in the way an individual matures as he or she grows up. As social development occurs, new insights are achieved: We will never be free until we are all equally free. We shall have no true democracy until all spheres of society are democratically constituted. We shall never be a wealthy society until we have abolished poverty and discrimination for everyone. We shall never know peace until we end the arms race and imperialist conquest and intervention in the affairs of others. We shall not live long unless we stop the death and destruction of the natural world. We have always had the power to end injustice; and although we have made reforms, we have so far lacked the social maturity to do so completely. For example, we have created public education and public libraries; and with the United States being the sole exception in the developed world, we have created national health plans that cover everyone. These coexist with private schools, private bookstores, and private health insurance. However, we have largely not extended, with few exceptions, that idea to the creation of government jobs with decent wages and benefits for all those who want and need to work, but whom the private, capitalist system cannot or will not employ. We have established Social Security and welfare systems, but not yet a negative income tax system that would guarantee that everyone would be above the poverty level. As society has developed, the movement for democratic socialism has gathered speed and force. More and more people in every nation have come to the realization that liberation is worth the struggle, that no price is too great to pay to be democratic, free, and equal. Time and time again, people have risen up against their oppressors, both domestic and foreign. The question in Isaiah 3:15, "What mean ye that ye crush My people, and grind the face of the poor?" is not just one of a single age or society, but an eternal one for all nations. From the democratic and the labor movements of Europe and North America to the fight against dictatorship and colonialism in Central America, South America, Africa, Asia, and the Middle East, people all over the world have fought for their rights. At times their societies have slid back into tyranny. Millions have died in wars against fascism and imperialism. But always the struggle continues. This work is the story of that struggle, of the democratic socialists and the political parties and the governments they have formed worldwide.

1

Defining Democratic Socialism

THE DIFFICULTIES IN DEFINING *SOCIALISM*

Many have tried to define *socialism*, but unfortunately, few have agreed on its meaning. Angelo S. Rappoport, for example, in his *Dictionary of Socialism*, listed some thirty-nine definitions of socialism as samples of the multitude to be found in the literature; and, yet, he still stated that he did not know what socialism was.[1] Albert Fried and Ronald Sanders found that histories of socialism have traditionally been saddled with the nearly impossible task of defining socialism.[2] In part, this has to do with the fact that there are so many forms of socialism, the adherents of each opposing each other, and in some cases violently so.

The difficulties in defining socialism also have to do with its everchanging and everevolving nature. Leszek Kolakowski noted that if we tried to find a general definition of socialism we would discover that any such definition would be lacking in precision and depth.[3] Indeed, socialism has not always meant the same thing to all people.

G. D. H. Cole remarked that while the impossibility of defining socialism had been often noted, the same could be said for other ideas, such as democracy and liberty. At best, stated Cole, we could try to find some common element to the many different schools of socialism and note the various additions to them.[4]

R. N. Berki described all the attempts to define socialism as leading to results that were reductionist, of which he described several forms.[5] Perhaps such oversimplification in making definitions is unavoidable. Yet a starting place is necessary to understand what socialism is and is not, despite these problems. Cole's approach seems to be the wisest: to find the common element in all forms of socialism and, from there, to explore the schools of socialism in all their variety.

THE COMMON ELEMENT IN SOCIALISM

Socialism may be defined as movements for social ownership and control of the economy. It is this idea that is the common element found in the many forms of socialism. Yet having stated this as the common definition of socialism, one must necessarily admit that there are a wide variety of views among socialists of various stripes as to just what constitutes social ownership and control of the means of production, distribution, and exchange. Additionally, these schools of socialism differ on a wide range of other, noneconomic issues, such as the form of political government sought.

THE FORMS OF SOCIALISM

The major political ideologies that comprise the socialist family are utopian socialism, social anarchism, democratic socialism, and communism. There are subforms of each of these major divisions. Additionally, there is the philosophy that underlies many of these ideologies, Marxism, and more recent schools.

Some of these socialist political ideologies belong to wider classifications. Utopian socialism, for example, forms a part of utopianism, not all of which is socialist in nature. The same may be said of anarchism: social anarchism—a nonstate form of socialism—may be distinguished from the nonsocialist and, in some cases, procapitalist school of individualist anarchism.

Utopian Socialism

Utopianism is largely a literary genre concerning perfect societies and/or attempts to form such perfect societies. Those that sought to do this by means of a socially owned economy are properly classified as utopian socialists.

This is the oldest form of socialism and is the breeding ground for the ideas of the later and more politically active schools of socialism. However, it is not a dead form; people are still writing about perfect societies, especially in the form of science fiction. There are also those living in communes trying to realize an ideal lifestyle, sometimes based on a utopian novel or work.⁶

Marxism

The outstanding philosophy underlying or at least having a major influence on all of the modern socialist family of political ideologies past utopian socialism is *Marxism*—the body of work by German philosopher Karl Marx (1818–1883) and his coauthor and popularizer Friedrich Engels (1820–1895). In many ways, Marxism is a competitor and critic of utopian socialism and has largely superseded the latter.

The key ideas of Marxism include dialectical and historical materialism, which have often been described as economic determinism—the view that economics determines all else and that the forces of economics inevitably are leading to a socialist revolution by the workers over the capitalist class. Combining the dialectical theory of German philosopher Georg Wilhelm Friedrich Hegel (1770–1831), the socialism of German Jewish publisher, author, and activist Moses Hess (1812–1875), and the materialism of German professor of religion turned atheist Ludwig Feuerbach (1804–1872), Marx developed the theory of *dialectical materialism*.⁷ This is a term that Marx did not actually use but that was invented by his coauthor Friedrich Engels to help explain and popularize Marxian ideas. Dialectical materialism is the theory that the most important thing about the world was not ideas but material conditions, especially economic classes, and that these conditions and classes were fundamentally in conflict with each other. The world of ideas is only of secondary importance, in contradiction to the dialectical idealism of Hegel.

The application of dialectical materialism to history gives rise to the theory of *historical materialism*, another term invented by Engels to give a label to a Marxian concept. Historical materialism is the theory that all of history is but the story of the struggle between material conditions, especially of economic classes. Down through the ages, one class has fought another: slaves versus masters in the ancient world, serfs versus lords in the feudal world, and the bourgeoisie (the middle class of capitalists) versus the aristocracy in such bourgeois revolutions as the American and French Revolutions. With the nineteenth century and the Industrial Revolution, a new class entered the stage of world history—the proletariat or the working class. Driven by poverty and unemployment, the workers became so oppressed that they inevitably rose up and overthrew the bourgeoisie and the capitalist system, thus ushering in socialism.

Marx did not speak in terms of a stage of socialism and a stage of communism to follow. For him, *communism* was merely a more radical and revolutionary sounding term for essentially the same movement as socialism. By the late nineteenth century, it became common to speak first of a stage of socialism immediately following the proletarian revolution in which the state would still be necessary to coin and print money and to defend the revolution against its enemies by means of the military, the police, the courts, and the prisons. Not yet quite free of the bourgeoisie or bourgeois ideas, it would be necessary to live by the old socialist slogan, "From each according to his ability, to each according to his work," implying that compensation would still be paid. However, after all bourgeois agents and ideas had disappeared, the state could "die out," in Engels's phrase, or "wither away," as V. I. Lenin would later translate Engels on this point; and money and the state would no longer be necessary. Then people would be ready for communism.

Marx had spoken only of crude communism versus a higher or upper phase of communism.[8] However, in later usage, communism meant a classless and stateless society, without government or organs for law and order; for there would be no one left to repress or to keep in check, and no compensation would have to be paid for work. Communism would mean free distribution of goods and services. The communist slogan, "From each according to his ability, to each according to his *needs*" (as opposed to "work") would then rule.

Marxism also has its own theories of economics, including the labor theory of value—the value of a good is solely determined by the amount of labor that went into making it. A corollary to this is the theory of surplus value, which holds that profit is literally robbed by the capitalists from their workers making goods.[9]

Social Anarchism

What all anarchists share in common is the opposition to government and a belief in the abolition of the state.[10] The principal division in anarchism, also known as libertarianism or antiauthoritarianism, is between the social anarchists, who believe in a nonstate form of socialism, and the individualist anarchists, who oppose socialism and favor capitalism or are opposed to any form of social organization whatsoever. Of the two, social anarchism is the far larger, although anarchism as a whole has never attracted as many adherents as the other ideologies. Often, anarchists have been the competitors and the opponents of the Marxists, while at the same time undeniably influenced by Marxist thought.

Social anarchism can be divided into several schools: The oldest of these is *mutualism*, founded by the man who was the first to call himself an anarchist, the Frenchman Pierre-Joseph Proudhon (1809–1865). Under mutualism, the state would be abolished, and factories would be owned and controlled by the workers in the form of producers' cooperatives. Compensation would be retained in the form of labor checks paid to workers by people's banks, corresponding to the number of hours they worked. Private property would be retained under this system.

Collectivist anarchism, or *collectivism*, would abolish the state and all forms of private property. All property would be owned by workers' collectives. The Russian Mikhail Bakunin (1814–1876), the chief advocate of this school of social anarchism, also believed in retaining some form of compensation paid to workers for their work. Although Bakunin scoffed at Proudhon's idea of labor checks and people's banks, he was vague as to how this compensation was to be paid. Other collectivist anarchists, however, merely adopted Proudhon's scheme.

Fellow Russian Peter Kropotkin (1842–1921) believed, however, in a form of social anarchism that would do away with compensation, called communist anarchism, anarcho-communism, or, as he preferred to call it, *anarchist communism*. Under this system there would be free distribution of goods and services, with everything being produced and given away for free without wages paid or prices charged.

Anarcho-syndicalism, revolutionary syndicalism, or simply *syndicalism* is a labor-union form of social anarchism.[11] One of the chief exponents of syndicalism was Frenchman Fernand Pelloutier (1867–1901). In it, the labor unions would own and control industry in the absence of the state. Most syndicalists would also do away with compensation, but some followed the collectivists' insistence that the principle of compensation for work performed be retained.

In Guild Socialism, an English school of socialism that was closely related to syndicalism,[12] workers' guilds, rather than labor unions, were to be the organ of ownership. Some Guildsmen argued for functional representation in government, in which representation would be based on industrial guilds, rather than on territorial divisions.

The New Left was a quasi-anarchist school of the 1960s and early 1970s. Largely a student movement, it rejected the Old Left ideologies of socialism and communism and believed in participatory democracy.[13] This quasi-anarchist idea argued for direct democracy in government and in company management.

There was also a belief in the New Left that people should not rely on politicians (who are all bought off) to make change, but instead should go out and make change for themselves, from stopping the war in Vietnam by demonstrations to setting up their own free-food distribution programs to deal with hunger.

Another anarchist related ideology is Green Politics, one of the newest to appear.[14] It largely grew out of the New Left, however. Whereas the latter was primarily concerned with stopping the Vietnam War, Green Politics took a relatively minor element in New Left thought, ecology, and made it into the primary focus. While still opposed to war, the Greens call for ecology, nonviolence, social responsibility, and grassroots democracy. This last idea is closely related to that of participatory democracy in the New Left. Greens advocate direct democracy and protesting for change, but there is less opposition to running for political office among most Greens.

The anarchists have differed widely as to means to achieve anarchy. The philosophical anarchists, such as Proudhon, were peaceful and believed in nonviolent means to achieve anarchism by philosophical persuasion. Terroristic anarchists, such as Bakunin, on the other hand, believed in "propaganda by the deed" rather than "propaganda by the word"; that is, they believed in violent acts of terrorism—bombings, shootings, and armed uprisings against capitalists, aristocrats, and politicians—to inspire the masses to rise up in a violent revolution.

This split was apparent in the New Left, some of whom engaged in violent acts of terror; however, the Greens oppose all forms of violence. Like many in the New Left, the Greens believe in civil disobedience and peaceful protests.

Still a third means to bring anarchism about was that of the anarcho-syndicalists, who believed in the power of the general strike by all workers to bring about the downfall of capitalism and the state.

Communism

In a modern sense of the word, *communism* refers to the ideology of Marxism-Leninism.[15] Unlike democratic socialism, communism is not eclectic, being primarily based on the ideas of just two main thinkers—Karl Marx and Russian revolutionary Vladimir I. Lenin (1870–1924).

To most people, communism is an undemocratic form of socialism, based on totalitarianism and either dictatorship or oligarchical rule. However, communists would hotly dispute this assertion and claim theirs to be the only truly democratic and socialist ideology.

Communists mainly believe in a nationalized economy with some agriculture collectives. In terms of management, they tend to favor a command economy, in which a government not only appoints all managers, but also plans all aspects of production, distribution, and exchange, as opposed to a market economy.

However, command economy is not always the case, as in Yugoslavia, which practiced before its breakup both workers' self-management and market socialism. Recently China and Vietnam have also been developing a market economy.

It is sometimes said that communism is revolutionary, whereas democratic socialism is evolutionary. Though there is some truth to this, it is something of an oversimplification, as attitudes toward violent revolution for any movement depend much on the local political and social conditions in a given country at a particular time. There are also several variants of communism, among them Eurocommunism found in some of the Western European nations and Maoism in China.

DEMOCRATIC SOCIALISM

One of the great ideologies of the world, and the subject of this work, *democratic socialism* combines the ideas of liberal-democratic government with that of social ownership and control of the economy. It is eclectic in nature, its ideas coming from many sources, including revised Marxism (revisionism), which adds or emphasizes elements of democracy to Marxism while playing down its violent revolutionary aspects, Fabian socialism and religious socialism. It is sometimes called social democracy or simply socialism, although this term is problematic. It tends to be evolutionary or peaceful revolutionary in seeking its aims.

In discussing European democratic socialism, we shall want to consider *fascism* and what is considered today to be a German variant, *National Socialism*, which in many respects are the opposites of democratic socialism.[16] Despite the name National Socialism, it can be considered to be largely a procapitalist movement, rather than truly socialist. Only a small wing of it was ever socialist in the sense of seeking social ownership of the economy. The name socialism was used largely because it was popular in Germany at the time of its rise.

Democratic socialism is the wing of the socialist movement that combines a belief in a socially owned economy with that of political democracy. Sometimes simply called socialism, more often than not, the adjective *democratic* is added by democratic socialists to distinguish themselves from Communists who also call themselves socialists. All but communists, or more accurately, Marxist-Leninists, believe that modern-day communism is highly undemocratic and totalitarian in practice, and democratic socialists wish to emphasize by their name that they disagree strongly with the Marxist-Leninist brand of socialism. Communists, of course, believe that they have the only truly democratic ideology, and almost never use the term *democratic socialism* for that ideology, for that would imply that they were, in contrast, the undemocratic socialists—something that they do not wish to admit. Instead they refer to democratic socialists as "social democrats," and mean this as an epithet. Communists have also used even worse sounding terms on occasion for democratic socialists, such as "social fascists."

Social democracy is a somewhat controversial term among democratic socialists. Many democratic socialists use *social democracy* as a synonym for *democratic socialism*, while others, particularly revolutionary democratic socialists, do not, the latter seeing social democracy as something less than socialism—a milder, evolutionary ideology that seeks merely to reform capitalism. Communists also use the term *social democratic* to mean something less than true socialism that sought only to preserve capitalism by reform rather than by overthrowing it and establishing socialism. Even revolutionary democratic socialists and Communists have at times, particularly in the past, called their parties "social democratic."

One popular way to conceive of democratic socialism is in terms of four kinds of democracy: (1) political democracy, (2) social democracy, (3) economic democracy, and (4) international democracy. This was the approach taken in the founding statement of the Socialist International, a post-World War II reincarnation of the Second International founded in 1889 in Paris. The Socialist International is an international organization of democratic socialist parties. Their 1951 founding statement, "Aims and tasks of democratic socialism," is commonly called the "Frankfurt Declaration."[17] These forms of democracy can be thought of as stages of development in achieving democratic socialism.

Political Democracy

Political democracy is the first goal on the road to achieving democratic socialism, according to the democratic socialists. Basic civil rights must be established—the freedom to participate in government and society without discrimination, meaning free elections, free political parties, and freedom to work and to use public amenities without racial or other forms of discrimination. Additionally, civil liberties must be established—the freedom from government and majorities, which would include the freedoms of speech, press, and peaceable assembly; the freedom to practice religion and from having state religions established; and the right to a fair trial. With respect to political democracy, the democratic socialists have borrowed heavily from the liberal-democratic philosophers and, out of a concern for democracy and freedom, have come to reject all dictatorial and totalitarian ideologies either of the extreme right, such as fascism, or of the extreme left, such as Communism.

Social Democracy

Social democracy is often used by democratic socialists to mean a second stage beyond the establishment of democratic government and civil liberties. This would be the stage in which an extensive and comprehensive social welfare system would be established, which would include a government system for old-age pensions, unemployment compensation, and a national health plan.

One may well ask how any of this differs from that proposed by liberals and conservatives? Social democracy would have far more inclusive social welfare plans than the liberals or the conservatives would be likely to propose or accept. For example, whereas health care planning in a country like the United States, which does not have a large democratic socialist party, would include government-subsidized health care insurance for the elderly and the poor, it would not provide public-paid coverage for everyone else in society. However, a social democratic system, which most other industrialized nations have, would have a national health insurance system in which nearly all citizens would be covered. In some countries, such as the United Kingdom, a national health plan would go beyond a nationalized health insurance system to a national health system in which the government directly owned hospitals and most health care workers were employed by the government.

Under social democratic governments, other programs besides health care, such as aid to the unemployed and the uneducated, would also be far more generous than those commonly found in nonsocialist governments, such as the United States. Naturally, taxes are often higher in these countries than in the United States in order to pay for these social programs.

Very few other industries besides the health insurance industry are likely to be socialized under the stage of social democracy. Only industries in fields such as transportation and communications are likely to be nationalized— uncommon in a nonsocialist nation such as the United States. Perhaps a few other major manufacturing industries will be nationalized under the stage of social democracy, but the bulk of companies will remain private capitalist owned. Even these are often denationalized by incoming conservative governments who strongly believe in privatization and the virtues of capitalism and less government ownership.

The majority of democratic socialists are evolutionary socialists—seeking a very gradual transition to socialism, leaving most industries for the time being in the hands of private capitalists. To go more boldly and declare for revolutionary change, especially if it involves the use of violence, is often viewed as adventurist and likely to lose votes.

The opposite problem for democratic socialists is being opportunist. In the name of winning elections, most of the socialist platform is shelved. When social democrats do come to office, however, they often find that their timid approaches to change and to the problems of government and society do not do much to address and correct pressing social problems such as unemployment.

The case of French Socialist president François Mitterrand in the 1980s is instructive. Expectations were raised when he was elected and a socialist majority was established in parliament; but in the end, most of the economy was left in private capitalist hands, and unemployment remained high in France. When the expectations for change were dashed, the socialists suffered a massive parliamentary defeat in 1993 and subsequently lost the presidency to the Gaullists in 1995 with the election of Jacques Chirac. That French conservatives may be no better in lowering France's high unemployment rate is beside the point. Moderate social democratic platforms may win elections, but by being insufficiently radical in effecting change, they can also cause disillusionment and the loss of elections.

Revolutionary democratic socialists are usually a minority in democratic socialist parties, except in some countries where peaceful, evolutionary reform is not permitted by authoritarian regimes. In Central American nations, for example, democratic socialists by necessity are more inclined to revolution than are their European counterparts and have joined forces with communists and radicalized liberals to overthrow dictatorial governments.

Revolutionary democratic socialists need not necessarily be advocates of violent revolution and the overthrow of governments. They can also be peaceful, revolutionary democratic socialists, who seek faster, more radical change than do most social democrats, including more extensive socialization of businesses and industries.

Economic Democracy

Beyond the stage of social democracy is the goal of achieving economic democracy—an economy that is socially owned and democratically controlled and that is thus an end to inequality, exploitation, and alienation of the working class under capitalism. To end these social ills is the reason why socialists are socialists and reject capitalism, which they see as a major source for these injustices. To the social democrat, economic democracy would be a goal that could only be achieved gradually and in the far future, whereas to the revolutionary democratic socialist, it would be the immediate goal to be established in the near future.

By "social ownership," socialists have meant many differing forms. Some conceive of it as nationalization, in which the national government takes over ownership of the major means of production, distribution, and exchange. Others conceive of socialism as meaning municipalization and local government or community ownership, with perhaps only some nationalized nationwide services, such as health care, transportation, and communications.

It is an error to equate socialism only with government or public ownership, although this has been the most common form of social ownership in the twentieth century. An alternative to government ownership is cooperative ownership. Cooperatives come in two basic forms: (1) the producers' cooperative, which involves worker ownership; and (2) the consumers' cooperative, which entails ownership of stores by consumers. Specialized forms of consumers' cooperatives exist, such as housing and food cooperatives, or "co-ops," and credit unions. Sometimes the term producers' cooperative is meant only to refer to collective ownership of a marketing operation that sells the products of private, capitalist producers, and the term workers' cooperative is reserved for situations in which the workers own their own factory; but the latter too is often referred to as a producers' cooperative. Also, it is possible to have a hybrid involving both worker and consumer ownership.[18]

Consumers' cooperatives have been more numerous and more successful than producers' cooperatives. Many of the latter have failed in the past, but this need not be the case. With government support, the Israeli kibbutz system has flourished; and the Mondragon cooperatives of the Basque region of Spain have shown that producers' cooperatives can succeed if they put back into their cooperatives much of their earnings.[19]

Still another form of worker ownership is that of socialist industrial unions—a centralized system in which nationwide labor unions own and operate all industries and elect representatives to an Industrial Congress that would take the place of legislatures elected on the the basis of territorial districts. Such a plan was envisioned by the outstanding American Marxist Daniel De Leon of the Socialist Labor Party.[20]

Hybrid forms of social ownership involving party government, part cooperative, part private capitalist, and part labor union ownership are also possible, and these may exist alongside a private capitalist sector. Some socialists have argued that only the "commanding heights of industry" should be socialized, whereas others would have a much more thoroughgoing socialist economy.

A separate question is: how are these forms of socialism to be managed? Economic democracy has often meant that democratically appointed legislatures appoint managers and exercise an oversight function. This is common in state-owned industries. However, the cooperative movement and other socialist movements have instead conceived of economic democracy as meaning worker and/or consumer election of management. Up to now, only one country has ever practiced workers' self-management as a national policy—Yugoslavia; but on a smaller scale, a number of cooperatives have successfully practiced workplace democracy.[21] Partial forms of workers' control have also been practiced in Germany under the name "co-determination," which involves the ability of workers to elect their own labor union representatives to the board of directors of companies.[22]

International Democracy

The foreign policy of democratic socialists has been called *international democracy*. One goal has been the establishment of worldwide, political democracy and socialism. Another goal has been universal disarmament and an end to war. Still another goal is the end of imperialism, both outright colonialism and neocolonial domination of powerful nations over the economies and politics of others.

Additionally, democratic socialists seek a new international economic order in which the world will no longer be divided by the north/south split between the wealthy nations mainly in the northern hemisphere and the desperately poor nations of the Third World, found mainly in the southern hemisphere in Africa, Asia, and Latin America. The democratic socialists urge greater foreign aid to help end this situation of international inequality.

All complex systems of thought carry the possibility that two or more elements might be in contradiction. Political ideologies have such built-in contradictions, which can be clearly seen between democratic socialists' goals of political democracy and their desire for international democracy. As political democrats, they oppose dictatorial and often aggressive fascist and communist states. This translates into a desire to be armed for the purposes of self-defense. At the same time, under the goal of international democracy, democratic socialists also declare for universal disarmament.

The social democratic parties of Western Europe were split over these conflicting goals when the United States began arming these nations with nuclear missiles in response to a Soviet buildup in nuclear and conventional forces in the 1970s and 1980s. The left wings of these social democratic parties joined with communist and Green parties to protest these Western, Soviet-matching buildups, whereas the right-wing social democrats tended to side with the conservatives in their nations in seeing the need for American nuclear arms on their soil in the name of protecting democracy from tyranny.

Similarly, in the name of opposing imperialism, the left wings of democratic socialist parties called for immediate United States withdrawal from the Vietnam War and, later, from conflicts in Central America, whereas the right-wing social democrats supported the Vietnam War and U.S. intervention in Nicaragua and El Salvador in the name of fighting communism. The Socialist Party, USA, actually split three ways over these and other issues in the early 1970s; democratic socialist parties elsewhere where badly hurt by these divisions of opinion.

This tendency to be divided over foreign policy is not new for democratic socialists. The most damaging divisions were over World War I. In 1907 the world's socialist parties of the Second International agreed to the Stuttgart Resolution opposing the coming conflict and pledged action against it when it came.[23] Indeed, the left-wing socialists led by Rosa Luxemburg (1871–1919) of Poland and Lenin got the Second International parties to declare that they would fight to end both the war when it came as well as capitalism, which had created the war. Yet when World War I actually began, nationalism and mutual fear led the majority of socialists to support their countries in the conflict. The German socialists split over the issue, with both revolutionary democratic socialists and moderate social democrats opposed to the war uniting to form their own breakaway Independent Social Democratic Party of Germany. The Russian Social Democratic Labor Party was already divided into moderate Menshevik and Marxist-Leninist Bolshevik wings, with the former supporting the war and the Bolsheviks in opposition. The American and Italian Socialist Parties opposed the war and suffered defections and repression because of it. The division in the Italian Socialist Party over the war led to Benito Mussolini quitting the party to form the fascist movement; the division over the war in Russia and elsewhere was one of the principal reasons for the emergence of communism from the old socialist movement as antiwar socialists in large numbers either broke away from socialist parties or were expelled from them. This was the beginning of a historical division in the socialist movement that has never been healed to date.

As the twentieth century wore on, new issues arose to divide the socialists. One of these issues is feminism. How far would democratic socialist parties go in supporting such contentious issues and men's/women's parity in party meetings and in elected party offices? Would the democratic socialists support prochoice positions on abortion? Generally, democratic socialists have moved to incorporate into their thinking elements of feminist theory, but not without strong differences of opinion and internal struggle.

Another of the relatively new issues with which democratic socialists have had to deal is the natural environment. Would they support measures to protect the environment, even when it meant sacrificing jobs? An even larger debate has concerned nuclear power. Many a social democratic government backed nuclear power generation as a key to economic development and to energy independence from imported oil.

However, in the wake of the Three Mile Island and the Chernobyl nuclear disasters, a growing number of people, including some democratic socialists, came to oppose nuclear power as an inherently unsafe technology and instead urged the development of safe, renewable sources of energy, such as solar power, geothermal energy, and biomass technology, as well as increased efforts at energy conservation.

Such disagreements over environmental and energy policies led to infighting among democratic socialists and played a major part, along with the argument over nuclear weapons, in the formation of the Greens.

NOTES

1. Angelo S. Rappoport, *Dictionary of Socialism* (London: Adelphi Terrace, 1924), pp. v, 34–41.
2. Albert Fried and Ronald Sanders, eds., *Socialist Thought—A Documentary History* (Garden City, NY: Anchor Books, Doubleday, 1964), p. 1.
3. Leszek Kolakowski, *Main Currents of Marxism,* trans. P. S. Falla, 3 vols. (Oxford: Oxford University Press, 1978), 1:182.
4. G. D. H. Cole, *A History of Socialist Thought,* 9 vols. (London: Macmillan, 1953–1960), 1:1.
5. R. N. Berki, *Socialism* (New York: St. Martin's, 1975), pp. 9–14.
6. Harry W. Laidler, *History of Socialism* (New York: Apollo, 1968), pp. 3–117.
7. Shlomo Avineri, *The Social and Political Thought of Karl Marx* (Cambridge: Cambridge University Press, 1968), pp. 8–40.
8. David McLellan, *Karl Marx: Selected Writings* (Oxford: Oxford University Press, 1977), pp. 88–89.
9. James Edward LeRossignol, *Backgrounds to Communist Thought—From Marx to Stalin* (New York: Apollo, 1968), pp. 162–226.
10. Atindranath Bose, *A History of Anarchism* (Calcutta: World Press Private Ltd., 1967).

11. Laidler, *History of Socialism*, pp. 277–315.
12. Ibid., pp. 316–343.
13. Alan Adelson, *SDS—A Profile* (New York: Scribner, 1972); Kirkpatrick Sale, *SDS* (New York: Vintage, 1974).
14. Fritjof Capra and Charlene Spretnak, *Green Politics—The Global Promise* (New York: Dutton, 1984); Jonathon Porritt, *Seeing Green—The Politics of Ecology Explained* (New York: Basil Blackwell, 1985); Brian Tokar, *The Green Alternative—Creating an Ecological Future* (San Pedro, CA: R. & E. Miles, 1987).
15. Leon P. Baradat, *Political Ideologies—Their Origins and Impact*, 2d ed. (Englewood Cliffs, NJ: Prentice-Hall, 1984), pp. 202–209.
16. Ibid., pp. 250–285.
17. "Aims and tasks of democratic socialism" (often called the Frankfurt Declaration), in Massimo Salvadori, ed., *Modern Socialism* (New York: Harper Torchbooks, 1968), pp. 279–287.
18. Martin Buber, *Paths in Utopia* (London: Routledge, 1949).
19. Alastair Campbell, *Mondragon 1980* (Los Angeles: CRSP, 1982).
20. *Socialist Industrial Unionism—The Workers' Power* (New York: New York Labor News, 1974).
21. Carole Pateman, *Participation and Democratic Theory* (Cambridge: Cambridge University Press, 1970).
22. Warren Lerner, *A History of Socialism and Communism in Modern Times: Theorists, Activists, and Humanists* (Englewood Cliffs, NJ: Prentice-Hall, 1982), pp. 228–229.
23. Ibid., pp. 82–83.

2

Democratic Socialism in Continental Europe

GERMANY

In Germany there arose two socialist parties in the nineteenth century.[1] Ferdinand Lassalle (1825–1864) had organized the General German Workingmen's Association in 1863 to fight for suffrage and state-aided producers' cooperatives. Most Association members, commonly called the Lassalleans, came from Prussia. A rival Marxist party was founded and led by August Bebel (1840–1913), who had known poverty and who had a genuine proletarian background as a lathe operator and labor leader, and by Wilhelm Liebknecht (1826–1900), a philologist and intellectual. This party was formally known as the Social Democratic Workers' Party, nicknamed the Eisenachers because they had held their first congress in the German city of Eisenach in 1869. Organized in Saxony and South Germany, the Eisenachers placed more emphasis on state ownership and less on political democracy than did the Lassalleans.

The two parties united in the unity congress of 1875 in the German city of Gotha to form the Social Democratic Workingmen's of Germany, later shortened to Social Democratic Party of Germany (SPD). Its Gotha Program contained Lassallean demands for winning working-class suffrage and political democracy.

In 1877 the SPD had reached a half million voters and had elected a dozen deputies to the Reichstag, alarming the government. Two unsuccessful attempts on Emperor Wilhelm I's life had been made in 1878, although neither of the assassins had any connection to the SPD. But Chancellor Otto von Bismarck saw the opportunity to convince the Kaiser that the socialists had to be suppressed, and Wilhelm supported the plan. Bismarck pushed for the Reichstag members to pass antisocialist legislation; and when they refused, the Reichstag was dissolved and new elections were called. The elections brought a majority favorable to Bismarck. He had told the parliament that Bebel's speech to them praising the Paris Commune of 1871 showed how dangerous socialism was, and the parliament concurred, passing the Anti-Socialist Laws, which banned socialist meetings and literature distribution. The party was not banned outright, however, and only in the Reichstag could socialists enjoy the freedom of speech. The socialists soon began publishing their newspaper, *The Social Democrat*, in Switzerland, with Eduard Bernstein (1850–1932) as editor, smuggling it across the border into Germany where they distributed it to thousands of workers.

Despite the repression, the socialist vote mounted. By 1890 it had topped a million votes, a 300 percent increase. Bismarck tried to appease the workers by enacting reform legislation beginning in 1882. Called "State Socialism," the Reichstag passed various accident, sickness, and old-age insurance legislation.

It was during this period that the SPD moved to the left. In 1891 the SPD adopted the Erfurt Program, purging itself of Lassallean demands for state aid to establish producers' cooperatives and, instead, adopting a Marxist program that stressed the growing gulf between the rich and the poor—the class struggle—and that called for nationalization of the means of production, distribution, and exchange.

Bernstein

Eduard Bernstein is the father of revisionism, that is, revised Marxism.[2] Born in Berlin, the son of a railroad engineer, he became a bank clerk and joined the SPD in 1872. By 1878 he was forced to go into exile by the newly passed Anti-Socialist Laws. He was editor of the party's paper until 1888 in Zurich, until the German government prevailed on the Swiss government to deport him. Bernstein went to London, where he was to serve as a correspondent for the Berlin *Vorwaerts* (Forward). It was in London that Bernstein came into contact with the Fabian Socialists, and began to rethink and revise his own revolutionary Marxist beliefs into an evolutionary socialism. He saw that the standard of living of the workers had risen, not fallen, and that the middle class was growing larger, not smaller, contrary to Marx's predictions. Bernstein made his criticisms of Marxism in a number of works, notably *Die Voraussetzungen der Sozialismus und die Aufgaben der*

Sozialdemokratie (The Presuppositions of Socialism and the Tasks of Social Democracy), which was published in 1899 and translated into English that year under the title *Evolutionary Socialism*.[3] It caused a major stir in socialist circles. The academic German socialists who advocated "Socialism of the Chair" agreed with Bernstein, but others, such as SPD leader Karl Kautsky (1854–1938), denounced it as heresy. They called Kautsky "the Pope of Marxism" for his defense of orthodox Marxian ideas.[4] When Bernstein returned to Germany in 1900, he led the revisionist faction of the SPD.

Luxemburg

Born in Zamosc, Poland, Rosa Luxemburg (1871–1919)[5] was a leader of revolutionary democratic socialism. A Jewish socialist as were Marx, Hess, Lassalle, and Bernstein (Kautsky is often presumed to be Jewish, but was not), she received a doctorate in economics from the University of Zurich, after frequently clashing with her professors. In 1898, she immigrated to Germany, using a false marriage to a German to gain entry, so she could join the German socialist movement. She thought that Bernstein was a sellout and that SPD leaders Bebel and Kautsky were too lacking in revolutionary ardor. She also attacked Lenin in her work *Marxism or Leninism* for his antidemocratic ideas.[6]

In 1907 the Second International parties adopted the Stuttgart Resolution, promising to work to prevent World War I and, if it came, to resist and turn it into a revolution against capitalism. When the war began in 1914, most of the Second International member parties did not remain true to their antiwar pledge and instead supported their governments in the war. As a result, the Second International was killed for a time.

In Germany, the antiwar socialists (Bernstein, Kautsky, and Luxemburg among others—strange bedfellows), spanning from the revisionists and evolutionary socialists on the right to the orthodox Marxists and revolutionary democratic socialists on the left of the party, organized their own Independent Socialist Party of Germany (USPD). Some of these members were later to join the German Communist Party (KPD), and others were to drift back to the SPD after the war.

The antiwar socialists held the Zimmerwald Conference outside the Swiss capital of Berne in 1915. Luxemburg supported it but did not attend because she was in prison charged with high treason. Karl Radek (1885–1939) a Polish-German socialist and journalist, supported Lenin's formation of the Zimmerwald Left, which called for turning the war into a proletarian revolution; but the majority of the Zimmerwald delegates did not endorse this revolutionary stance. Perhaps there would have been no Marxism-Leninism—split in the socialist movement with the emergence of a separate Communist movement hostile to the traditions of liberal democracy—had all of the Second International parties upheld their prewar Stuttgart Resolution to oppose the war.

After the war, Luxemburg-inspired "Spartacists," the Bremen Left-Radicals, and the Berlin Shop Stewards founded the German Communist Party in Berlin in 1918. Luxemburg and Radek warned that the time was not ripe for a revolution in Germany, but the KPD, nevertheless, launched the Spartacist uprising in Berlin in 1919. Luxemburg and Karl Liebknecht (1871–1919), the son of Eisenacher founder Wilhelm Liebknecht, reluctantly supported the uprising. The majority social democratic reformists, now in control of the German government after the war and the abdication of Wilhelm II, had appointed Gustav Noske as commander-in-chief of the German army and, along with the help of the Free Corps that had been created and led by former Imperial German officers, moved to crush the Spartacist Rebels. The Free Corps also assassinated Rosa Luxemburg and Karl Liebknecht.

A similar revolt in Bavaria led by Kurt Eisner (1867–1919) created a short-lived Socialist Republic of Bavaria, but it too was put down, and Eisner was assassinated in February 1919.

Ironically, the head of the postwar German government that had crushed these revolts was a socialist himself—a moderate social democrat who feared Communism—Friedrich Ebert (1871–1925). He became the first president of the Weimar Republic, serving from 1919 to 1925. He had hoped that the new German republic with its capital at Weimar would be a democratic state that would peacefully evolve toward socialism. This reformist state socialism was influenced by the "Socialism of the Chair"—a form of socialism advocated by German professors such as Adolph Wagner and Gustav Schmoller among others. Rejecting revolution and utopian experiments, they called for the state to improve the lot of the working class by slow, evolutionary reforms.[7]

National Socialism

With the defeat of Germany in World War I and the abdication of Kaiser Wilhelm II, the leaders of the Weimar Republic attempted to form a stable, democratic government; however, it was in trouble from the very beginning.[8] The Treaty of Versailles was particularly harsh on Germany, which had to pay very heavy war reparations and was not permitted to have a large or modern military. Also the Great Depression hit Germany hard. People dreamed of the good old days of glory and strength under the old Empire and tended to blame their problems on the democratic government.

During times of great political and economic crises in any country, people begin to turn to more radical alternatives, both left-wing and right-wing. If the governments in these countries seem to be dealing effectively with a crisis, they will likely retain enough popularity to maintain control. For example, the New Deal in the United States and the National Government in Britain made enough progress against the ravages of the Great Depression to keep the Communists and the fascists from gaining too much support. If a government does not deal effectively with a crisis, then radical opponents of either the left or the right may well rapidly gain enough strength to threaten a revolution.

In Germany, the Weimar Republic was coping with the depression so badly that the National Socialists grew by leaps and bounds. Prior to the onset of the Great Depression, the Social Democrats had become the strongest party in the Reichstag, by 1928 increasing their representation from 135 to 153 seats and their popular vote to over nine million. Ebert had been in office as president until his death in 1925 and was replaced by conservative Field Marshal Paul von Hindenburg (1847–1934), who served as president from 1925 to 1934. In the 1928 election, the Social Democrats were able to elect Hermann Muller as chancellor. Soon after the election, the rising unemployment during the Great Depression, as well as the mounting cost of the war reparations, put the Social Democrats in the government in a perilous position. The nonsocialist parties in the cabinet wanted cuts in spending, and the right wing of the Social Democratic Party, including Finance minister Rudolf Hilferding, agreed to reduce unemployment compensation because of the escalating taxes they were requiring.

The left wing of the Social Democrats opposed this reduction, along with the trade unions. In 1930 the Social Democrats withdrew from the coalition government over the compromise with the other parties to reduce unemployment compensation. Heinrich Bruning, a Centrist, succeeded Muller as chancellor in 1930 as the head of a conservative government, and in turn, he was succeeded by Colonel Franz von Papen in 1932.

Meanwhile, the National Socialist German Workers' Party (NASDAP), nicknamed "the Nazi Party" as a contraction of the words National Socialism, was rising to power under Adolf Hitler (1889–1945). Winning a third of the Reichstag seats in the 1932 election, von Papen offered Hitler the position of vice-chancellor, as no party alone could form a parliamentary majority. As head of the largest party, Hitler refused and instead demanded the chancellorship for himself alone. A second election that year saw the

National Socialists lose some of their votes but still retain about a third of the vote. Von Papen, as did Bruning before him, proposed the breakup of the large Prussian landed estates to settle the unemployed on small farms; but Hindenburg and the large landowner class refused to go along with this, and Von Papen resigned. Kurt von Schleicher was now appointed chancellor; but running into the same problems as von Papen and Bruning, he too resigned on January 28, 1933. Hitler was then appointed chancellor with a cabinet made up of National Socialists and members of the Nationalists. The Reichstag building was destroyed in a fire on February 27, 1933. The fire, set by the Nazis, was blamed by them on the Communists and used as a pretext to suppress them. The Nazis and their Nationalist partners won a majority of the votes in the election of March 4, 1933, and on March 23 they and the Nationalists placed dictatorial power in the hands of Hitler. The Social Democrats protested, but it was to no avail; and they along with the trade unions were suppressed for the duration of the Nazi regime, functioning as an underground movement.

The National Socialists were certainly more nationalist than socialist. Only one wing of their movement had any sort of socialist, proletarian character—the Storm Troopers (SA).[9] Also known as the Brown Shirts, they were led by Ernst Rohm (1887–1934). Having suppressed the Communists and the Social Democrats, the Brown Shirts now moved to create a "Second Revolution" to eliminate the capitalists, the aristocrats, and the Prussian military officers. Hitler, threatened by Rohm's popularity and needing the support of the ruling class who were threatened by the Brown Shirts, moved against them, executing Rohm and his followers in June and July of 1933 in the so-called "Blood Purge."

The Nazis under Hitler were actually very procapitalist, although it was a highly regulated form of capitalism they had in mind. An extreme right-wing ideology, Nazism sought to conquer the world, to enslave all non-Germans, and to exterminate the Jews. After Hitler came to power, the Third Reich was proclaimed, the First Reich, or Empire, being considered the Holy Roman Empire, and the Second Reich being the German Empire from 1871 to the formation of the Weimar Republic in 1919. Now under the Third Reich, more and more emergency powers were granted to Hitler, creating a dictatorial and totalitarian state. Also, a series of anti-Semitic laws were passed barring Jews from participating in political or cultural life. A vast public works program was launched, including the building of spectacular highways (Autobahnen)—perhaps the only socialist aspect of the Nazis' program. Vast military production also helped lift the economy out of depression, as it was to do in the United States.

Hitler repudiated the Treaty of Versailles, rapidly rearmed Germany, and embarked on a series of territorial demands and coups that brought Austria and the Sudentenland of Czechoslovakia into the Nazi Empire with the approval of the Western powers at the Munich Conference.

Germany invaded Poland on September 1, 1939, starting World War II. Hitler made a pact with Stalin to partition Poland, and Britain and France declared war on Germany. With the defeat of France and the near defeat of Britain, Hitler suddenly decided to double-cross Stalin and launched an invasion of the Soviet Union on June 22, 1941. With the entry of the United States into the war in December 1941, the Germans found themselves crushed between two allied fronts, with millions perishing in the war and in the Nazi death camps. After the war, Germany was divided into two nations: West Germany allied with the Western democracies, and a Soviet-dominated East Germany.

The SPD after the War

On May 23, 1949, the "Basic Law" of the Federal Republic of Germany (West Germany) was published; and on October 17 of that year, the German Democratic Republic (East Germany) was created. Under the Basic Law, West Germany had its first election that August 14, and Konrad Adenauer, a conservative, became chancellor. Bonn was the seat of the new government, with West Berlin as part of West Germany, although the old capital city of Berlin was within the borders of East Germany.

The Soviets forced a fusion of prewar remnants of the Communist and the Social Democratic parties in East Germany into the Socialist Unity Party in 1946, which, dominated by Moscow, became the ruling Communist party of that nation.

In West Germany, three major parties developed—the Social Democratic Party; their conservative competitors in the Christian Democratic Union (CDU) along with their Bavarian affiliate the Christian Social Union (CSU); and a smaller liberal party called the Free Democratic Party (FDP).

The Adenauer Era (1949–1963) was a time of political stability and rapid economic growth for Germany. With the help of the Marshall Plan, German industry was soon booming again. Under these conditions, the CDU/CSU coalition scored victory after victory over the SPD in federal elections.

Meanwhile, the SPD was deciding what it could do to halt this losing trend. At the Bad Godesberg Conference in 1959, the SPD leader Herbert Wehner, a tough, ex-Communist, got the SPD to drop its Marxist slogans and program adopted with the 1891 Erfurt program and instead to call for nothing more radical than reformist social democracy.[10] This was a defeat for the left wing of the party, and the new, moderate program proved popular with the voters. In abandoning Marxism, the SPD also abandoned Marx's theory of history, leaving something of a philosophical vacuum in the party.[11] Socialism increasingly came to mean to the SPD and other social democratic parties not an inevitable revolution toward a socially owned economy, but the immediate goals of creating and managing a social welfare state.

After 1959, led by the dynamic mayor of West Berlin Willy Brandt (1913–1992), the SPD began to make a strong comeback. Brandt, originally born Herbert Ernst Karl Frahm, had become a socialist at age sixteen and had used "Willy Brandt" as a pen name while a journalist for the socialist cause. Fleeing Germany for exile in Norway and Sweden when the Nazis came to power, he returned after the war, serving in the Bundestag (1949–1957) and then as mayor of West Berlin (1957–1966). He became vice-chancellor in the Grand Coalition government between the SPD and the CDU/CSU in 1964 and chancellor in 1969 with the victory of the SPD and its new coalition partner, the liberal FDP. Brandt remained chancellor until 1974, at which time he resigned after taking responsibility for a scandal involving an East German spy who was discovered serving as his aide to party affairs.

Brandt received the Nobel Peace Prize in 1971 for his policy of *Ostpolitik* —relaxing tensions between East and West. In 1970 West Germany signed nonaggression pacts with the Soviet Union and Poland, allowing free traffic between the East and West Berlin. Brandt went onto serve as president of the Socialist International in 1976 and as a member of the European Parliament (1979–1983).

Social Democrat Helmut Schmidt followed Brandt as chancellor of West Germany between 1974 and 1982. During these years of SPD rule, the social welfare state was expanded. However, there had been continuing infighting between the left wing of the SPD, led by its youth affiliate *(Jusos)*, and the dominant right wing, led by Schmidt. The left wing wanted more nationalizations of industry, while the right wing of the party was opposed to such radical demands. About 10 percent of West German industry is state-owned.

German trade unions had fought for co-determination in industry since before World War I. In 1951 the right of worker representation in management decisions on shutdowns and other changes in enterprises was established by law for the coal mining and iron and steel industries. Half of the Boards of Supervision of these companies are representatives of the workers. In 1971 the law was amended to provide for works councils to be established for all enterprises with more than twenty workers. In these industries, worker representatives hold one-third of the seats on the Boards of Supervision.

The FDP in 1982, feeling that its long-standing coalition with the SPD was submerging its own independence and identity and opposing an SPD plan to spend even more on social programs, broke with the SPD. Five FDP members of the Schmidt cabinet resigned; and on October 1, 1982, there was a successful vote of no confidence in the parliament, causing the Schmidt government to fall. The FDP formed a coalition with the CDU, and the CDU leader, Helmut Kohl, became the new chancellor. On November 9, 1989, the Berlin Wall, built in 1961 to prevent the escape of East Germans to West Berlin, was opened. Finally, on October 3, 1990, as East Germany's communist government collapsed, Germany was unified, and the former East Germany became part of the Federal Republic of Germany. On September 27, 1998, SPD candidate Gerhard Schroeder, age fifty-four, beat Helmut Kohl, age sixty-eight, in an election for Chancellor, running as a center-left candidate in coalition with the Greens. Schroeder campaigned as a probusiness candidate in favor of cutting business regulations, as did Kohl. The SPD platform called for not cutting social welfare programs, although Schroeder has said that he will not be bound by it. Some blamed Germany's high unemployment rates of over 10 percent on its generous welfare state programs and high taxes to pay for them. However, the strong SPD left wing is opposed to any further reductions in social welfare spending and programs and wants to restore those that had been modestly cut by Kohl's government. Both Schroeder and Kohl sounded much the same, with Kohl emphasizing stability and Schroeder saying he was for change, although vague about the specifics.

The former Communists (now called the Party of Democratic Socialism), led by civil rights lawyer Gregor Gysi, have done well in what was East Germany.

FRANCE

France has had five republics, in addition to several periods of intervening monarchist and dictatorial rule. A stable democracy did not arise until 1870 with the founding of the Third Republic. It arose out of France's defeat in the Franco-Prussian War (1870–1871). Emperor Napoleon III (Louis Napoleon) was taken prisoner by the Prussians during the war, which had been a disaster for France, and the Third Republic was declared. Under president Louis Adolphe Thiers, the French continued the war with Prussia but eventually lost. Reacting against this defeat and the possibility of another monarchist restoration, the people of Paris rose up in what some consider to be the first socialist revolution in history and created the Paris Commune of 1871. This fledging socialist state was crushed two months later by the French army in bloody house-to-house fighting.

The Third Republic was dominated by conservatives, and the French left largely turned from revolutionary action to open campaigning for political office in the wake of the defeat of the Communards. In 1895 the Radicals (as the liberals were called) and the Socialists had gained enough strength to elect Socialist Léon-Victor-Auguste Bourgeois (1851–1925) as premier. He attempted to establish a social welfare program and a progressive income tax; but the shocked conservatives, after a sharp struggle, defeated those social democratic proposals, and Bourgeois was out of office the following year.

The Marxists and the Possibilists

In the Congress of Saint-Étienne held in 1882, the French Socialists split, with Jules Guesde (1845–1922) founding a Marxist Parti Ouvrier Français (French Workers Party, often called Guesdists) and Paul Brousse, M.D. (1844–1912), founding the Parti ouvrier socialiste révolutionnaire Français (French Revolutionary Socialist Workers Party.) [12] Later on, the word *revolutionary* was dropped from their title. This latter group was often called the Broussists, or less flatteringly the "Possibilists" or "Opportunists," by their Marxist opponents, for unlike the French Marxists, the Possibilists were a reformist party that would seek out cooperation with other parties for possible reforms. Still other groups were the Allemanists—a split from the Possibilists led by J. Allemane because the Possibilists were charged with being too interested in parliamentary politics and not enough concerned in building up the Socialist movement. The Blanquists—followers of veteran Socialist conspirator Louis Auguste Blanqui (1805–1881) formed the Comité Revolutionnaire Central (Revolutionary Central Committee); they also formed a legal political party and abandoned revolutionary action. Another group was the Independent Socialists, which came as an outgrowth of the Society for International Economy, founded in 1885 by theoretician Benoit Malon, publisher of the monthly *Revue socialiste* (Socialist Revue). This group produced such outstanding socialists as Jean Léon Jaurès (1859–1914) and Alexandre Millerand (1859–1943). The Possibilists derided the Guesdists for their refusal to work with other parties, especially when the Third Republic was threatened in the 1880s by a possible right-wing coup by General Boulanger.[13]

The French Marxists at first ignored the imprisonment of army Captain

Alfred Dreyfus in 1894 on phony charges of treason, which were brought about by anti-Semitism, as irrelevant to the workers' struggle.[14] But by 1898 with the supporters of Dreyfus—the Dreyfusards—fighting to save the Republic against the anti-Dreyfusard monarchists and other haters of democracy, even the Marxists were moved to openly join with the Dreyfusards in defense of the Republic.

Alexandre Millerand (1859–1943) was the first socialist to join the cabinet of a Third Republic nonsocialist government, that of Waldeck-Rousseau, in order to save the Republic—a decision sharply opposed by Guesde, now the leader of the Socialists in parliament. Guesde opposed such participation, arguing that Socialists should hold out from becoming part of the government until they could capture office for themselves alone. Guesde denounced Millerand as a sellout to capitalism; and indeed, in time, Millerand did abandon the Socialist cause. However, Jean Jaurès, the most outstanding French Socialist of this period, supported Millerand in attempting to create a revisionist Marxism that could place the cause of democracy high on the list of goals, even if it meant cooperation with nonsocialists. Jaurès also argued for a dualist conception of history—both materialist and idealist.[15]

Both the Marxists and the Possibilists wanted to celebrate the one-hundredth anniversary of the French Revolution in 1889, and each party called for an international Socialist meeting in Paris on Bastille Day, July 14, for that year. Karl Liebknecht tried to get the two French groups together to hold a join meeting, but failed. Most of the foreign delegates came to the Marxist meeting, and they then declared it to be the founding congress of the Second International, successor to the First International (1864–1876) in which Marx had participated. In 1905, various French Socialist groups merged to form the Section française de l'international ouvrière (French Section of the Workers' International, SFIO),[16] also known as the Unified Socialist Party.

French Socialism during World War I

When the French government declared war on Germany in 1914, Jaurès was ready to organize a general strike to stop the mobilization for what he considered to be an imperialist war. However, he was shot to death by a nationalist fanatic in a Paris cafe on July 31, 1914, which Leszek Kolakowski has wryly called the last day of the nineteenth century.[17] Without the leadership of Jaurès, the SFIO ended up supporting the war. As with many other socialist parties that pledged in the Stuttgart Resolution of 1907 to oppose the coming war, when the war actually came, the ideology of nationalism proved to be a stronger attraction than socialist internationalism for many of the socialists including the French, and they rallied to the defense of their nation in time of war. The tragedy is that the French, British, German, Austrian, and other socialist parties might have stopped the war before it started, but they failed to do so. They could have saved the lives of millions of people, prevented the historic split in the socialist ranks between social democrats and Communists, and prevented World War II, which was based, at least in part, on unresolved conflicts of World War I.

The Popular Front

French Marxist-Leninists split from the SFIO to form their French Communist Party (PCF) in 1920. The Socialists had only briefly been able to form a government in 1895. Refusal to enter coalition cabinets led Marcel Déat of the SFIO's right wing to form his own nationalistic Neo-Socialist Party. Léon Blum (1872–1950), the SFIO leader since 1923 who had at one time resigned in 1933 because the parliamentary Socialists had voted for war credits, became the premier in 1936 in a Popular Front electoral alliance and coalition cabinet formed to oppose the rise of fascism.[18] Under this government, a social democratic program was enacted, and laws were passed to reduce the workweek to forty hours, to ensure paid vacations and the right to collective bargaining, and to nationalize the munitions industries and the Bank of France. Blum adopted a foreign policy of nonintervention; but at the same time, with the growing fascist threat, he led the way in increasing military spending. In mid-1937, he requested emergency powers from the parliament to deal with a financial crisis but was denied this by the conservative dominated Senate; and so he resigned from office. He returned to the premiership in March 1938 amid another crisis, but this government only lasted a month. Edouard Daladier formed a "Government of National Defense" in 1938, but the Socialists quit the Popular Front after Daladier signed the Munich Pact with Germany, Britain, and Italy.

With the outbreak of war and the defeat of France, Blum was arrested by the puppet Vichy government, controlled by Germany, and was tried for responsibility for the defeat of the French in the war. However, Blum's defense at his trial was so eloquent that the Vichy government was too embarrassed to put him to death. Instead, he was sentenced to a concentration camp. Freed by Allied forces in 1946, Blum went on to head a caretaker government from December 1946 to January 1947 when ill health forced him to resign. He died on March 30, 1950, in Jouy-en-Josas.

France after World War II

The French Fourth Republic was established in 1946 as a parliamentary system. Economic conditions at the time were troubled. The government also tried to reassert French control over their colonies, which were resisting this. Using borrowed warships, the French Navy shelled the port of Haiphong, starting the French-Indochinese War (1946–1954). By 1947 it was necessary for the United States to rescue the war-shattered economies of France and other European nations with the Marshall Plan, to prevent communists from coming to power.

Politically, France was divided between the conservatives led by Charles de Gaulle, who had been the provisional premier from 1944 to 1946, and the French Communist Party, which had eclipsed the Socialists as the leading party of the French left, largely due to their popularity garnered by their strong, activist role in the resistance to the Nazi occupation. The clash between the French left and right reached its peak in 1951, leading to a stalemate situation; and a coalition government was unable to get much of anything done. It is a wonder that this stalemate between the left and the right lasted so long—until 1958.

Meanwhile, French forces had been defeated by the Vietnamese by 1954, despite the United States paying 80 percent of its war costs toward the end of the war. Just as war in Indochina was ending, the French colony in Northern Africa revolted, and France was plunged into another colonial war. The ensuing Algerian War would take a quarter of a million lives. The failure of the French government in this war, too, was the final straw. The French government was paralyzed as six consecutive premiers had failed to end the Algerian rebellion, and the French army was left without any direction or control. The Socialists had supported the French government in the Algerian War; and joining with the Radicals (a liberal party) to form the Republican Front of 1956, they were able to elect Socialist Guy Mollet as premier the following year. Antiwar Socialists split from the SFIO in 1958 to form their own minor party, the Unified Socialist Party (PSU).

In this confusion, a conspiracy in the military, called the Secret Army Organization (OAS), seemed on the verge of making a coup. On May 16, 1958, Charles de Gaulle agreed to establish an emergency government to save the republic. De Gaulle insisted on a new constitution that would establish a presidential system with an executive elected by the people, not the parliament, with strong, independent powers. Some members of parliament opposed this and wanted to retain the parliamentary system of the Third and Fourth Republics with a premier elected by the parliament. The Fifth Republic, established under a new constitution, was a compromise, with a dual executive system being established, having a popularly elected president with strong powers and a premier elected by the parliament.

De Gaulle cautiously strengthened his control over the military command and negotiated an independence treaty with the Algerian rebels in 1962. Something of a maverick, de Gaulle was domestically conservative but followed a liberal foreign policy, early on recognizing Red China; withdrawing French forces from the North Atlantic Treaty Organization (NATO) control, although technically remaining in NATO; and criticizing the U.S.-led war in Vietnam.

The Revival of the French Socialists

Political movements often rise and fall in cycles, and so it was true of the French Socialists. The early years of the Fifth Republic had been dominated by the conservative party under changing names, but commonly called the Gaullists. By 1968 an upswing in the fortunes of the French left wing had begun what would in a few years bring the French Socialists back to power.

In May 1968 French students joined by workers went on a general strike against conservative rules and low pay that nearly toppled the Gaullist government. The SFIO and the PCF played almost no role in this strike, although the PSU and the New Left were deeply involved. Although the Gaullist government did not fall, as some of the strikers had hoped for, the strike certainly put the government on the defensive and forced its leaders to promise reforms to end the strike. Now with the strike over, the Gaullists campaigned on the threat of the strike being a communist revolution in the making and won a decisive majority in the parliamentary elections of June 1968.

This victory was a reaction to fear, but it was short-lived. With an economy troubled by serious inflation, by the next year, the French people turned away from de Gaulle and defeated a referendum to abolish the French Senate, replacing it with a new body based on functional representation, and to create new, regional institutions.

De Gaulle had staked his personal prestige on this referendum, and when it was defeated, he resigned as president on April 28, 1969. That year the Socialists changed their name from the Section française de l'international ouvrière to the Parti Socialiste (Socialist Party) and got a new, dynamic leader, Francois Mitterrand (1916–1996). The party was reorganized to try to get more of the working class to join instead of being only a middle-class party. The changes paid off. An electoral alliance called the Union of the Left, between the Socialists, the Communists, and the Radicals, was organized in

1973 and did quite well at the polls. The Socialists now eclipsed the Communists, who had earlier surpassed them as the main party of the French left; and this in turn led the Communists to quit the Union of the Left in 1978.

In 1981 the Socialists won a smashing victory in the parliamentary elections. Then Gaullist Georges Pompidou, who had succeeded de Gaulle as president in 1969, suddenly died in office in 1974. The Gaullists at the time had no strong candidate of their own to run against a powerful challenge by Mitterrand. With Gaullist support, the rightist Independent Republican candidate Valéry Giscard d'Estaing won the presidency in a close election in 1974. Giscard's failure to stimulate the weak French economy and his autocratic manner brought twenty-three years of conservative rule to an end with the election of Mitterrand as president in 1981 amid street celebrations.

The French Socialists in Office

The Socialist program included the nationalization of all the banks and many key industries. Money was pumped in to beef up the social welfare system. Local governments were strengthened by decentralizing many functions formerly handled by the central government in Paris. Capital punishment was abolished, and the workweek was reduced in hours.

The six main industries that were nationalized—CGE, Rhone-Poulenc, Thomson, Saint-Gabain, Pechiney, and Bull—were saved from probable bankruptcy by nationalization, with the government pumping new funds into them for modernization, turning them around into again profitable companies. At first, the Socialists tried government spending to create jobs, but this only resulted in people buying mostly foreign goods and in a large trade deficit, while the French economy remained in recession.

By the early 1980s, the Mitterrand government was abandoning socialist orthodoxy and adopting policies of austerity and the German model of low inflation and high interest rates. In the name of modernization, thousands of workers were laid off. The gamble was that once French industry was returned to health, these workers would be rehired. Unfortunately, unemployment remained high. The policy of fiscal austerity was highly unpopular, and large protests against it erupted. The government of Socialist premier Pierre Mauroy resigned and was replaced by that of fellow Socialist Laurent Fabius on July 17, 1984.

The "French Watergate Scandal" broke on July 10, 1985, when the *Rainbow Warrior*, a ship of the antinuclear Greenpeace organization, in the

Pacific to protest French underwater nuclear tests, was sunk off the coast of New Zealand by an explosion that killed one of the crew. New Zealand police arrested two Frenchmen for the bombing, who turned out to be officers in the General Direction of External Security (DGSE), France's foreign intelligence service (formerly the SDECE). The French government finally admitted that the DGSE ordered the bombing; and the head of the DGSE, Admiral Pierre Lacoste, was fired, and the Defense minister, Charles Hernu, resigned.

On March 16, 1986, the conservatives won a narrow majority in the National Assembly elections; and for the first time in the history of the Fifth Republic, different parties controlled the presidency and the parliament—what the French call "cohabitation." Gaullist leader Jacques Chirac became premier on March 20, 1986, while Socialist Mitterrand remained as president. The reasons for the Socialist loss were high unemployment, despite some improvement in the economy, and government mismanagement, particularly in foreign affairs.

The conservative government pursued the privatization of some of the industries nationalized under the preceding socialist government at this time. Chirac's rule provoked massive protests and strikes. On November 27, 1986, leftist and rightist students clashed in Paris in major street battles over a new government plan by Education minister Alain Devaquet to raise university fees and limit enrollment. On December 6, 1986, French police beat up and killed Malik Oussekine, a twenty-two-year-old law student, touching off protests against police brutality and racism, with the protesters demanding the resignation of Premier Chirac and Interior minister Charles Pasqua. Then on December 14 of that year, a nationwide rail strike began. On January 7, 1987, government electrical and Parisian subway workers joined the strike, blacking out Paris and threatening to bring down Chirac's government.

In the presidential election on May 8, 1988, Mitterrand was reelected on the second ballot, beating Chirac by a ratio of 54 to 40. Two days later, with the resignation of Chirac as premier, Mitterrand named Socialist Michel Rocard as Chirac's replacement, heading a minority government. Rocard at this time called himself a "free enterprise socialist," indicating a break with the recent Socialist past when they had called for a coming rupture with capitalism when they first came to power in 1981.

Mitterrand was not going to press for renationalizing the industries that the Chirac government had privatized. At the most, he promised to bring back higher taxes on the wealthy. Why this retreat from nationalization? In part, because it was an unsustainable form of socialism. State socialism, unlike producers' cooperatives favored by the cooperative movement—Ferdinand

Lassalle and Louis Blanc before him—can only last as long as the Socialists remain in power. The Marxist-Leninist solution was to not permit free elections so that the communists could not be voted out of power. Even this would not work forever: we have seen the fall of the Soviet Union and its allied Communist states in Eastern Europe. In democratic countries, there is virtually no way to prevent the conservatives from sometimes winning elections, and when they do, they are sure to dismantle state ownership as a matter of course. In this particular case in France in the late 1980s, the Gaullists, after privatizing the industries that had been previously nationalized by the Socialists, had enough power in the minority government to block any return to nationalization. Even the Socialists had lost their taste for more nationalizations. It had cost a great deal of money and did not buy popular support, as it turned out. Mitterrand's government had laid off thousands of people to modernize nationalized industries; and when they were not rehired by a resurgent economy, many people turned against nationalization and the Socialists. These layoffs might have been prevented if the Socialists had listened to the trade union most closely associated with them, the Confédération française démocratique du travail (the French Democratic Confederation of Labor, CFDT). The CFDT had argued for *autogestion*— the French term for workers' self-management. If the workers were given a say in the management of these industries, very likely they would have not engaged in the mass layoffs and would have sought another method of improving industrial performance. The Socialists had discussed this idea and had made promises to support autogestion before they came to power; but once they had arrived, they feared workers' control would mean power to the Communists who dominated the Confédération générale du travail (General Confederation of Labor, CGT), France's largest trade union organization. Additionally, perhaps the bureaucrats in government feared loss of control to any workers, Communist or not.

Rocard had promised a moderate government, doing little more than raising the minimum wage. On May 15, 1991, he was sacked by Mitterrand in an attempt to restore the Socialists' sagging popularity and was replaced by Edith Cresson, France's first female premier. She advocated a policy of protectionism as a way to halt the decline of French industry. Her remarks calling a quarter of Englishmen homosexuals and the Japanese "ants" made her highly unpopular. On April 4, 1992, Mitterrand dismissed her because of the persistence of high unemployment and of Socialist losses in local elections in France. She was replaced as premier by Pierre Bérégovoy, the former Finance minister noted for his tight money policies.

On March 21, 1993, the French Socialists suffered huge losses in the parliamentary elections because of high unemployment and because of scandals in which the premier was accused of taking interest-free loans from someone linked to an insider trading and the Health minister was accused of taking bribes. The conservatives won 80 percent of the seats in the National Assembly; and on March 29, Mitterrand was forced to name a former Gaullist Finance minister, Edouard Balladur, as the new premier. The Union for the Republic—the conservative coalition of the Gaullist party known formally as the Rassemblement pour la République (Rally for the Republic, RPR) and its partner, the Union pour la démocratie française (Union for French Democracy, UDF)—captured 461 out of the 577 seats in the National Assembly.

Together with other rightists, the conservatives controlled up to 484 seats—some 84 percent of the lower house. Meanwhile, the Socialists only won a mere 54 seats, just 9 percent; and together with 16 other leftist members of parliament, the left could command only 12 percent of the parliamentary seats. Balladur shortly announced plans to privatize twenty-one state-owned firms, including Renault, Air France, Bull the computer maker, electronics manufacturer Thomson, Aeropatiale in aerospace, Rhone-Poulenc in chemicals, and Elf Aquitaine in oil. Balladur said that this would breathe new vigor into France's sagging economy. At the same time, president Mitterrand vowed to protect France's "social achievements" and worried that "savage capitalism" would throw tens of thousands of people out of work from denationalized companies as new, private owners sought to slash operating expenses. France's unemployment rate reached a postwar record in 1993—three million out of work, or 11 percent of the workforce. Only rail and telecommunications were to be left as state-owned enterprises, but the eventual change in the French economy would be the greatest since the Industrial Revolution. On March 31, 1994, thousands of French students protested plans to cut minimum wages for youth, the protests ending in violence. These protests went on for a month and forced premier Balladur to repeal these cuts the day before the protests began.

By 1995 Mitterrand was dying of cancer; but despite calls to quit early, he remained as president until he finished his term of office. On April 23, 1995, the Socialist presidential candidate Lionel Jospin, given little chance to win, surprised the voters by coming out first in the presidential, first-round elections against the Rally for the Republic (RPR, Gaullist) candidate Jacques Chirac. Coming in third was another RPR candidate, Premier Balladur, followed in fourth place by Jean-Marie Le Pen of the neofascist National Front. Jospin called for the introduction of a proportional representation system, which would help minority and women candidates but would also help the National Front who had been demanding this for the parliamentary elections.

On May 7, 1995, Chirac won the presidency, beating Jospin by about 5 percent of the vote. Gaullist Alain Juppe was elected premier. The economy continued to stagnate, and the government planned steep cuts in spending, provoking strikes by public employee unions. Failing to lower unemployment, the Gaullists lost the second-round parliamentary election of June 1, 1997. A Socialist-Communist coalition won a majority in the National Assembly. Jospin then replaced Juppe, who resigned, as premier. The Socialist and other splinter parties captured over 11 million votes and jumped from 75 seats in the National Assembly to 273 seats. The conservative coalition of the RPR and UDF gained 249 seats, the Communists 38 seats, the Greens 8 seats, the National Front a single seat, and other rightists 8 seats. On March 31, 1998, the National Assembly passed a Socialist-backed bill that would cut the work week in France from 39 hours to 35 hours as a way to reduce unemployment, then above 12 percent in the nation. It was the largest such plan since the Popular Front government of 1936 had cut the workweek to 40 hours and introduced paid vacations.

SWEDEN

Organized in 1889, the Swedish Social Democratic Labor Party (SAP) has enjoyed the longest period in power of any democratic socialist party.[19] Hjalmar Branting (1860–1925) was the Swedish Social Democrats' only member of parliament from 1897 to 1902. He was elected party leader in 1907. During World War I, he and the Social Democrats followed a policy of neutrality and largely through their efforts kept Sweden out of the war, despite strong pressure to join Germany and the Central Powers against the Allies. Branting and his fellow Social Democrats also supported the peaceful separation of Norway from Sweden. Initially opposed to joining a coalition cabinet, the Swedish Social Democrats reversed this decision during the crisis of World War I, leading to a split in the party in 1917 and the left wing leaving to form their own party. Yet despite this split, the Social Democrats emerged as the strongest party in Sweden in the elections of that year and joined the cabinet for the first time in 1918 as the minority party in coalition with the Liberals, with Branting becoming the minister of Finance, although resigning a few months later. With the rising power of the Social Democrats, one of the most remarkable increases in the history of democratic socialism, Branting was able to become prime minister in 1920, in 1921 to 1923, and again in 1924 to 1925 in a series of socialist-led governments.

Branting was succeeded as prime minister by Richard J. Sandler (1884–

1964), the former Finance minister, who remained in power until 1926. The Social Democrats came back to power in 1932 with Per Albin Hansson (1885–1946) as prime minister. The rising unemployment of the 1930s was dealt with by the Hansson government by a policy of deficit spending, including a large public works program.[20] Hansson resigned in 1936 when the Swedish parliament refused to pass legislation to strengthen the old-age insurance system and to raise pensions with cost-of-living adjustments. The Social Democrats increased their seats in the parliament in the 1936 election, and again Hansson was asked to form a government. He continued to serve as prime minister in the wartime coalition cabinet created in 1939. The Swedish government held to the policy of neutrality but increased military spending.

Following Hansson's death in 1946, SAP leader Tage Erlander (1901–1985) succeeded as prime minister until his retirement in 1969. He was in turn succeeded by Olof Palme (1927–1986), the former Education minister. After forty-four years in office, the Social Democrats finally lost in the 1976 election to a coalition of liberal, conservative, and center parties. The new government headed by prime minister Thorbjörn Fälldin (1926–) began a policy of austerity measures designed to control inflation and to encourage the sale of Swedish goods abroad. He resigned in 1978 over the growing popular resistance to nuclear power in the country. The following year, he returned to head a minority liberal government.

It was during this period that the idea of wage-earner funds was born. The idea came originally not from the Social Democratic Labor Party, but from the Swedish Trade Union Confederation (LO).[21] The Meidner Plan, as it was initially called, was developed by the LO's chief economist in the early 1970s, Rudolf Meidner. He proposed that a tax would be imposed on the excess profits of Swedish companies, with the revenues being used to buy shares in the companies collectively on behalf of the workers. Under this plan, Swedish workers would come to eventually control enough shares to take over their companies in twenty to seventy-five years, depending on the level of which the tax on excess profits was set. Thus, an evolutionary form of socialism with greater equality in income would be introduced over a period of time.

Swedish industry reacted strongly to these proposals, denouncing it as "pure and unadulterated socialism." The employers' federation poured millions of kronor into the antifunds campaign, which undoubtedly helped contribute to the Social Democrats' defeat in 1976.

The Meidner Plan was accepted in a modified form by the LO in 1976 and by the SAP at its congress in 1978. However, the Social Democrats gave it only lukewarm support and presented no proposals to the Swedish voters on how to implement the wage-earner funds in the 1979 election. Again, the employers' campaign against the wage-earner funds, as they were now being called, contributed to the Social Democrats' defeat that year.

The Social Democrats did not adopt any firm proposals on the wage-earner funds until 1981, but by then, the scheme was significantly different from the original plan proposed by Meidner. The tax on excess profits would not be paid into regional funds belonging to all the workers in a region. These funds would be invested in companies, not necessarily the ones paying the tax, and would not give workers control over their own companies at any time in the future. The funds would be controlled by regional boards initially appointed by the government, although eventually they would be elected. When a board bought shares in a company, the workers in that company would have half voting rights if they wanted them, but only up to 20 percent.

The policies of the minority liberal government provoked a ten-day general strike in Sweden in May 1980. The government barely survived a vote of no confidence that October by just one vote. Another strike the following May by white-collar workers caused the government to split, and a general strike was barely averted.

As the 1982 election approached, the Social Democrats found that the wage-earner funds were controversial enough that it was badly hurting them in the polls. They had a choice: either stick to their plan to promote this form of evolutionary socialism with the hope of educating the voters into eventually accepting it, even if it meant losing this election; or else moderate the wage-earner plan, which might allow them to win the next election and get back into power where, even if they could not directly promote socialism, at least they could do some good. The Swedish Social Democrats chose this latter course. Olof Palme announced three limitations on the wage-earner funds: (1) the funds would collect money only until 1980; (2) a maximum of 40 percent of any company's stock could be held by the wage-earner funds, and (3) the funds would be expected to return a yield of 3 percent on investments. This took the bite out of the employers' campaign against the funds; and so, in the parliamentary elections of 1982, the Social Democrats returned to power with Olof Palme as prime minister. The wage-earner funds formally came into being on January 1, 1984.

Besides the wage-earner plan, accomplishments of the Swedish Social Democrats in their long tenure in office include one of the most comprehensive social welfare systems yet to be created. Sweden enjoys one of the highest standards of living in the world. More than 80 percent of Swedish industry is privately owned, but Sweden also has a large cooperative sector—the "middle way" to socialism, as it has been called. The coordinating agency of these cooperatives founded in 1899 is the Ko-operativa Forbundet (KF).[22] Highly successful in both distribution and manufacturing, the KF consumers' and producers' cooperatives account for nearly a quarter of the total retail trade and the food trade. Luma, a lightbulb producer, became the first cooperatively owned international factory and the largest enterprise in all of Scandinavia.

Sweden also has a large housing cooperative movement. Two national housing associations are the National Association of Tenants' Savings and Building Societies (HSB) and the Cooperative Building Organization of the Swedish Trade Unions (SR). Together, they assisted in the construction of over a quarter of the new homes in Sweden. The agricultural cooperative movement is also quite large in Sweden, with four-fifths of the sales of all agricultural imports.

The Social Democrats won again in 1985, but tragedy struck on February 28, 1986, with the assassination of Palme as he walked down a street in Stockholm. Palme was the first European head of government to be assassinated in office in forty-seven years. Succeeding Palme as prime minister was Social Democrat Ingvar Carlsson (1934–), and the Social Democrats were retained in power in the 1988 election. However, Carlsson resigned in 1990 after the parliament refused to go along with his demand for a temporary wage, price, and rent freeze. Later forming a new government, Carlsson was able to get parliament to pass a modified austerity plan, which allowed limited wage increases. The drift to the political center with these demands backfired on the Social Democrats. Many voters who had voted in the past for them were alienated by this retreat to the right and did not vote, while those who had never voted for them in the past continued to do so. Thus the Social Democrats went down to defeat in the 1991 elections. A nonsocialist coalition government led by Carl Bildt (1949–) of the Moderate Party was formed, which slashed public jobs. Combined with layoffs from the private sector, unemployment was pushed up to 14 percent, leading to an electoral victory for the Social Democrats in September 1994 with Ingvar Carlsson returning as prime minister. In 1995 Mona Sahlin (1957–), the deputy prime minister, was elected as the new leader of the Swedish Social Democrats, and Carlsson announced he would resign as prime minister in March 1996, paving the way for Sahlin to become Sweden's first woman prime minister.

Later that month, she was succeeded by Social Democrat Goeran Persson, a fiscal conservative who will have to find a way to get Sweden's high public debt down, while retaining its social welfare system and dealing with high unemployment.

DENMARK

Danish socialism has been said to have begun on May 21, 1872, with the Danish Section of the First International calling a meeting on the Copenhagen Commons to support striking bricklayers.[23] When the meeting was broken up by the police, the organizers were arrested, and the Chief of Police assured the minister of Justice that socialism had been stamped out in Denmark. However, in 1876, a conference of trade unionists and socialists resulted in an organization that united union organizing with political action. Then on February 12, 1878, the Danish Social Democratic Party was born. The party grew rapidly, building both membership and representation in the Danish parliament. Prior to World War I, the Social Democrats refused to join coalition cabinets on principle; but by 1916 the international situation was so grave that their party leader, Thorvald Stauning (1873–1942), did agree to become a minister without Portfolio, and later the minister of Labor.

The Danish Social Democrats increased their representation in the parliament after the war; and in the 1924 election, following an economic depression, they were able to form a cabinet of their own members with Stauning as prime minister. Out again in 1926, they were defeated by a coalition of nonsocialists led by the Liberals. Yet the Social Democrats made a comeback in 1929 after bickering between the nonsocialist parties over industrial and military policies led to the resignation of the cabinet. Again the Social Democrats were able to form a cabinet, which included three Radical ministers, with Stauning returning as prime minister. The Social Democrats remained in power until the Nazi invasion in April 1940.

In 1935 the left-wing parties were able to capture a majority of the upper house of the Danish parliament, and for the first time they controlled both houses. The Social Democrats and the Radicals were then in a position to pass a long list of social democratic measures, including comprehensive social welfare and insurance legislation and public ownership of some industries.

Denmark had tried to stay neutral in the days prior to World War II, even signing a nonaggression pact with Germany in May 1939, but to no avail. Invaded and occupied by Germany, the Germans allowed the Danish government to remain in place but stripped it of most of its authority. The leaders of Danish political parties issued a joint statement on July 3, 1940, pledging to abandon all points of disagreement to work for the common cause of Danish independence.

There were several demonstrations against the occupation, all brutally broken up by the Germans with many arrests. Prime Minister Stauning died in office in May 1942. For a few months, his successor, Vilhelm Buhl, was prime minister, but the Germans insisted that the collaborationist foreign minister Erik Scanvenius, whom they had forced on the Stauning government, become the new prime minister on November 8, 1942, with a shakeup in the cabinet.

During the occupation, the Social Democrats did their best to resist, supporting an underground press and a campaign of sabotage. The Nazis responded by declaring martial law and arresting thousands. Riots were crushed, and many Danes, including a number of ministers in the cabinet that had resigned, fled the country.

After the war, the Social Democrats resumed office in Denmark. In 1946 after winning another election, the liberal leader Knud Kristensen resigned. He had replaced a short-lived government headed by Vilhelm Buhl upon liberation as prime minister. The Social Democrat Hans Christian Hedtoft (1903–1955) became the new prime minister.[24] His government was in office until 1950 and again from 1953 to 1955 when he died in office. In 1951 and 1952, there had been a liberal and conservative coalition headed by Erik Erikson. Succeeding Hedtoft in 1955 was Social Democrat H. C. Hansen (1906–1960). Under his government, the old-age pension system was strengthened, and agricultural price supports were enacted.

Hansen also died in office and was succeeded by Viggo Kampmann (1910–1976) in 1960. The voting age was lowered from twenty-three to twenty-one, and Denmark sought entry into the Common Market.

The 1964 election brought a new, all-Social Democratic minority government to power under Jens Otto Krag (1914–1978). Protests against rising prices and higher taxes brought four decades of Social Democratic dominance in Denmark to an end in the 1968 election. Hilmar Baunsgaard (1920–), the leader of the Radical Liberal Party, formed a nonsocialist coalition government that year, which lasted until 1971 when Krag returned to office as the head of a Social Democratic government.

Denmark's entry into the Common Market was approved in 1972, and Krag resigned shortly thereafter, being replaced as Social Democratic Party leader and prime minister by Anker Jørgensen (1922–). However, the Social Democrats suffered losses in the 1973 election, and the Liberal Poul Hartling (1914–) formed a minority government. Jørgensen was to return to office as prime minister at the head of a minority Social Democratic government in 1975. Greenland was granted home rule in 1979. In 1982, a Conservative, Poul Schlüter (1929–) formed a center-right government and remained in office in the 1984, 1987, 1988, and 1990 elections.

NORWAY

The Norwegian Labor Party (originally called the Social Democratic Party) was for many years considered to be one of the most left-wing of socialist parties, and for a time it worked closely with the communist Third International.[25]

The party was founded in Christiana in 1887. At first, the Norwegian socialists worked to form labor unions, but after 1899 they left that work to the unionists themselves and instead concentrated exclusively in the political arena. The Norwegian socialists first ran candidates in 1894; and by 1903 they had won their first seats in parliament, succeeding in electing four members. In 1905, Norway broke from Sweden, and the party lost its seats; but the following year it increased its number to ten and thereafter continued to grow.

During World War I, the party held to the antiwar position that most other socialist parties had abandoned and participated in the antiwar Zimmerwald Conference in 1915. The party in 1919 voted to affiliate with the communist Third International; and in 1921, its executive voted to accept the latter's twenty-one points of affiliation.

A split in the party, with moderates quitting to form their own Norwegian Social Democratic Labor Party, occurred at this time (1921). However, the controversy would not die down, and the Norwegian Labor Party began expelling individual communists for alleged violation of party rules, without consulting the executive of the Third International in Moscow. The latter took the position that no party member could be expelled without its consent. A majority of the Norwegian Labor Party members denounced this in the party congress the following year, and the minority formed the Norwegian Communist Party.

In 1927 the split-away Norwegian Social Democratic Labor Party reunited with the Labor Party; and in January 1928 this united party, as the nation's largest, for the first time was able to form an all-socialist government headed by Christian Hornsrud.

The socialists introduced a bill calling for the redistribution of wealth. The strong reaction to this bill by the nonsocialist parties caused the socialist government to fall; and for the next several years, the Labor Party was in opposition. However, in 1932 it was again called to form a cabinet, this time in coalition with the Agrarian Party. Labor's Johan Nygarrdsvold (1879–1952), a former railroad worker in the United States, was elected premier.

The Labor government launched an extensive program of public works projects, which reduced unemployment below the 1931 level, and passed a series of social security and unemployment compensation acts. The Labor government lasted until the outbreak of World War II, at which time the country was invaded by the Germans. The Nazis set up a puppet regime under Vidkum Quisling (1887–1945); but in 1940 many of the Labor government members formed an "official Norwegian government" in exile headquartered in London. So hated was the puppet government that *quisling* became a noun denoting a traitor.

Norwegian Labor leaders refused to cooperate with the German commissioner Josef Terboven (1898–1945). Instead, the Resistance movement, in which Labor party members were prominent, cooperated closely with the government-in-exile to sabotage and to spy on the Nazi invaders. With the liberation of Norway in 1945, Terboven and other German collaborators committed suicide, and Quisling and twenty-five others were tried and executed for treason.

In the election of 1945 the Labor Party again won, and the transition government headed by Nygaardvold was replaced by that of Einar Gerhardsen (1897–1987), the former General Secretary of the party, who, on his return from a German concentration camp, was elected party chairman.[26]

Following Gerhardsen was Labor premier Oscar Torp (1893–1958) in 1951, with Gerhardsen returning as premier in 1953. The parliamentary elections of 1961 failed for the first time since World War II to produce a Labor majority, although Gerhardsen remained as premier. A left-wing Socialist Party made up of dissenting Labor Party members had drained enough votes away from Labor to prevent it from capturing a majority. This new party adopted a more radical economic agenda and called for Norway to pull out of the North Atlantic Treaty Organization (NATO), which it had joined in 1949.

In 1963 the Socialists voted to join others in voting no confidence in the parliament for the Labor government, after the latter was severely criticized for a fatal accident in the state-owned King Coal Company. Gerhardsen remained as premier in a new cabinet; but in 1965, Labor suffered a defeat at the polls, and Center Party leader Per Borten (1913–) formed a government of nonsocialist parties.

However, Norway's policies did not dramatically change. Norway applied for membership in the European Community in 1970. In 1971 Labor returned to power in a minority government headed by Trygve Bratteli (1910–1984). The Norwegian voters in 1972 failed to approve a referendum on their country joining the European Community. The Bratteli government resigned that year, and a centrist coalition government headed by Lars Korvald (1916–) of the Christian People's Party was formed. Bratteli returned as the head of a minority government in 1973, and although he resigned in 1976, Labor remained in power until 1981, at which time Gro Harlem Brundtland (1939–) of Labor became Norway's first female premier.

By September of 1976 the nonsocialist parties formed a majority government under Kare Willoch (1928–) of the Conservative Party. He was reelected in 1983 and 1985. With dropping oil prices in 1985 and 1986 costing Norway revenues from its North Sea oil and gas wells that were exploited by a state-owned company in the 1970s, Willoch was forced to call for higher gasoline taxes and lost a vote of no confidence on this in 1986. He was succeeded as premier by a minority government headed by Labor's Brundtland. She resigned with the inconclusive elections of 1989, and Jan Syse (1930–) of the Conservative Party formed a minority government; but this center-right coalition collapsed in 1990 over disagreements on economic policies. Brundtland was again asked to form a new minority Labor government in 1990 by King Olaf V (1903–1991), who died the following year. Olaf was succeeded by his son Harald V (1937–) as king.

FINLAND, RUSSIA, AND THE FORMER SOVIET REPUBLICS

The Finnish social democratic movement began in 1895 with the founding of the Työmies (Worker). By 1898 a local labor party was organized in Helsingfors; and the following year, at a trade union convention, the Finnish Labor Party was founded.[27] At first a reformist party, it adopted a specifically socialist platform in 1903 and changed its name to the Social Democratic Party of Finland. They played an active role in the general strike in 1905 against oppressive Russian control. In 1906 women's suffrage was granted, and a one-house parliament or Diet was created. The Social Democrats successfully elected a number of representatives and offered a number of social and labor legislative bills for consideration. The Czar, however, refused to agree to most of this legislation, and in 1911 the Russian Duma transferred most of the decision-making powers from the Finnish Diet to itself. All progressive legislation was halted, workers' organizations were suppressed, and heavy duties were placed on Finland.

With the outbreak of World War I, the Czar sought to dissolve the Finnish regiments and tried to draft them to serve in the interior of Russia. This violated the Finnish Constitutional ban on the use of its army outside Finnish borders, provoked a strike by the troops, and led to thousands of young men refusing to appear at enlistment centers, many of them fleeing to America. Although the strike itself was successful, Czar Nicholas II (1868–1918) soon retaliated with ever more repressive measures. Despite this oppression, the Finnish Social Democrats increased in power; and by 1916 they had a majority in the parliament—the very first socialist or labor party, worldwide, to do so.

With the outbreak of the Russian Revolution in 1917 and the removal of reactionary Russian officials from the Finnish Diet, a new government was created in which the Social Democrats had half of the cabinet posts, and Finland declared its independence from Russia on December 6, 1917. The newly formed Bolshevik government had no power to stop this and no choice in granting recognition. Finnish radicals in 1918 formed Red Guard units and launched a revolution reacting to government orders to expel all Russian troops; conservative White Guards units counterattacked. In January 28, 1918, the Red revolution spread across the country, with much death and destruction being unleashed. A workers' revolutionary government was proclaimed in Helsingfors, and state buildings were seized. The Social Democrats, who had opposed the use of violence, felt, nevertheless, that they had to support this government; but it proved to be short-lived. With the conservative government having fled to Vassa, the White Guards under General Carl G. Mannerheim (1867–1951), with the assistance of German troops, attacked and captured Helsinki, instigating a wave of terror against all Red sympathizers. By April 1918 the German Army occupied Helsingfors, causing the Red government to flee, and soon the revolution was over. The Diet adopted a new republican constitution in July 1919, and the Finnish Communist Party, for a time, was dissolved.

The Social Democrats bounced back and were able to form a government in 1926 with Vaino Tanner as premier. Lasting until 1929, this minority socialist government passed a number of pieces of social reform legislation, which included pension and health insurance laws, reduced duties on imported foods, and a liberal amnesty law.

In November 1929 the Communists had organized an antireligious campaign and held a demonstration at Lapua, a stronghold of Lutheranism. This provoked a vigilante movement called "the Lapuans" that demanded the suppression of the Communists as well as the Social Democrats. Together with another reactionary force, the Lock movement, the Lapuans marched on Helsingfors. Before they reached the capital, the Finnish parliament passed legislation permitting the suppression of Communist newspapers, and replaced the Agrarian-led coalition government by a more inclusive government that met with the Lapuans when they reached Helsingfors and agreed to their demands to deprive the Communists of their seats in parliament.

When new elections were called, the Communist and Social Democratic leaders were kidnapped, and a terror campaign was waged against all leftists. The result was that sixty-six Social Democrats were elected and a new, sweeping, anti-Communist law was passed.

The Social Democrats remained in opposition until 1937 when they joined the cabinet, Tanner becoming the minister of finance, and after the 1939 election the minister of foreign affairs, and still later, the minister of food supplies.

Finland had signed a nonaggression pact with the Soviet Union in 1932. At the outbreak of World War II, Finland declared its neutrality: nevertheless, they were attacked by the Soviets on November 30, 1939, after they had refused to cede certain areas of their territory that the Soviets wanted for security on the eastern border, in trade for certain parts of Soviet Karelia. The Finns fought back valiantly in the Russo-Finnish War, but after some initial successes, they were overcome by superior Soviet forces.

When the Germans attacked the Soviet Union in June 1941, again the Finns declared their neutrality, only to find themselves again thrust into war. Sizable German forces crossed into northern Finland, leading the Soviets to attack Finnish cities. Finland declared war on the Soviet Union, and Great Britain declared war on Finland, even though the Finns insisted that they were not the allies of the Germans, but merely co-belligerents. After a long standstill, Finland signed an armistice in 1944 and a peace treaty with the Soviets in 1947. As a result of this treaty, the Finnish Communist Party was again legalized.

The relationship of a more powerful country imposing its will on a weaker nation (as in the case of the Soviet Union over Finland) became known as "Finlandization." Finland was forced to display a certain sensitivity to Soviet interests to assuage their fears, and this policy became known as the "Paasikivi Line" and later the Paasikivi-Kekkonen Line, for Finnish president Juho K. Paasikivi and his successor Urho K. Kekkonen (1900–1986), who broadened it. Finland had been forced to cede the Petsamo area to the Soviets and to lease them the Porkkala Peninsula in 1944 in return for $300 million in reparations paid off fully by 1952 in the form of commodities. The Soviet returned the Porkkala Peninsula to Finland in 1955, but Finland had to agree to a policy of strict international neutrality and friendly relations with the Soviet Union in return for their continued, recognized independence. None of the Finnish political parties in the postwar years had had a majority in the parliament, leading to a series of coalition governments.

The Social Democratic premier Mauno Pekkala (1890–1952) led such a coalition cabinet from 1946 to 1948, followed by the minority socialist government led by August Fagerholm from 1948 to 1958, when he was forced to resign partly as a result of Soviet opposition and the threat of the loss of Soviet trade.[28] The Social Democrats remained out of the cabinet until 1966 when their leader, Raphael Passio, was asked to form a government in coalition with the Communists and the Agrarian Center Party. Attempts by the Soviets to interfere with the Finnish elections usually had a negative effect on Finnish Communist fortunes, and the latter's support declined in the 1980s. Since 1987 Finland has had its first conservative-led governments since World War II, but in 1995 the Social Democrats scored their biggest electoral victory in fifty years.

The post–Soviet Union Russian Communist Party today pledges its support for multiparty democracy and may be moving in a social democratic direction. Azerbaijan, Estonia, Georgia, Latvia, and Lithuania all have social democratic parties today.

BELGIUM AND LUXEMBOURG

The Belgian Labor Party was founded in Brussels on April 15, 1885, and adopted a socialist platform.[29] Uniting the trade unions, the cooperative societies, and other progressive groups, the party campaigned for universal suffrage and called for general strikes in 1893, 1902, and 1912 on behalf of this cause. The party also worked for social reform and labor legislation. With the outbreak of World War I, the Belgian Labor Party, as did most other European socialist parties, supported their government in the war. The Belgian socialists even entered a coalition, prowar government. After the war, the Belgian government finally agreed to grant suffrage to men age twenty-one years and older, although they still denied women the right to vote. In the election of 1919, the Belgian Labor Party captured 36 percent of the vote and increased their representation in the parliament from thirty-four seats to seventy—enough to deprive the Catholic Party the majority that they had held since 1884. The Catholic Party now formed a cabinet containing Labor members. Labor used this opportunity to demand and to have passed such reform legislation as a graduated income tax, inheritance taxes, old-age pensions, the eight-hour workday, and the repeal of a law that prohibited picketing.

The Labor Party was in and out of coalition governments until 1936, when it won the highest number of seats in the parliament, and party leader Émile Vandervelde (1866–1938) was asked then to form a government. The king, however, insisted on a coalition National Union cabinet consisting of members of the left, right, and center parties, as had existed the previous year under Paul Van Zeeland (b. 1893). Vandervelde found that he was unable to organize such a cabinet, and so Van Zeeland again formed a National Union cabinet.

In the 1930s the Belgian Labor Party adopted a "plane of economic transformation," developed by Henri De Man (1871–1947), that called for the nationalization of the banks and key Belgian industries. The stress was on winning people to socialism and away from fascism.

In 1938 Henri-Paul Spaak (b. 1899) of the Labor Party became the premier, retaining his position as foreign minister in the previous government. This coalition government was reshuffled in 1939 and 1940. With the invasion of Belgium by Germany in 1940, Spaak and most of the other Labor leaders fled the country and formed a government-in-exile in London. During the course of the next several years, Labor Party and trade unionists waged a campaign of sabotage against their Nazi occupiers.

With the end of World War II and the return of the Belgian government-in-exile, Spaak once again became foreign minister in a coalition cabinet headed by one of the famed resistance leaders, Achille Van Acker (b. 1898), a socialist.[30] In August 1945 Van Acker was replaced as premier by the socialist Burgomaster of Antwerp, Camille Huysmans (1871–1968), who in turn was replaced in a coalition government headed once again by Spaak in 1947 and lasting until 1949.

The socialists lost three seats in the parliamentary elections of 1949, coming in second to the Social Christians, the latter forming a coalition government with the Liberals. Out of office, the socialists vigorously opposed the return of King Leopold III in 1950, and he decided to transfer his powers to his son, Prince Baudouin.

In the 1954 election, Labor increased its number of parliamentary seats to 86, up from 77 in 1950, and subsequently formed a coalition cabinet with the Liberals, with Van Acker as premier and Spaak as foreign minister. Initiatives were take under this government to expand social spending in education, employment, housing, and pensions. Steps were also undertaken to reduce the term of compulsory military service from twenty-one to eighteen months and to shorten the workweek. Reduction of state subsidies to Roman Catholic parochial schools and greater restrictions on how those funds were to be spent angered the Roman Catholic bishops. Launching a campaign against the socialists in 1955, the bishops were able to hurt the Labor Party at the polls, with a loss of two seats in parliament, forcing Van Acker to resign and the socialists to again go into opposition to the government.

In 1960 the Congo was granted independence from Belgium, and Labor was again invited to join a coalition government with the Christian Socialists in 1961, with Spaak serving as deputy premier and foreign minister. The long-standing ethnic conflicts between the Flemings and the Walloons of Belgium resulted in frequent riots.

A 1963 law established three official languages: Flemish in the North, French in the South, and German along the eastern border of Belgium. In 1966, the socialists quit the coalition government over the insistence of the Social Christians that fees should be charged at seven medical clinics run by socialist-affiliated mutual insurance associations. The government collapsed in 1969 due to continuing clashes between Flemings and Walloons; Christian Socialist leader Gaston Eyskens (1905–1988) formed a new coalition government with the socialists, which lasted until 1972. The socialists were briefly leading a three-party coalition, but it fell in 1974.

Since then, the Christian Socialists have formed a succession of coalition governments, usually under the leadership of Wilfred Bartens, and since 1991 under Jean-Luc Dehaene (1940–). There is a French and a Flemish Socialist Party in Belgium today.

The Grand Duchy of Luxembourg has a constitutional monarchy with three major political parties. They are the Christian Social Party, the Socialist Workers' Party, and the Democratic Party. In 1974 the Socialists and the Democrats won enough seats in the unicameral chamber of deputies to form a Democratic-Socialist coalition government with Gaston Thorn (1928–), a Democrat, as prime minister, which lasted until 1979. The Socialist Workers' Party was to return to power in a coalition government, this time with the Christian Socialists in June 1984 under prime minister Jacques Santer (1937–), a Christian Socialist. In 1995 Jean-Claude Juncker of the same party became prime minister in coalition with the Socialist Workers. Luxembourg has a modest volunteer army and enjoys one of the highest standards of living in the world.

THE NETHERLANDS

The Dutch Social Democratic Union was formed in 1878 under the leadership of Romela Nieuwenhuis (1846–1919), who was elected to the States General the following year.[31] After receiving a hostile reaction in the Dutch parliament, he became discouraged of the possibilities for socialism to be advanced by parliamentary means and soon quit to join with the anarchists. By 1894, the anarchists had broken away from the socialists. That year the Social Democratic Labor Party was formed, led by such leaders as Pieter J.

Troelstra (1860–1930). This party steadily grew in the years before World War I and by 1913 had been invited to join a coalition government. At a party congress, the membership voted down this proposal on the grounds that the socialist movement was diametrically opposed to capitalism and, thus, could not in good faith join a capitalist government. The Dutch socialists continued to fight for universal suffrage and old-age pensions and for keeping Holland neutral in the coming war.

The Dutch Social Democratic Labor Party split in 1920—a radical group within it, angered over the party's voting for war appropriations among other issues, left to join the Third International. Despite this loss, the Social Democratic Labor Party continued to grow. In 1920, a program was adopted calling for nationalization of industries, starting with large monopolies and progressing to smaller, competitive companies, with the former owners being paid compensation raised by means of income and inheritance taxes.

A further split occurred in the 1930s when the left wing of the party led by Edo Fimmen (1881–1943), feeling that the capitalist system was about to collapse in the worldwide depression, believed that extraparliamentary actions were called for to secure power. This group formed the Independent Socialist Party, with Fimmen as its president. He later withdrew from it, and this splinter has played only a minor role in subsequent Dutch politics.

In the mid-1930s, the Social Democrats campaigned vigorously against the Dutch National Socialists. To meet this fascist threat and to deal with the crisis of the depression, the Social Democratic Labor Party congress of 1935 reversed the party's earlier rejection of participation in coalition governments—a change that virtually every other social democratic party was to make in the course of time. In 1939, they joined their first coalition cabinet with the Catholic, Christian Historical, and Liberal Democratic parties.

Holland was invaded by Germany on May 10, 1940, and a government-in-exile was formed in London. The Social Democrats and other anti-fascist parties were suppressed in Holland by the Nazis, who set up a puppet government.

With the return of the government-in-exile after the war, Queen Wilhelmina appointed former professor of geodesy and leader of the People's Movement, socialist Willem Schermerhorn (b. 1894), as premier.[32] In 1946 the People's Movement merged with the Social Democrats, Liberal Democrats, and members of other progressive Catholic and Protestant groups to form the Dutch Labor Party. The program of this party called for nationalization of the Bank of the Netherlands, the mines, railroads, steel, and other monopolistic industries. In the election of May 1946, the Labor Party received the second largest vote, coming in behind the Catholic People's Party, and Schermerhorn stepped down as premier. Labor formed a coalition government with the Catholic People's Party on the condition that a conciliatory policy on their colony in Indonesia be implemented. Schermerhorn became the Commissioner General of the Netherlands Indies.

Labor served in a number of coalition government in those years. In 1954 a controversy broke out between Labor and the Archbishop of Utrecht, who issued a statement declaring that a Catholic could not be a member of socialist organizations such as the Netherlands Federation of Trade Unions and could not attend socialist meetings, read the socialist press, or listen to the socialist radio network. Labor premier Willem Drees (1886–) attacked the archbishop for this pronouncement. Within a few years, the Church reversed itself on this ban on socialist and trade union activity.

The Labor Party was part of coalition governments in the 1950s and 1960s. In 1973, Joop den Uyl (1919–1987), the leader of the Labor Party, became premier as the head of a five-party coalition government, which lasted until 1987. He was replaced by Christian Democratic premier Andreas van Agt (1931–) and, after 1982, by Ruud Lubbers (1939–).

SWITZERLAND

Swiss social democracy can be traced back to the Grütli Union, a working-class organization that began as a progressive party in 1838 and in 1878 adopted socialism.[33] In 1901 it joined the Marxist-oriented Social Democratic Party, which elected seven members of the National Council in 1902. The party's vote increased in the years before World War I. The Swiss Social Democrats took a strong stand against the war and afterwards veered to the left, voting in 1919 to quit the Second International and join the communist Third International. However, they did not repudiate parliamentary activity, causing a minority to break away from the party to form their own Communist Party of Switzerland.

The vote to join the Third International was unpopular with much of the rank and file, who rejected it in two party referendums, causing another communist breakaway, this splinter fusing with the Communist Party of Switzerland in March 1921.

The Swiss Social Democrats then joined the International Working Union of Labor and Socialist Parties, commonly known as the "Second-and-a-Half International," and later in 1926 became a member of the Labor and Socialist International of the interwar years.

After World War I, the Swiss Social Democrats gradually grew in strength and increased their representation in the National Council; however, unlike other European socialist parties, they were unable to muster enough votes to form a government. In the 1930s the party had at first been steadfast against military spending; but as the threat of Nazism arose, the membership, in time, modified their views.

By the late 1930s, it was necessary for the Social Democrats to give considerable effort to fighting fascism in their country. In 1938 the Social Democrats joined the Movement of Guiding Principles, an antifascist front consisting of the Swiss Trade Union Federation and other progressive forces.

To deal with the Great Depression, the Swiss Social Democrats developed a labor plan to help reduce unemployment, to protect wages and consumer buying power, and to regulate financial markets and monopolies. This was defeated by the Swiss people in a referendum. The party also fought for public works projects and a referendum allowing direct election of members of the cabinet called the Federal Council, instead of election by the parliament.

With the outbreak of World War II, the Swiss Social Democrats played an active role in keeping the Nazis from invading one of the few remaining democracies in Europe. In 1943 the Social Democrats were given one representative in the Federal Council, Ernest Nobs (1886–1957) as minister of Finance and Customs, and remained in coalition government for another ten years.[34] The party adopted in 1943 a program known as the New Switzerland, calling for an extension of social security, public ownership of monopolies, and a planned economy. Quitting the government coalition in 1953 over what it considered to be reactionary policies, the Social Democrats soon returned, and in 1963 Social Democrat Dr. Willy Spühler (1902–) served as the Federal Council's president.

In those years, the Social Democrats opposed Switzerland's development of atomic energy and advocated the use of the initiative in federal legislation and progressive taxation. In February 1971 women's suffrage was granted in Switzerland's federal elections—one of the last nations to do so. The cantons also extended suffrage, with the process of extension being completed in 1990. An equal rights amendment was added to the Swiss constitution in 1981, and women were granted legal equality in marriage in a 1985 referendum. Another referendum the same year rejected attempts to restrict the right to an abortion and on some forms of contraception. However, a referendum to abolish the Swiss military was defeated in 1989.

AUSTRIA AND EASTERN EUROPEAN NATIONS

In 1888, the Austrian Social Democratic Party was organized.[35] In 1897, workers were allowed, for the first time, to send representatives to parliament; and over the course of the next four years, the Austrians elected ten Social Democrats. Universal suffrage was won in 1907, following which the Social Democrats captured about a third of the vote.

On June 28, 1914, Archduke Francis Ferdinand (1863–1914), heir to the Austro-Hungarian Empire's throne, was assassinated by a Serbian nationalist, Gavrilo Princip (1893–1918), while on a visit to Sarajevo, the capital of Bosnia-Herzegovina, which had been annexed by Dual Monarchy of Austria-Hungary during the Turkish Revolution in 1908 against the strong wishes of Serbia. Despite diplomatic attempts and conciliatory moves on the part of Serbia to avoid war, they were not able to meet two of Austria-Hungary's ten demands, and Austria-Hungary declared war on Serbia on July 28, 1914. Russia, supporting Serbia, began to mobilize, and when they refused Germany's demand that they stop the mobilization, Germany, in support of Austria, declared war on Russia on August 1. France also began to mobilize, entering the war on August 3. When Germany declared its intentions to march across Belgium to fight the French, and Belgium refused this passage, Britain declared war on Germany on August 4 in support of Belgian neutrality. Soon other nations were swept up into the worldwide war.

With the outbreak of World War I, the Austrian Social Democrats opposed their government's declaration of war on Serbia; but when the war started in earnest with other European powers, the majority of the Social Democrats voted to defend the nation against Russian militarism by supporting the declaration of war. Thus, nationalism has often competed and won out over the antiwar elements of democratic socialism, even among the socialists themselves. Pressure from the antiwar minority within the party resulted in the Social Democrats issuing a manifesto calling for peace. A famous debate between Social Democratic leader Dr. Victor Adler (1852–1918) and his son Dr. Friedrich Adler (1879–1960), the party secretary, took place at the national Conference of the Austrian Social Democracy held in Vienna on March 25 to 28, 1916. The father held that the Social Democrats had to put the interests of their own proletariat above all else, while still striving for a union of the workers of the world, and thus support their nation in war. His more radical son, however, took the position that this view was responsible for the disunity among workers internationally and that Austrian socialists should recognize as binding the decisions of the international socialist congresses on international questions, such as opposing the world war. The elder Adler's position, however, won by a wide majority at the conference. Democratic socialists have debated these issues of war and peace again and again in countless countries in the succeeding years.

As the war continued, conditions worsened. The government refused now to convene parliament and ruthlessly suppressed socialist and radical newspapers. Many radicals were imprisoned. By September 1916, the Social Democrats were demanding peace negotiations to be commenced. Shortly afterward, the premier, Count Karl von Stuergkh, was assassinated by Friedrich Adler for his refusal to attend a conference called by the leaders of all of Austria's political parties with the goal of restoring constitutional government. In the subsequent trial, the Social Democrats declared that they had nothing to do with the assassination. The younger Adler was sentenced to death; his sentence was later commuted, and he was released in 1918.

At the end of World War I, riots broke out in favor of peace; and on November 3, 1918, Emperor Charles I abdicated. In the following elections of 1919, the Social Democrats became the largest party in the Constituent National Assembly. They formed a coalition government with the reform Christian Social Party, with Social Democrats Karl Seitz (1869–1950) elected president and Karl Renner (1870–1950) chancellor. The Social Democrats also headed the Foreign Ministry, the War Ministry, and the Ministry of the Interior. A democratic constitution was adopted, and reform legislation was passed by the new government. This government lasted until 1920 when the Christian Socialists took over, although the Social Democrats retained control in Vienna and other large Austrian cities.

The Social Democrats played the role of the opposition in the parliament until 1927. On July 15 of that year, a riot broke out in Vienna as the Austrian military attacked protesters who demonstrated against the acquittal of an accused defendant in the killing of an invalid socialist veteran. The police shot into the crowd; and the Social Democrats declared a one-day general strike, while the Communists called for a revolutionary war. Following these events, a private, reactionary army called the Heimwehren, made up of the sons of prosperous peasants and led by officers of the Imperial Army and the German Free Corps, began to grow. Supported by the government, big business, and the Church, the Heimwehren started a campaign to establish a fascist regime. The Social Democrats organized counterparades to those of the Heimwehren but urged that the private armies of both the right and the left (such as Schutzbund, labor's own military) be disbanded. However, the chancellor, Father Seipel, refused to listen to these pleas, supporting the victory of the Heimwehren over the left.

In the election of 1930, the Social Democrats won a stunning victory and became the largest party in the parliament. But the growth of Nazism in Germany strengthened the fascist forces in Austria. The movement for *Anschluss*—unification with Germany—which was prohibited by the peace treaties, was revived and grew stronger. Dr. Engelbert Dollfuss (1892–1934) had become chancellor in 1932, and with the resignation of Karl Renner as president of the Lower House, Dollfuss declared that only the president could convene the House and because there was no longer any president, the Parliament could not meet. Dollfuss used this excuse to rule by decree, attempting to form an alliance with the Nazis. In 1934 the Heimwehren, with the help of the government, crushed the Social Democrats in a civil war lasting four days. Many Social Democrats fought, but secret stores of weapons could not be found because the leaders who knew of their location had been arrested. The Social Democrats also were unable to send out an official call for a general strike this time around because they had neglected to make arrangements beforehand with the electrical workers for the use of socialist printing presses.

Many of the Social Democratic leaders fled to Czechoslovakia, while others were hanged; and the labor movement was driven underground. This underground movement, the Revolutionary Socialists (RS), worked to bring together many socialist groups, becoming a strong force in the years to come.

As for Dollfuss, he was assassinated during a Nazi putsch in July 1934. He was replaced as chancellor by the minister of Culture and Education, Kurt von Schuschnigg (1897–1977). At first he had the promise of Benito Mussolini to help preserve Austrian independence; but with the 1936 formation of the Rome-Berlin Axis, Mussolini reversed himself and supported the unification of Germany and Austria. Now, desperate to preserve his nation, Schuschnigg turned to the socialist underground. In return for fighting to keep Austria independent, the underground was promised freedom of press, freedom to express socialist ideas, and self-determination for the trade unions.

On March 7, 1938, the trade unionists were able to meet openly for the first time since 1934. The socialists supported Schuschnigg in a plebiscite on Austrian independence set for March 13 of that year. Schuschnigg also reached an agreement with Hitler that had brought the Austrian Nazi leader Artur von Seyss-Inquart (1892–1946) into the government as minister of the Interior in charge of the Austrian police. On March 12, Hitler declared his native Austria to be part of Germany, and German troops invaded Austria, forcing Schuschnigg to give his radio farewell address to the nation. Austria lost its independence and its name, being called Ostmark, and was divided into seven administrative districts under the rule of the Third Reich. Again socialist forces were driven underground, and many of their leaders escaped the country to continue the fight against fascism.

The Moscow Declaration signed by Roosevelt, Stalin, and Churchill in October 1943 committed the Allies to the restoration of Austrian independence after World War II. On April 29, 1945, with the defeat of Germany imminent, a provisional government was set up in Vienna under the leadership of the Social Democratic statesman Karl Renner.³⁶ In the elections of November 1945, the Social Democrats captured seventy-six seats in the parliament, with the Catholic People's Party getting eighty-four seats and the Communists winning five seats. The following month Renner was elected president, and Leopold Figl of the Catholic People's Party became chancellor. At the same time, the Social Democrats changed their name to the Austrian Socialist Party but rejected a proposal to merge with the Communists. A coalition government was formed that was made up of representatives of the Catholic People's Party, the Socialists, and the Communists. At the urging of the Socialists, the Austrian parliament passed a bill in 1946 to nationalize the banking, oil, electric, metallurgy, and shipping industries. The Soviet military arrested several Austrians attempting to carry out this decree, declaring that the property had been forcibly Germanized and belonged to the occupying Soviet forces. This issue caused much controversy, which was not resolved until the formal reestablishment of the Austrian Republic in May 1955 and Austria's agreement to buy back from the Administrator of Soviet Property in Austria many of these assets confiscated from the Germans. The Austrian Communist minister in the coalition government resigned in November 1947 in protest over a financial reform measure, leaving the Socialists in coalition with the People's Party. This coalition lasted for many years, usually with the Socialists providing the presidents and the People's Party providing the chancellors. The Socialists more and more often adopted a revisionist platform, dropping old antireligious slogans and stressing individual rights. Socialist Party leader and Mayor of Vienna Theodor Koerner (1973–1957) succeeded Renner as president in May 1951. The Socialists pushed for the nationalizing of industry, whereas the People's Party resisted them, favoring private capitalism. The coalition between the Socialists and the People's Party broke down in 1966 with the Socialists going into opposition. In 1970 the Socialists won a narrow victory that brought Bruno Kreisky (1911–1990) into office as chancellor. He served as chancellor until 1983, when the Socialists lost their majority. The new chancellor, Fred Sinowatz (1929–) also a Socialist, headed a Socialist-Freedom Party coalition government. The presidential elections of 1986 brought the People's Party candidate Kurt Waldheim, the former Secretary-General of the United Nations, to office. Waldheim was dogged, however, by continuing controversy over his role as a German officer in World War II and what connection he may have had to Nazi atrocities; he did not run for a second term. Sinowatz also resigned in 1986 and was replaced as premier by fellow Socialist Franz Vranitzky (1937–), who retained his office at the head of coalition government in 1990. Thomas Klestil (1933–) of the People's Party replaced Waldheim in 1993 as Austria's president.

Post-Communist Albania, Bosnia and Herzegovina, Bulgaria, the Czech Republic, Hungary, Macedonia, Moldavia, Montenegro, Poland, and Romania, Slovakia, Slovenia, and Serbia all have social democratic parties today.

ITALY

Originally it was anarchists that represented Italy in the First International, but by 1892 the Italian movement had separated into anarchist and socialist wings, the latter under the leadership of Philipo Turati (1857–1932).[37] As suffrage was expanded in the early twentieth century, so did the votes of the Socialists. As Italy entered World War I, the Italian Socialists were one of the few parties of the Second International to remain true to their pledge to oppose the war. This opposition caused Benito Mussolini (1883–1945), the editor of the socialist newspaper *Avanti* (Forward), to resign, even though he had at first been associated with the extreme left wing of the party, In the early days, he had leaned toward anarchism and had published editorials at the outset of the fighting calling it a "bourgeois war." He had argued that the workers should prepare to bring about the socialist revolution as the war precipitated the "crisis of the capitalist system." However, by October 1914, following the visit of the French Radical and later Communist leader Marcel Cachin, Mussolini suddenly shifted ground and declared himself in favor of Italy's entrance into the war on the side of the Allies. Shortly after resigning as editor of *Avanti,* he was expelled from the Socialist Party and, the following month, founded his own, prowar paper, *Il Popolo d'Italia* (The People of Italy).

At the conclusion of the war, returning soldiers and war workers found no jobs available. Some of the unemployed joined the Socialists, but in times of economic crisis, not everyone is attracted to the left. Many in such dire circumstances are attracted to the extreme right, which promises easy solutions to complex problems. In the case of Italy, the extreme right-wing solution was offered by the new Fascist Party that Mussolini had founded.

The Italian Socialist Party's National Executive Committee, strongly influenced by the Bolshevik Revolution, had moved to the left during this crisis and had endorsed the manifesto of the Third International in March 1919; by January 21, at the party's national congress, all sections of the party had declared their acceptance of the twenty-one points decreed necessary for joining the Third International. However, right-wing and center groups in the party claimed national autonomy in interpreting and applying some of these conditions for affiliation. A representative of the Third International at this congress demanded that there be complete acceptance of the twenty-one points and that reform elements be expelled from the party. The party congress voted this down by a wide margin, causing a minority to secede from the party to form their own Italian Communist Party.

Fascism

Meanwhile, with all Italy in economic and political turmoil, Mussolini had founded his first Fascist groups, the *Fasci di Combattimento*, in March 1919 in Milan. This was a highly nationalistic, anti-Communist, and anti-liberal movement that attracted support from the lower middle class. If one considers nationalism to be an ideology, it is certainly the most powerful, the cause of most wars, and the chief competitor to socialism. The name of Mussolini's group came from the *faces*, a bundle of sticks tied together with an axe, which had been the ancient, Roman symbol of the authority of magistrates to punish wrongdoers. It was the desire for authority among the people to which the Fascists appealed, and it was clear that the "wrongdoers" that they sought to punish were the Communists, the Socialists, and all liberals.

The Fascists called for a single-party, totalitarian regime. On the economic level, Italy would become a corporative state in which workers and employers were organized into party-controlled groups representing differing sectors of the economy.

Capitalism would be preserved, businesses would be given free rein, and free labor unions would be abolished, as would the right to strike. Social services were to be expanded, but a smaller share of national income was spent on them compared to other European countries. As a result of these policies, living standards declined under Fascist rule, and hunger and child labor became widespread.

The role of women in Fascist society was to become mothers and to increase the birth rate. Birth control education was banned, and women were to be under the complete domination of their husbands.

The Fascists' foreign policy was militaristic and imperialist, and their aim was to rebuild the Roman Empire, starting with the conquest of Ethiopia.

Originally, the Italian Fascists were not anti-Semitic; but after they had forged an alliance with the Nazis, they adopted anti-Semitism as a doctrine, although they never carried it out with quite the genocidal fervor of the Germans.

The black-shirted Fascists repeatedly clashed with the Communists throughout Italy. Mussolini demanded that the government be turned over to the Fascists. On October 24, 1922, he led the Fascists on a march on

Rome, and three days later the Italian premier Luigi Facta resigned. King Victor Emmanuel III (1869–1947) now gave Mussolini a free hand in forming a government. Public anger over the murder of a Socialist deputy, Giacomo Matteotti (1885–1924) by Fascist mobs now gave Mussolini the excuse he needed to suspend constitutional rights and liberties in the name of law and order. The Italian parliament was forbidden to initiate legislation, and Mussolini was given dictatorial powers. The press was censored, and all political parties except for the Fascists were outlawed. By 1929 the old parliament was transformed into a Fascist chamber, its deputies selected by the Fascist Grand Council, the ruling group of the state. In 1934 some twenty-two corporations were organized that represented workers and their employers, with Fascist Party members serving on their governing councils. These corporations were united into a National Council of Corporations, with Mussolini serving as the president. In 1939 the Chamber of Deputies was ordered to vote itself out of existence and to be replaced by a Chamber of Fasci and Corporations composed of 800 appointees of the National Council of Corporations. In each of their industries, these corporations were given the power to regulate wages and prices and to engage in economic planning.

Italy attacked Ethiopia on October 3, 1935, formally annexing it on May 9, 1936. Mussolini then entered into a Rome-Berlin Axis, agreeing to cooperate with Hitler on common goals. Although Mussolini had refused to join Germany at the start of World War II, German military successes convinced him to reverse himself and to lead Italy into the war on the side of the Germans. It was this decision that proved to be the Fascists' undoing. Italian forces in Albania invaded Greece on October 28, 1940, but encountered strong Greek resistance that drove the Italian army from both Greece and Albania. A succession of military defeats and growing economic hardships at home led to rising anti-Fascist sentiments among the Italian people. German intervention offset these military losses, and almost all of Greece was occupied by Italian forces with the aid of the Germans, who remained the real masters. The price of helping Italy had been sending increasing amounts of food and other goods to the Germans from Italy, which further increased the hardships among the Italians. In return for German coal and oil, Italy joined Germany in declaring war on the Soviet Union on June 22, 1941. Meanwhile German officials increasingly took over Italian life, weakening Mussolini's power and prestige at home.

Allied victories in Africa and the invasion of Italy forced Mussolini to be summoned to a meeting of the Fascist Grand Council in Rome to consider the crisis. After a stormy debate, a vote of no confidence was taken against

Mussolini, who once had been called *Il Duce* (The Leader). Then, on July 25, 1943, King Victor Emmanuel III ordered Mussolini to resign and Marshal Pietro Badoglio to form a new government. Mussolini was arrested, and all Fascist organizations were ordered to be liquidated. The Germans stepped in, rescuing Mussolini and forcing him to head a puppet Social Republic in Northern Italy. In the closing days of the war, Mussolini attempted to escape to Switzerland, was caught by Italian partisans, and executed on April 28, 1945.

The Italian Socialist Party during the war had organized an antiwar week, April 1 to 7, 1942, under the call, "Enough of war! Enough of fascism!" They remained active during the rest of the war, organizing a campaign of civil disobedience.

With Mussolini's fall, the Italian Socialists joined the Italian Communist Party and other anti-Fascist organizations in demonstrating for peace and a restoration of democracy. With the occupation of Italy by Allied forces, the Socialist, Communist, and other anti-Fascist groups formed a Committee of National Liberation. From this group, in July 1944, the former Socialist Ivanoe Bonomi was chosen as premier.

The Italian Socialist Party after the War

The Italian Socialist Party was led by Pietro Nenni (1891–1980) in the post-World War II era. In these years the Socialists believed that the interests of the working class would be best served by supporting a joint Socialist-Communist list of candidates. Nenni was closely tied to the Soviet Union, receiving the Stalin Peace Prize in 1952, and he generally supported Soviet foreign policy and opposed Italy's entry into NATO. However, he was critical of the Soviet invasion and crackdown in Hungary in 1956. From that point onward, the Socialists began to restrict their political cooperation with the Italian Communists.[38]

The Socialists had suffered a split in their ranks as a result of their collaboration with the Communists. In 1945 the more moderate wing of the party, opposed to political alliances with the Communists, split to form the Social Democratic Party, which became a member of the Socialist International along with the larger, parent Italian Socialist Party.

Bonomi had agreed to resign as premier after the liberation of Northern Italy. The next two Italian premiers were Ferruccio Parri (1890–1981) of the Action Party and Alcide de Gasperi (1881–1954), a Christian Democrat. Italians had voted to declare themselves a Republic in 1946, and King

Humbert (1890–1981) abdicated and left Italy. Enrico de Nicola (1890–1981) of the Liberal Party was elected president in 1946 with de Gasperi remaining as premier. Nenni served as foreign minister in de Gasperi's cabinet but resigned in 1947, followed by the entire cabinet. De Gasperi then formed another coalition cabinet involving both Socialists and Communists. However, an armed band of rightists attacked a Communist May Day parade in Greci, Sicily, in 1947, killing eight people and precipitating a cabinet crisis that month, which resulted in de Gasperi forming still another cabinet, this time without the Socialists or Communists participating.

The Socialists would remain out of the cabinet until 1963, although the centrist Social Democrats, who had fused with other socialist groups and changed their name to the Democratic Socialist Party in 1951, would participate in a coalition cabinet with the Christian Democrats in 1958 under Amintore Fanfani (1908–). In 1963 the Socialists joined the left-center government of Christian Democratic premier Aldo Moro (1916–1978), with Nenni serving as vice-premier. A minority of the Socialists objected to this and left the party, forming their own Party of Proletarian Unity.

As for the Democratic Socialist Party, for years they had argued for reuniting with the larger Socialist Party, as long as there were to be no alliances with the Communists. Finally, they had their way, with the reunion between the Democratic Socialists and the Socialist Party being formalized on October 30, 1966, in a Congress in Rome. Nenni was chosen to be the president of the new Italian Socialist Party. This reunion was made possible by the gap between the old Socialist Party and the Communists that had greatly widened over the years and by the Socialists losing their taste for united action with the Communists. The new Socialist Party soon became the Italian representative in the Socialist International.

In 1968, New Left students clashed with police in Rome and other Italian cities and demanded educational reforms, while workers called a general strike to demand reform of the social security system. The period of the late 1960s and early 1970s found Italy experiencing a number of short-lived coalition governments led by the Christian Democrats. As economic and social conditions worsened, the Communist Party, headed by Enrico Berlinguer (1922–1984), increased in size.

The Italian Communists had announced in 1975 a "historic compromise" with democracy. Rejecting Stalinism, the Italian, Spanish, and French Communist parties had adopted to varying degrees a variant of communism known as Eurocommunism that was critical of the Soviet Union's totalitarianism and militarist foreign policy. Both the Socialists and the Communists may be thought of as moving to the democratic center and away from revolutionary socialism in these years. Where the Socialists may have moved too far to the right so as to be hardly distinguishable from the Christian Democrats, and not terribly inspiring or exciting, the Communists had moved just enough to gain new adherents without alienating their radical core. In any event, the Communists made gains under this new policy and eclipsed the Socialists as the leading party on the Italian left. With newfound strength, the Communists were permitted a voice in policy making in the government formed by Christian Democratic leader Giulio Andreotti (1919–) in 1977. However, loss of Communist support led to the resignation of Andreotti in January 1979.

The decision of the Communists to participate in a bourgeois government angered extreme left-wingers and led to terrorist factions attacking businessmen, politicians, and other establishment figures. One of the best known of these terrorist groups is the Red Brigades, which kidnapped former premier Aldo Moro in March 1978 and demanded that their comrades be released from jail in return for Moro's freedom. However, the government refused to agree to this deal, and Moro was found murdered.

In the early 1980s, Italy had its first non-Christian Democratic premier in the post-World War II era. He was Giovanni Spadolini (1925–) of the small Republican Party. One of Italy's frequent cabinet crises then brought the country's first Socialist premier, Bettino Craxi (1934–2000) to office in August 1983. He served until March 1987—the longest term for any postwar Italian premier. High unemployment and inflation were reduced on his watch and he fled Italy after being charged with corruption.

Following Craxi, there was a return to short-lived governments under Fanfani, Giovanni Giuseppe Goria (1943–), Circiaco de Mila (1928–), and again Andreotti of the Christian Democrats in the late 1980s to early 1990s. Another cabinet crisis in 1992 brought Italy's second, postwar, Socialist premier, Giuliano Amato (1938–), to office. A widespread corruption scandal involving top leaders of the Christian Democrats and the Socialists, including Craxi, badly hurt both parties. Picking up support they had lost was the conservative Freedom Alliance of media tycoon Silvio Berlusconi, which was made up of his own *Forza Italia* (Go, Italy), the separatist Northern League, and the neo-Fascist National Alliance. In the elections of March 1994, Berlusconi's coalition was able to beat the former Communist Party, renamed the Democratic Party of the Left, and its allies. Berlusconi had his own scandal not long afterward and was forced to resign. The pattern of short-lived coalition governments continues in Italy. The left-center Olive Tree coalition, which includes ex-Communists and ex-Christian Democrats, was the victor in the April 1996 parliamentary election; and their leader, economics professor Romano Prodi, was chosen as prime minister. There is also a small Italian Democratic Socialist Party, and San Marino has a Socialist Party.

SPAIN AND PORTUGAL

The origins of the Spanish Socialists date back to 1869 and the formation of the Spanish Section of the First International.[39] This body, however, soon fell under the control of the anarchists, and it was not until 1879 that the Social Labor Party was formed. Among its founders was Pablo Iglesias (1850–1925). He was the Secretary of the International Proletarian Federation in 1871, founder of the Typographical Societies in 1872, and elected its president in 1885. Becoming editor of *El Socialiste* in 1886, Iglesias was elected a Socialist deputy in the Spanish parliament in 1910 and became leader of the parliamentary Socialists in 1923.

The Socialists fought hard for a democratic government in those years, continuing the struggle after the coup d'état and the establishment of a military dictatorship under General Miguel Primo de Rivera (1870–1930) in September 1923 followed by dictator General Damaso Berenguer (1873–1953), who came to power in January 1930 after de Riviera's resignation.

Attempts by the Socialists and Republicans to revolt that year were crushed, however, and many thousands were arrested. Popular discontent increased, and in 1931 the Socialists and the trade unionists were able to force King Alfonso XIII (1886–1941) to abdicate and to install a Provisional Republican Government led by Niceto Alcalá Zamora Torres (1877–1949) as president. A new constitution that year established a republican form of government, men's suffrage, and, for the first time, women's suffrage, freedom of speech and press, and separation of church and state. Zamora selected a cabinet containing a number of Socialists and Republicans headed by Don Manuel Azaña. Under this government, large, landed estates were broken up, and public schools created.

Many of these reforms provoked a strong, conservative backlash; and following the elections of 1933, a center-right government came to power that was intent on reversing these reforms. State stipends to the clergy were reintroduced, land reform held up, autonomy for Catalonia postponed, and the substitution of public schools for parochial ones delayed. A revolt broke out in Catalonia, and Azaña was jailed on suspicion of aiding the revolt. As opposition to the center-right government grew, the president suspended the Spanish parliament and called for new elections.

The election of 1936 brought an electoral alliance of Socialists, Communists, Trotskyists, syndicalists, anarchists, Republican Leftists, and Republican Unity groups together under the name the Popular Front. United, these progressive forces won a smashing victory against the right and center parties. Azaña was again elected president by the parliament, and Casares Quiroga was chosen as prime minister.

Shortly thereafter, a fascist revolt in the army began in Spanish Morocco led by General Francisco Franco (1892–1975). The revolt quickly spread to the mainland, plunging the nation into civil war. Most of the army went over to Franco's Nationalists. The Loyalist army supporting the Popular Front government was staffed mainly with untrained men. By the end of 1936, Germany and Italy were providing large-scale military aid to Franco's Nationalists.

Following the fall of Irein to the Nationalists, a new Loyalist government was formed under Don Francisco Largo Cabellero (1869–1946) including Socialists, Communists, and Republicans. The anarcho-syndicalists joined this government later when Madrid became threatened.

With the removal of the Loyalist government to Valencia, Franco assumed control as dictator of a Nationalist Spain on October 1, 1936. Suffrage and autonomy were abolished. On April 29, 1938, two main Nationalist groups, the Falangists and the Traditionalists, were merged into a single Falangist party, with all other parties being outlawed. Vertical syndicates of employers and workers were created, and a National Council of fifty members was formed.

Meanwhile, the anarcho-syndicalists staged an uprising in Barcelona, May 3 to 10, 1937, and the Loyalist forces were joined by an International Brigade made up of supporters of many countries. A new Loyalist government was formed that was headed by Juan Negrin as prime minister and that excluded the anarcho-syndicalists. A counteroffensive was launched by Loyalist forces on December 5, 1937, capturing Teruel, an insurgent stronghold, on December 19. Franco's forces retook Teruel on February 18, 1938, and advanced toward the Gulf of Valencia. A counterattack from the rear stopped Franco's army for several months; but the insurgents were able to resume their offensive by December of that year and captured Barcelona on January 26, 1939. Four rebel columns now converged on Madrid, where a fifth column of Franco's supporters prepared to rise against the Loyalist defenders. Madrid fell on March 28, 1939, and the Loyalist government, badly split by internal dissension, fled the country.

Franco had announced his support for the German-Italian-Japanese, Anti-Comintern Pact in 1939 and withdrew Spain from the League of Nations. When World War II began, Spain declared its neutrality. With the fall of France to the Germans in 1940, Spain moved to a position of nonbelligerency, meaning that it would provide aid to Germany and Italy, but it would not join them in the fighting. After the Allies successfully invaded North Africa in 1943, Franco moved Spain back to the policy of neutrality. During the last months of the war, Spain broke diplomatic relations with Germany and Japan. It was this caution and refusal to throw his fate in with the warring fascist states that would allow Franco to outlast his dictatorial counterparts in Germany, Italy, and Japan. While they and their regimes were all destroyed by the end of World War II, Franco and his Falangists lasted until Franco's death on November 20, 1975. Indeed, the United Nations General Assembly in 1950 lifted its ban and allowed Spain to fully join the UN in 1955, despite its long history of fascist repression. The United States also overcame objections from other North Atlantic Treaty Organization (NATO) countries to the signing of U.S.-Spanish pacts in 1953 that allowed the United States to use and expand several Spanish air and naval bases in exchange for $226 million in economic and military aid to the Spanish dictatorship. Despite this aid, economic conditions remained bad in Spain for most of the late 1940s and the 1950s.

In the late 1950s, popular challenges began to unravel dictatorial rule in Spain. Student demonstrations and labor unrest in early 1957 forced Franco to reduce the Falangist representation in the parliament, to increase that of business and labor organizations, and to reorganize his cabinet. Later that year, it was announced that government controls over trade would be reduced and that closer economic relations with other countries would be sought. Fighting in 1957 and 1958 led to Spain returning Spanish Morocco to its native people and the Spanish enclave of Ifni to Morocco, brokered by the United States. Strikes, beginning with that of the coal miners in 1958, finally led the Franco regime to recognize the right of labor to collective bargaining with employers, although strikes remained illegal. Despite this, workers continued to strike for better pay and working conditions, and college students protested rising costs, overcrowding, and government control in the late 1960s and early 1970s.

The Franco regime met all such challenges to its authority with brutal repression. Protesters were shot, and martial law was declared to force workers back to work. A campaign of terrorism to win Basque independence led to the Spanish government passing a law requiring military trials for terrorists and the death penalty for killing police officers. Economic growth in the 1960s was choked off in the 1970s as unemployment, inflation, and the foreign debt all increased. To placate the people, plans were announced for a new, bicameral parliament to be popularly elected, and the ban on forming political associations was lifted in 1974. Additionally, Spain agreed to cede Spanish Sahara to Morocco and Mauritania, which both had claims to it in 1975 as a result of a peaceful march of Moroccans into the Spanish colony.

The death of Franco opened the way for gradual, democratic reform to take hold in Spain. King Juan Carlos I succeeded to the throne and granted amnesty to 650 political prisoners, excluding, however, the Basque terrorists. A Political Reform Law was approved by referendum in December 1975, and the first democratic elections since the Civil War were permitted in June 1977. A plurality of seats in the lower house was won by the moderate Union of the Democratic Center (UDC), and its leader, Adolfo Suarez Gonzales, became the new premier. High unemployment, inflation, and debt plagued the government, and taxes were increased while wages and prices were frozen. However, Spain was allowed to join the European Community in 1986.

With a new constitution adopted in 1978 establishing Spain as a constitutional monarchy, pressure increased for regional autonomy, especially the pressure applied by the Basque terrorists. In 1981 armed Civil Guards invaded the parliament and attempted to seize power. The coup failed, however, when King Juan Carlos successfully ordered troops back to the barracks.

In October 1982 the Spanish Socialist Workers' Party (PSOE) swept to power, electing their leader, Felipe González Márquez (1942–) as premier and he was succeeded in 1996 by Jose Maria Aznar of the conservative Popular Party.

Like Spain, Portugal also had its fascist period under a professor of economics appointed as minister of finance in 1928, António de Oliveira Salazar (1889–1970). Under General António de Fragoso Carmona (1869–1951), the military junta that seized power charged Salazar with the job of putting the Portuguese economy on a sound basis. Salazar succeeded at this task and soon became the most powerful figure in the country. In 1930, he organized the National Union, a political organization based on authoritarian principles. After becoming prime minister and dictator in 1932, he set out to create Portugal as a corporative "New State." Opposition parties were banned, and a planned economy instituted. Salazar, naturally, supported his fellow fascist Franco, and in 1939 Portugal signed a friendship and nonaggression pact with Spain. Like Spain, Portugal also stayed neutral in World War II. Only when it looked as if the Axis might lose did Portugal allow the Allies to base ships and planes in the Azores. It was this foreign policy that allowed fascist Portugal and Spain to last as long as they did, long after Nazi Germany and the fascist regimes in Italy and Japan were defeated in war and overthrown.

In the postwar years, Portugal suffered severe unemployment and poverty. This stimulated resistance to the regime, but all such movements were suppressed. In May 1947, the Salazar government deported rebellious labor leaders and army officers to exile in the Cape Verde Islands.

In the 1960s Portugal increasingly faced rebellion in its overseas possessions. Anticolonial warfare broke out in Angola in 1961, in Portuguese Guinea in 1962, and in Mozambique in 1964. Additionally, India had annexed Portuguese Goa in 1961. These wars lasted well into the 1970s and would play a key role in the eventual overthrow of the fascist regime.

Salazar had become incapacitated by a cerebral stroke and was succeeded in 1968 as prime minister by Marcello Caetano (1906–1980), a law professor, businessman, and Salazar associate. While calling for reforms when he first took office, he, nevertheless, continued Salazar's repressive and colonialist policies at home and in Africa. The success of the African independence movements and the decline of the Portuguese economy led to the overthrow of the Caetano government on April 25, 1974. A seven-member junta was installed under General António de Spinola (1910–) which promised to bring democracy at home and peace in the colonies. Over the next two years, Angola, Mozambique, Guinea-Bissau, São Tomé and Principe, and the Cape Verde Islands all became independent. In 1975–1976 Portuguese Timor was occupied by Indonesia. The return of Portuguese troops and settlers to the home country only aggravated the nation's problems with unemployment.

General Spinola stepped down as president in 1974 and was replaced by General Francisco da Costa Gomes (1914–) with Vasco Gonçalves (1921–) who had become prime minister in July of that year, remaining in office.

In early 1975 the Movement of the Armed Forces (MFA) assumed a formal role in the Portuguese government. Steps were taken to reform the military, and laws were passed nationalizing certain heavy industries and banking. Large agricultural estates were expropriated and the land redistributed. Additionally, by law a single trade union confederation was established.

A rightist coup was attempted, reportedly led by Spinola, but was put down. In the election for a constituent assembly in April 1975, the Portuguese Socialist Party (PSP) led all others.

Gonçalves attempted to form a new government, but it lacked stability. The Socialists were fighting the Communists, and there were violent anti-Communist demonstrations, particularly in the north. The MFA established a ruling triumvirate of Costa Gomes, Gonçalves, and General Otelo de Carvahlo (1934?–), the security chief.

At the army's insistence that September, Gonçalves was replaced as prime minister by Vice Admiral Jose de Azevedo (1917–1983), whose government succeeded in reestablishing some measure of stability.

In the parliamentary elections of April 1976, the Socialists won a plurality of the vote, and their leader, Mario Soares (1924–) became the new prime minister. That June, General Antonio Ramalho Eanes (1935–) was elected president. Portugal experienced severe economic troubles in the 1970s, and Soares was replaced as prime minister in 1978 by two, consecutive, interim governments. Then in December 1979, the Democratic Alliance won a majority of the vote in the parliamentary elections, and their leader Francisco Manuel de Sá Carneiro (1934–1980) took office as prime minister in January 1980. However, he was killed in a plane crash that December and was succeeded by another conservative, Francisco Pinto Balsemão (1937–), in January 1981. A constitutional amendment instigated and adopted at his urging abolished the military Council of the Revolution in 1982. Parliamentary elections in April 1983 brought Soares back into office as prime minister. His government was forced to adopt an austerity program.

The elections of October 1985 brought a minority government to office under Aníbal Cavaco Silva (1939–) of the rival Social Democratic Party. Soares was elected president in 1986 and was reelected to a five-year term in January 1991. Meanwhile the Social Democrats won a majority in the 1987 parliamentary elections and retained that majority in the 1991 elections. The Socialists won the parliamentary elections of October 1995. The former mayor of Lisbon, Socialist Jorge Sampaio, succeeded Soares as president, defeating in January 1996 the former prime minister Aníbal Cavaco Silva, whose government had been burdened with an economic recession in recent years. The Portuguese people had often elected a president of a party different from that of the prime minister as a counterweight, but in this election they gave a single party, the Socialists, control of both the presidency and the parliament for the first time since 1974.

GREECE AND MALTA

Between 1900 and 1918, several Greek socialist organizations existed, which united in 1918 to form the Socialist Labor Party of Greece.[40] The majority of this party at their Second Congress held in 1920 voted to join the Third International and became the Greek Communist Party. The sizable minority that did not go along with this broke away to establish the Greek Socialist Party led by A. Sideris.

The latter Socialists took an active part in the trade union movement, with one of the Socialist leaders, D. Stratis, being elected the General Secretary of the Greek Trade Union Confederation.

The Socialists joined the National Liberation Front to resist the occupation of Greece by German, Italian, and Bulgarian forces in World War II. The National Liberation Front had its own army. A smaller and less effective resistance force was the conservative National Democratic Greek Union. These two groups began to battle each other following the Allied invasion of Italy and the near prospect of Greek liberation by the end of 1943. The British at first gave support to the leftist National Liberation Front but, fearing Communist participation and domination in it, switched to supporting the National Democratic Greek Union.

In October 1944 the German army abandoned Greece. The prime minister of the coalition government established in this period, Georgios Papandreou (1888–1968), ordered the National Popular Liberation Army to disarm and disband, but they refused; and by December 1994, civil war between the government and the National Liberation Army erupted in Athens, touched off by Athenian police firing on a demonstration of the latter. The British provided aid to the government forces and allowed them to gain military superiority. In February 1945 a truce was reached, according to which, in return for dissolving its army, the National Liberation Front would be allowed the freedom to campaign, and a nonpartisan army would be established.

In the first postwar election in March 1946, the royalist Populist Party gained a majority, although the National Liberation Front claimed that the election had been rigged.

The socialists, which had cooperated with the Communists in the National Liberation Front, eventually broke ties with the latter over the Communists' use of violent tactics. Insurgent Communist forces in Northern Greece became a serious threat to the Greek government in the late 1940s. After several major rebel bastions in the Grammos mountains were captured in 1949, the rebel leadership declared that they were stopping military operations to avoid the destruction of the country.

In the early 1950s, the National Liberation Front merged with the Democratic Party of the Working People. In 1953 a socialist education and propaganda center was established in the merged party, which was called the Socialist League. This group was admitted into the Socialist International in 1955 with observer status.

In 1952 the rightist Greek Rally Party won the parliamentary election, and their leader Field Marshal Aleandros Papagos (1883–1955), became the prime minister. He died in 1955 and was succeeded by Constantine Karamanlis (1907–). The following year, Karamanlis announced the formation of a new, rightist party, the National Radical Union, to replace the Greek Rally Party, which had fallen apart on Papagos's death. This new party won a majority of the parliament, in the elections of 1956.

In 1961 Karamanlis's party again won a majority in the parliament, but a new party, the moderate Center Union, refused to recognize the results, charging that voters had been coerced. Center Union supporters clashed with Athens police in a rally in 1962, and Karamanlis stated that further disorder would not be tolerated. In the elections of 1963, the Center Union won a narrow majority, and its leader, Georgios Papandreou, was elected prime minister. He announced his intent to purge the Greek army of all political cells, including the leftist Aspida (Shield) group, and this led to a decree in which the prime minister took over the Ministry of Defense. King Constantine II (1940–), however, fearing that changes in the army command might deprive him of military support, refused to sign this decree, and Papandreou threatened to resign. However, even before he could do so, the king attempted to appoint a new prime minister, although he could not win parliamentary support.

Other attempts were made to form a government, all of which failed. Finally, on September 25, 1965, the deputy prime minister, Stephanos Stephanopoulos (1898–1982), was able to win parliamentary support and become the new prime minister. He only served a little more than a year before he lost the support of the National Radical Union and resigned; he was replaced by Ioánnis Paraskevopoulos (b. 1900). Some twenty-eight army officers involved in the Aspida group were court-martialed for conspiracy to overthrow the government. The Center Union tried to shield Andreas Papandreou (1919–), son of the former prime minister, implicated in the plot. He could not be tried because of parliamentary immunity, and the Center Union introduced a bill extending the period of parliamentary immunity between the time of the dissolution of the parliament and the holding of the new elections. When the National Radical Union would not support this bill, the resulting fight in parliament led to the Radical Union's withdrawing support from the prime minister, who was replaced by Panayiotis Kanellopoulos (1902–1986), the leader of the Radical Union, on April 3, 1967. He dissolved parliament because of popular discontent and ordered elections for that May.

Before those elections could take place, a group of army officers rose up and overthrew the government on April 21, 1967. Constantine Kollias (b. 1901), the chief prosecutor of the Supreme Court, was appointed prime minister, and the junta issued decrees to arrest thousands of leftists and other political figures, to suspend all political parties and many political organizations, to suspend civil liberties, and to censor the news media. After an abortive attempt to overthrow this junta failed, the king went into exile in Italy, and a new prime minister was chosen, Colonel Georgios Papadopoulos (1919–). It was a disastrous time for the Greek socialist movement and for all of Greece.

Criticism over widespread reports of arrests and torture of prisoners led

Greece to withdraw from the Human Rights Commission of the Council of Europe before the latter acted to expel Greece from the organization. On June 1, 1973, the junta abolished the monarchy, proclaiming Greece to be a republic, and named Papadopoulos as president. After his inauguration, he proclaimed amnesty for political prisoners and promised new elections. However, student demonstrations against the government that autumn led to the reimposing of martial law. Failure to maintain order resulted in a military coup against Papadopoulos on November 25, 1973, and he was replaced as president by General Phaidon Gizikis (1917–).

The failure to prevent the Turkish invasion of Cyprus led the junta to step down in July 1974, and Karamanlis was recalled from exile to form the first civilian government in Greece since the 1967 coup. Heading a political party named New Democracy, Karamanlis was able to win the election that November. The next month, a referendum to restore the monarchy was defeated, and a new republican constitution was proclaimed in June 1975. In the election of November 1977, the ruling party saw its majority shrink, and the Panhellenic Socialist Movement (Pasok) founded in 1974 by Andreas Papandreou came in second.

Greece had withdrawn its military from NATO over the Cyprus crisis in 1974, but it now rejoined its military forces in 1980. Continued confrontation with Turkey, as well as troublesome inflation, plagued Greece in these years. Karamanlis was elected president in May 1980, and his post as prime minister was filled by the former foreign minister Georgios Rallis (1918–), also a member of New Democracy. Under Rallis, Greece was permitted entry into the European Community in January 1981.

In the parliamentary elections of October 1981, Pasok scored a decisive victory, and Andreas Papandreou was elected Greece's first, socialist prime minister. Running with Pasok's support, Supreme Court justice Christos Sartzetakis (1929–) was elected president in March 1985. After suffering so many years in the war, and the 1967 coup, the Socialists had finally achieved victory. Women's rights and social security improved under the Socialists, and for this they deserve much credit. However, the Greek economy remained stagnant under their time in power. This was not entirely the fault of the Socialists, for like most European nations that have social democrats come to power, the economy remained largely capitalist, and therefore prone to recessions and economic depressions. That the Socialists did not do more to socialize the economy has much to do with fact that the public, by in large, is not ready for such radical measures and often will not vote in Socialist candidates who run on such platforms.

Papandreou lost his parliamentary majority over charges of corruption and was replaced by New Democracy candidate Tzannis Tzannetakis

(1927–) following the elections of June 1989. Following a period in which the parliament was deadlocked, the elections of April 1990 produced a slim majority for New Democracy leader Constantine Mitsotakis (1918–), who replaced Tzannetakis as prime minister. In 1993 Papandreou returned to power; but he resigned in 1996 due to poor health and was succeeded by Constantine Simitis (1936–).

Prior to independence from British rule, a new constitution that became effective on November 1, 1961, gave Malta self-government. The Nationalist Party, which advocated independence within the British Commonwealth, won the first election under the new constitution, and their leader, George Borg Olivier (1911–1980), became prime minister. Malta gained independence on September 21, 1964.

In the June 1971 election, the Nationalist Party was defeated by the Labor Party, a democratic socialist party that had urged independence outside the British Commonwealth of Nations. Dominic Mintoff (1916–), the leader of the Labor Party, became the new Maltese prime minister. Mintoff's socialist government moved more to the left in the next few years, creating violent, political polarization in the island nation.

The Mintoff government declared itself to be nonaligned in foreign affairs and in 1979 declined to renew an agreement that would allow British troops under NATO command to rent facilities on Malta. Mintoff also cooperated with Libya in the 1970s, although relations became strained in 1980 over a dispute regarding oil-drilling rights in the Mediterranean Sea. Mintoff won a third five-year term in office in December 1981 but resigned in December 1984 and was succeeded by Labor education minister Carmelo Mifsud-Bonnici (1933–). In May 1987 the Nationalists returned to power, and their leader, Eddie Fenech Adami (1934–), became prime minister. Cyprus also has the EDEK (*Ethniki Dimokratiki Enosi Kyprou*—Cyprus National Democratic Union) Socialist Party.

ICELAND

In 1916, the Social Democratic Party of Iceland was founded.[41] The first chairperson was Jón Baldvinsson, who died in 1938 and was succeeded by Stefán Jón Steffansson.

The Social Democrats have been represented in Iceland's parliament since 1921. Until 1940 the party and the trade unions had been members of the National Federation, whose supreme executive was the head of both, but the political party has since been separated from trade unions. The Social

Democrats suffered splits in the years before World War II, as did many such parties. First, in 1930 a group broke off to form the Communist Party of Iceland. Joining a popular front with the Communists at the latter's invitation in 1938 led to another split. One group of Social Democrats united with the Communists to form the Socialist United People's Party, which was soon controlled by the Communists, and provided the only government opposition during the war years to the ruling, national coalition of the conservative Independence Party, the Progressive Party, and the Social Democrats, who did not join with the Communists.

In 1942, the United People's Party had won more votes than the Social Democrats; but after the end of World War II, the United People's Party declined, and the Social Democrats were able to poll 16 percent of the vote, the same as the United People's Party, in the 1953 election.

In 1959, the Social Democrats again became part of the government in coalition with the Independence Party. The latter has maintained its lead since that time with the Progressives and the Social Democrats as smaller parties. Other Icelandic parties of note are the People's Alliance, the Marxist party, the Citizen's Party, and the Women's Alliance.

NOTES

1. Harry W. Laidler, *History of Socialism* (New York: Apollo, 1968), pp. 223–256.
2. Peter Gay, *The Dilemma of Democratic Socialism—Eduard Bernstein's Challenge to Marx* (New York: Collier, 1962); Leszek Kolakowski, *Main Currents of Marxism*, trans. P. S. Falla, 3 vols. (Oxford: Oxford University Press, 1978), 2:98–114.
3. Eduard Bernstein, *Evolutionary Socialism* (New York: Schocken, 1961).
4. Kolakowski, *Main Currents of Marxism*, 2:31–60.
5. Ibid., 2:61–97.
6. Rosa Luxemburg, *Leninism or Marxism?* trans. Ken Eaton (Leeds, UK: I.L.P. Square One Publications, 1971); "Organizational Questions of Russian Social Democracy," *Die Neue Zeit* 22(2) (Stuttgart, 1904): 484–492, 529–535.
7. Laidler, *History of Socialism*, pp. 505–509, 738–739.
8. Ibid., pp. 509–513.
9. Leon P. Baradat, *Political Ideologies—Their Origin And Impact*, 2d ed. (Englewood Cliffs, NJ: Prentice-Hall, 1984), p. 271.
10. Harry B. Ellis, *Ideals and Ideologies—Communism, Socialism and Capitalism* (New York: Mentor, 1972), pp. 139–140.
11. Otto Kallscheuer, "Philosophy and Politics in the SPD," *Telos*, 53 (Fall 1982): 83.

12. Laidler, *History of Socialism*, pp. 284–286.
13. Warren Lerner, *A History of Socialism and Communism in Modern Times: Theorists, Activists, and Humanists* (Englewood Cliffs, NJ: Prentice Hall, 1982), p. 68.
14. Ibid., pp. 76–77.
15. Jean Jaurès, "Idealism In History," in Albert Fried and Ronald Sanders, eds., *Socialist Thought—A Documentary History* (Garden City, NY: Anchor, 1964), pp. 405–415.
16. Stanley Rothman, Howard Scarrow, and Martin Schain, *European Society and Politics: Britain, France and Germany* (St. Paul, MN: West Publishing, 1976), pp. 178–181.
17. Kolakowski, *Main Currents of Marxism*, 2:120.
18. James D. Forman, *Socialism—Its Theoretical Roots and Present-day Development* (New York: Dell, 1972), p. 37.
19. Laidler, *History of Socialism*, pp. 534–539.
20. G. D. H. Cole, *A History of Socialist Thought*, 5 vols. (New York: St. Martin's Press, 1953–1958), 5:170–178.
21. Martin Linton, "The Swedish Road to Socialism," *Fabian Tracts* (London: Fabian Society, 1985), no. 503, pp. 26–29.
22. Laidler, *History of Socialism*, pp. 687–690.
23. Ibid., pp. 529–533.
24. Ibid., pp. 805–807.
25. Ibid., pp. pp. 539–543.
26. Ibid., pp. 808–811.
27. Ibid., pp. 543–547.
28. Ibid., pp. 811–812.
29. Ibid., pp. 494–499.
30. Ibid., pp. 795–798.
31. Ibid., pp. 500–504.
32. Ibid., pp. 798–800.
33. Ibid., pp. 525–528.
34. Ibid., pp. 804–805.
35. Ibid., pp. 513–519.
36. Ibid., pp. 803–804.
37. Ibid., pp. 548–558.
38. Ibid., pp. 812–814.
39. Ibid., pp. 558–562.
40. Ibid., pp. 814–815.
41. Ibid., pp. 815–816.

3

Democratic Socialism in Great Britain and Ireland

Britain has been a major source of democratic socialist movements and thought. Some of the forerunners of British democratic socialism were the utopians Thomas More and Robert Owen. However, by the mid-nineteenth century, two main wings of the British democratic socialist movement had developed: (1) the cooperative movement and (2) the parties that would eventually unite to form the Labour Party.

THE COOPERATIVE MOVEMENT

The first cooperative movement was organized by the Fenwick Weavers in Ayrshire, near Glasgow, Scotland, in 1769. During the next half century, several more consumers' cooperatives were organized in the Glasgow district.[1]

One of the earliest cooperators was Dr. William King, a Brighton physician and editor of *The Co-operator* (1828–1830), which enunciated the basic principles by which consumers' cooperative stores should operate.[2] In 1826, the Brighton Society was founded and opened its first store. Within a few years, they had opened some three hundred more stores throughout England. Unfortunately, many of these early stores failed.

Real success did not come until the founding of the Rochdale cooperatives.[3] In 1843 twenty-eight weavers, after an unsuccessful strike, met in the Chartist Reading Room in Rochdale, England, near Manchester, to discuss what could be done to improve their conditions. They had been inspired by Robert Owen's ideas on socialism, and they decided to set up a retail store to be owned and operated by their members. After saving up their money, in December 1844, they opened on Toad Lane the food cooperative store of the Rochdale Society of Pioneers. Ownership was by each member who bought one or more nominally priced shares. It was run by a board of directors, but every member got one vote in all important decisions, regardless of the number of shares they owned. The shares did not pay dividends, as this was a not-for-profit corporation. Rather, the cooperative made refunds to every member out of the surplus over costs made by the cooperative, based on how much each member had bought in a year's time.

The cooperative movement (also hyphenated *co-operative* or abbreviated *co-op*) was a great success. By 1895, the Rochdale Society of Pioneers had 12,000 members, and new cooperatives were opened. Today, Britain has 13 million co-op members, some 24 percent of the population, with millions more throughout the world. British Liberal Prime Minister William Ewart Gladstone (1809–1898) had hailed cooperatives as the greatest economic invention of the nineteenth century.[4] It can well be argued that cooperatives are the most successful form of socialism. They are a more sustainable form than is state socialism, surviving changes in government in a way that state ownership is not able to do when conservatives come to power and engage in privatization of previously nationalized enterprises. Although cooperatives certainly benefit from governments friendly to their aid, especially in times of economic distress, they do not necessarily need socialist governments to survive in the way that state-owned industries do.

CHRISTIAN SOCIALISM

British Christian Socialism was founded by Frederick Denison Maurice (1805–1872), a minister and professor, and by Charles Kingsley (1819–1875), also a minister and a professor as well as a novelist, and John M. Ludlow (1821–1911).[5] Son of a Unitarian minister, Maurice took an active interest in his father's philanthropic work with the poor. He became an ordained minister in 1834, a professor of English literature and history at Kings College, and later a professor of moral theology at Cambridge University. He also inaugurated the Working-Men's College, founded with Kingsley the weekly *Christian Socialist* magazine, and wrote *The Kingdom of Christ* and *Moral and Metaphysical Religion*. Kingsley, a minister at Eversley, was the author of the children's classic *Water Babies* and a professor of history at Cambridge.

Maurice's socialism was a mild appeal to logic rather than emotion, whereas Kingsley's ardent brand of socialism was filled with passion. Both derived their belief in socialism out of a radical interpretation of Christian ethics. They attacked class inequality, the inaction of the clergy, and the use of the Bible to justify holding the poor in their place. On the contrary, they considered the Bible to be the poor man's book and the word of God against tyrants and idlers. Kingsley particularly attacked the Manchester school of laissez-faire economics as an abomination.

Kingsley's novel *Alton Locke*, the story of a tailor-poet who works himself up from poverty, was published just as opposition to the Christian Socialists was developing. Bookstores refused to sell it, and the newspapers also refused to carry advertisements for the book. Maurice and Kingsley's magazine, *The Christian Socialist*, was banned in France, and a committee from King's College was established to investigate Maurice. Along with Kingsley and Ludlow, Maurice published a short-lived weekly paper, beginning in 1848, *Politics for the People*. In 1852 *The Christian Socialist* was superseded by *The Journal of Association*, edited by Thomas Hughes. Backing away from political criticism, all articles that were political in nature were excluded, and only the ones about cooperatives were carried. That year, partly as a result of work by Maurice, Kingsley, and others, a law was passed by the British Parliament, the first of its kind in the world, that recognized and protected cooperatives. Also in 1852, the Christian Socialist society changed their name from the Society for Promoting Workingmen Associations to the Association for Promoting Industrial and Provident Societies. This latter association supported the engineers' strike of 1852 and helped bring the public a better understanding of the aims of trade unionism.

Unfortunately, many of the producers' cooperatives began to fail by 1853. Internal bickering and indifference, as well as outright embezzlement of funds, all contributed to their demise.

In 1854 the Workingmen's College was founded, and the leaders of the Christian Socialist movement kept up instruction there for many years. However, the Christian Socialist movement began to decline after 1855, but from time to time there would be revivals of the movement in Britain and in Continental Europe. In the 1880s, the Reverend Stewart D. Headlam (1847–1924) founded the Guild of St. Matthew and edited its organ, the *Church Reformer*, which espoused Christian Socialism.[6] In 1889 the Christian Social Union was formed; and by the early 1920s, the Socialist Christian League was founded, with its members pledged to work and pray for the spiritual and economic emancipation of people and the establishment of the Commonwealth of God on earth.

In 1942 the Council of Clergy and Ministers for Common Ownership was founded, objecting to the vagueness of some earlier Christian Socialist pronouncements. The Bishop of Bradford was president, and the Bishop of

Malmesbury and the Dean of Canterbury were vice-presidents of this council calling for socialism at home and the defeat of Fascism abroad. Also in the 1940s, the Catholic Crusade attacked inequality and class exploitation in Britain and called for common ownership.

MILL

John Stuart Mill (1806–1873), the great philosopher of liberalism, late in life became an advocate of socialism.[7] In his *Principles of Political Economy*, he declared that communism with all its difficulties was preferable to the present system of suffering and injustice under capitalism.[8] However, he did not believe any increase in the standard of living due to a communist system would be worth the price of restrictions on liberty that communism might bring about.[9]

He was midway through writing a book on the subject of socialism at the time of his death and had completed the first four chapters, which subsequently were published in 1879 in the *Fortnightly Review*.[10] Mill argued that the advent of manhood suffrage would inevitably lead to a public discourse on the nature of the system of private property and that this discussion had already begun. Mill believed that socialism deserved study as it afforded the guiding principles of necessary social improvements.

THE SOCIAL DEMOCRATIC FEDERATION

G. D. H. Cole remarked that it was often said that socialism died out in Britain between the last Chartist Conference in 1858 and the founding in 1881 of the Democratic Federation.[11] However, he pointed out, and quite correctly, that this was not entirely true—there had been some socialist activity in Britain in the 1860s and 1870s, although not a true movement until the 1880s. The renamed Social Democratic Federation was one of the principal organizations in the formation of the British Labour Party, and the Federation was at the beginning of the revival of socialism in Britain and its emergence as a mass movement.

Hyndman

In 1881 Henry Mayers Hyndman (1842–1921) helped found the Democratic Federation.[12] Its origins are to be found in a suggestion of the Radical/Liberal workingmen's clubs of the 1880s. Their newspaper, *The Radical*, was critical of the Liberal Party leadership and in 1881 called for the formation of an independent party.[13] This led to a conference that was called for June 8, 1881, out of which emerged the Democratic Federation. Although the Federation's platform called for more attention to be paid to labor interests, it was largely based on the old Radical one.

The first leader of the new group was Joseph Cowen, a member of Parliament from Newcastle-upon-Tyne. The organization did not take on a specifically socialist cast until Hyndman began taking an active role. Hyndman had originally been in the radical wing of the Liberal Party, but he had quarreled with Gladstone over the question of what to do about the Ottoman Empire in the wake of its decay and the threat of Russian expansion into the region. Hyndman quit the Liberals, and ran as a Conservative in 1880. However, in 1881 he converted to Marxism.

There are historical reasons why someone like Hyndman should appear in the 1880s to lead a socialist party. The Reform Bill of 1867 allowed many British workingmen for the first time in history to vote.[14] This right was further granted to more people with the Reform Bill of 1884, giving impetus to the labor and socialist movements in Britain.

Having been converted to Marxism after reading Marx's *Capital* in a French translation during an American cruise, Hyndman visited Marx in London and told him of his plans to establish the Democratic Federation as a revival of the Chartist movement to win democratic rights for the working class in Britain.[15] His plan, as he described it to Marx, was not to immediately set up an explicitly socialist group, but rather to attempt to stimulate a working-class, mass movement via the Radical Working Men's Clubs that existed in large numbers in the working-class areas, especially in London.[16] However, Hyndman did not agree with Marx's views on violence and revolution. Although Marx did believe that the conditions in Britain might allow for a peaceful, democratic transition to socialism, he would not rule out violence and revolution.[17] Hyndman, on the other hand, wanted no part of violent revolution at this time as a means to establishing socialism and wanted to retain parliamentary institutions if at all possible. His democratic sentiments led him to hope for constitutional reforms that would forestall the need for revolution.[18] It must be remembered that this nonviolent, evolutionary view was part of the early thinking of Hyndman and his associates. There would come a time when he and his followers would sour on the peaceful, parliamentary road to socialism and adopt the revolutionary view held by Marx. At this time in the early 1880s, Hyndman and Marx were at odds over the issue of peaceful versus violent revolutionary change. Marx wrote to Hyndman saying that although revolution was not absolutely necessary in Britain, it, nevertheless, was a possibility.[19] It should be noted that Marx was not being dogmatic on this point. He was not insisting on revolution; he saw it only as a possibility, and one for which he was not eager. Indeed, Marx was willing to put the blame on his beloved proletariat as well as on the bourgeoisie should it come down to killing. Hyndman agreed that revolution could conceivably happen; but, as a matter of good politics, he did not want to even mention that possibility publicly, preferring to downplay the whole question with the voters. He may have been in better touch with the sentiments of his countrymen than was Marx, the revolutionary exile, and had instinctively understood that the majority of English voters would be repelled by any mention of revolution. Perhaps Marx, by virtue of his temperament and his status as an exile in a foreign country, may not have grasped the reality of the essentially nonrevolutionary nature of Victorian England.

One may also question whether the argument existed between Marx and Hyndman for reasons completely different from those stated. Marx did not get along with many of his fellow socialists and had a particularly bad feeling for Hyndman. They may have been arguing for argument's sake, not really over political differences, which were relatively minor in this case. One is reminded of the fighting between Stalin and Trotsky, which involved more personal dislike, egotism, and ambition than differences over building socialism in one country versus advancing world revolution.

We can further see the democratic sentiments of Hyndman in the program of the Democratic Federation, which called for:[20]

1. Adult Suffrage.
2. Triennial Parliaments.
3. Equal Electoral Districts.
4. Payment of Members and Official Expenses out of the Rates.
5. Bribery, Treating, and Corrupt Practices, to be made acts of Felony.
6. Abolition of the House of Lords as a Legitimate Body.
7. Legislative Independence for Ireland.
8. National and Federal Parliaments.
9. Nationalization of the Land.

This program was really an extension of the democratic reforms sought by the earlier Chartist movement. The emphasis is clearly on achieving a democratic form of government.

Morton Cowden explained that the results of the Depression of 1878 and 1888—high unemployment and falling wages, greater competition from abroad, and the end of sweeping political reforms—all combined to call into question the capitalist system itself. With inspiration from Owen, Marx, Mill, the Chartists, and other socialists and anarchists, British intellectuals began to form small, socialist groups by the 1880s, such as the Democratic Federation. However, at this time, the trade union movement rejected the appeals of these movements and remained married to the Liberal Party.[21]

Marx was discouraging about the idea of reviving the Chartist movement and he and Engels thought poorly of Hyndman and his abilities.[22] Nevertheless, Hyndman went ahead with his plans to form the Democratic Federation and wrote a book, *England for All: The Text-book of Democracy*,[23] published in 1881. He made a Marxian argument for socialism in England without mentioning Marx's name or giving Marx credit for the theories that were expressed in the book.[24] Hyndman argued that power was based on ownership and that capitalists should be replaced by the worker-controlled state.[25]

Hyndman purposely avoided mentioning Marx by name because he feared that the prejudice that his fellow British had against foreigners, particularly radicals like Marx, would alienate his potential readers.[26] Of course, it is also possible that this plagiarism was done merely for Hyndman to falsely claim credit for a greater man's ideas. Whether Hyndman's reasons were only a rationalization for stealing Marx's ideas or, as he claimed, for good politic for Marx, this was the final straw.[27] On December 15, 1881, Marx wrote to a friend, F. A. Sorge, living in the United States, that "a little book" published by Hyndman "pilfers *Capital*," making for good propaganda but lacking as a thorough study. Marx ranked Hyndman as a middle-class writer out to make money and a name for himself and to make political capital out of new ideas he had gotten as a windfall.[28] Indeed Geoffrey Foote commented that Hyndman's Marxism contained a crude, national chauvinism and a belief that socialism could be brought about by the existing state. Although Marx found Hyndman personally objectionable, Engels considered the Hyndmanites to be a sect that had turned Marxism into a dogma and had rejected all labor movements that were not Marxist.[29]

The Democratic Federation, in fact, failed to attract much of a working-class following but instead gained a small number of like-minded, middle-class radicals.[30] It was not revolutionary at all. Hyndman had written in *England for All*, for example, that perhaps only the English alone could carry out by peaceful means the changes that the revolutionaries in Continental Europe had sought to achieve by means of anarchy and bloodshed.[31] Indeed, he placed more hope in the actions of the middle and upper classes than in the working class to win reforms. If the reforms were to be peaceful, the upper class, Hyndman believed, would have to lead.[32]

With such elitist views, the Hyndmanites only succeeded in alienating the support of the working class. By denying that the labor unions had any right to speak for the workers and by demeaning them as having no other goals than winning pay hikes and shortened hours, the Hyndmanites also alienated the organized union movement.[33]

Hyndman was not without sympathy for the struggles of workers, their trade unions, and their strikes, yet he felt them, ultimately, to be ineffective in changing society.[34] He classified strikes, syndicalism, and anarchism as aspects of working-class ignorance and despair. Strikes could not end exploitation by seeking higher wages; they only legitimized the wage system and capitalism.[35] This sectarian attitude prevented Hyndman from playing a major role in the labor movement and even led to the withdrawal of the Social Democratic Federation from the Labour Party only a year after the latter was formed because it would not accept the class-war ideology that the Hyndmanites had adopted by that time.[36]

Hyndman's view was that deliverance from capitalist tyranny could only come about from outside of the working class by an educated elite. Trade unions, he believed, had essentially played out their effectiveness.[37]

Carl F. Brand, in writing about the Democratic Federation's view of socialism, noted that they first used the word *nationalization* in 1882 and that Hyndman used it with reference to nationalizing land, not industry. This had happened after the American Henry George (1839–1897), the originator of the single-tax theory of land, had visited England and raised the whole issue of the land question.[38]

This is not to say that Hyndman was the first to call for public ownership of land. Marx and Engels in *The Communist Manifesto* (1848) listed as the first of their proposed, socialist measures the abolition of private property in land.[39] Indeed, it was quite common in earlier utopian socialist writings to see land rather than manufacturing as the kind of property to be socially owned, largely because there were far fewer such manufacturing industries and because land was more important in these economies still based on agriculture.

In 1883 the Democratic Federation came out with its first explicitly socialist pamphlet, *Socialism Made Plain*.[40] It called principally for public ownership of capital and land, and it denounced monopolies.[41] It also called for a minimum program, which Hyndman referred to as stepping stones to a happier period, including better housing for artisans and agricultural workers, free and compulsory education for all social classes, free meals for school children, the eight-hour workday, cumulative taxation, state ownership of the railroads and banks, the abolition of the national debt, and the organization of agricultural and industrial armies.[42] These ideas were clearly based on *The Communist Manifesto*. The pamphlet proclaimed that because the creation of wealth had long become social, it was high time for the exchange of goods to also become social.[43] All of the remaining nonsocialist members of the Democratic Federation resigned with the adoption of this manifesto.[44]

In 1883 Hyndman published *The Historical Basis of Socialism in England*.[45] With this Marxist exposition, he did finally acknowledge Karl Marx and the influence Marx had on his ideas.[46] It was a chauvinist work, by Hyndman's own admission.[47] To his mind, he stated, the first real socialism was based on the interests of "the great Celto-Teutonic peoples" of Britain, America, Australia, and possibly Germany.[48]

British artist, craftsman, poet, and socialist William Morris (1834–1896) joined the Democratic Federation in 1883 and quickly became its coleader, along with Henry Hyndman.[49] They continued to lead the evolution of the organization into an explicitly socialist group; and in 1884, they changed the name of the organization to the Social Democratic Federation (SDF).[50]

The program of the SDF called for, among other things, nationalizing the means of production, distribution, and exchange by a democratic state; equality for women; compulsory as well as secular and free education; the abolition of child labor; and a forty-eight- hour workweek.[51]

How did Hyndman define *socialism*? For him, socialism meant national ownership of natural resources, land utilities, and factories.[52] He saw socialism as a historical theory that accounted for human progress in society by the growing command over the forces of nature, by mechanical developments, and by the power of producing wealth—a progress that substituted the struggle for existence by cooperation. However, Hyndman did not think that mere state ownership meant socialism. If the bureaucrats ran the system and the workers had not democratic control over industry, it was not socialism at all, in Hyndman's opinion, but rather state capitalism.[53] Hyndman believed that a bureaucratic, state capitalism was likely to be corrupt and that it could not completely reverse the degeneration of a capitalist society even with the vigorous application of state intervention. Hyndman was thinking of imperial Germany, which had developed such a state capitalist system, but his view seems both appropriate and prophetic with respect to the history of the Soviet Union.

In 1884 Hyndman and Morris wrote a pamphlet entitled *A Summary of the Principles of Socialism*.[54] The work sketched the history of slavery, serfdom, capitalism, and socialism from a Marxist perspective, although this view did not become a major one in the SDF until later on. Also, the official organ of the SDF, *Justice*, was established that year.

The Marxist viewpoint was strong in the SDF. This was a rigid form of Marxist theory, placing the main emphasis on the labor theory of value and Marxian economic theory.[55] The ethical appeal of socialism was not at all emphasized, but rather was a "scientific" appeal—Marx's economic theories on the nature of how the capitalists exploited the workers. The Hyndmanites, however, placed very little emphasis on Marx's speculative philosophy of history—the view that history was the story of class struggles, culminating in the superstruggle of the proletariat against the bourgeoisie and leading to the socialist revolution.

SDF Factions

Hyndman's Marxist faction was but one of five that existed in the early SDF. Hyndman's faction wanted to establish a Marxist party in Great Britain along the lines of the German Social Democratic Party, and he regarded socialism largely as a matter of political reform, placing special emphasis on electoral campaigning.[56]

A second faction, led by John Burns (1858–1943), was composed mainly of trade unionists who were politically minded, but less Marxist oriented than the Hyndman faction and more interested in industrial questions.[57]

A third faction, led by Joseph Lane, was anarchist. It had come out of the Labour Emancipation League and had affiliated with the Democratic Federation in 1884 when the latter was becoming more openly socialist. As anarchists, they were in sharp disagreement with the electorally oriented Marxism of the Hyndman faction and demanded that the program of the Labour Emancipation League be adopted as the party program of the renamed SDF at its conference in 1884. This was done, and many of the political reforms of the program of the Democratic Federation, such as calling for proportional representation and payment for elected representatives, were dropped from the new program of the SDF.[58]

A fourth faction was made up of socialists who were mostly intellectuals but who did not have a clearly defined school of socialism such as Marxism.[59] Some of them were active in establishing the Fabian Society, also begun in 1884. William Morris belonged to both groups, as did Ernest Belfort Bax (1854–1926), a frequent writer on German socialism.[60] The latter's criticism of Marxism was representative of this fourth faction's views: Marxism was economic determinist and failed to understand the roles of moral, religious, political, and other noneconomic factors in determining social affairs.[61]

A fifth faction existed in Scotland, which formed the Scottish Land and Labour League in 1884 and affiliated with the SDF that same year.[62] It developed largely from the Scottish farmers influenced by Henry George.[63] The Irish League also was part of this faction, and their agitation had so frightened the English government with the threat of more unrest in Ireland that the English government arrested Henry George while he was on a speaking tour of England, although he was soon released.

By the end of 1884, these factions split the SDF, finding little basis for ideological unity.[64] The split began when charges were made that Hyndman and his faction were dictatorial, were using undemocratic means to run the SDF, and were being opportunists. Hyndman denounced his opponents in the SDF, particularly Andreas Scheu (1844–1927), as being anarchists. The anarchists in the SDF were fundamentally opposed to parliamentary politics, while Hyndman's main goal was to establish a parliamentary, social democratic party. Between these two ideological poles was a third group, one that while not opposing establishing a parliamentary party on principle nevertheless disagreed with the Hyndmanites that the time was right to run candidates for office on a socialist ticket. Instead, they favored a program of educational work among the working class before a serious, socialist, political party could be launched successfully.

Another argument between the Hyndmanites and the anarchists concerned the Scottish Land and Labour League faction. Scheu had been in favor of this group being only loosely affiliated with the SDF rather than being full members. The anarchist Labour Emancipation League was also only an affiliate of the SDF. Hyndman objected to such anarchist decentralization. He thought in terms of a highly centralist and disciplined party. Denouncing Scheu and another member on the Executive, William J. Clarke (1852–1901), as being anarchists, Hyndman demanded their expulsion from the SDF. The motion was defeated nine to sixteen.

At this point, William Morris began to lead a schism by the left wing of the SDF against the Hyndmanites. Morris criticized Hyndman for the way in which he considered the SDF his own personal property and for his arbitrary rule. Morris's faction founded a rival group, the Socialist League, and started their own paper, the *Commonweal*. The anarchists in the Labour Emancipation League as well as in the Scottish Land and Labour League now detached themselves from the SDF, leaving the latter solely in the hands of the Hyndmanites, who sought to establish a Marxist parliamentary party.[65]

The SDF ran candidates in the parliamentary elections held in November 1885 but did so poorly that it nearly finished the organization, which had been badly weakened by the splits of the year before. The electoral failure caused a great loss of its remaining membership and of the subscriptions to its paper, *Justice*.[66] The SDF was also badly hurt by the Tory Gold Scandal connected with this election. It had accepted money from an unknown source for its campaign. It was later revealed that the money was given to the SDF through Henry Hyde Champion (1859–1938), a supporter, but it was supplied, in fact, by a Tory journalist, Maltman Barry. The "Tory Gold" was given to the SDF in the hopes that it would split the Liberal vote and result in a Conservative victory. When the truth came out, the Socialist League denounced the SDF. Most of the Fabians who had joined the SDF resigned and thereafter concentrated in working to build the Fabian Society.[67]

However, the SDF overcame these setbacks and put itself at the head of the movement, protesting the rising unemployment that began in Britain that year.[68] Demanding the "right to work," the SDF agitated for "Home Colonization," in which the government would take land not in production out of the hands of private owners and settle the unemployed there in Cooperative Colonies, as well as setting them up in businesses with the most modern production techniques.[69]

Hyndman and his followers in the SDF used a Marxist analysis of the sudden rise in unemployment in Britain and laid great stress especially on Marx's theory that capitalism needed an industrial reserve army of unemployed labor in order to keep wages low and to supply a constant source of complacent workers who could be used as replacements for strikers.

Demanding immediate relief programs from the government, the SDF agitation took the form of demonstrations and processions at Trafalgar Square and Hyde Park, organized mainly by John Burns and culminated in 1887 in a great procession and open-air address at St. Paul's Cathedral in London.[70] These demonstrations led to clashes with the police. In 1885 the police tried to put a stop to mass meetings on Dod Street and arrested several speakers. The next year, many SDF leaders, including Hyndman and Burns, were arrested and tried for inciting riots, but they were acquitted.

The SDF and the Labour Party

These years had been the high point of SDF activity. On February 27, 1900, the SDF, together with the Independent Labour Party, the Fabian Society, and the unions of the Trade Union Congress, met at the Congregationalist Memorial Hall in London to form the Labour Representation Committee, which changed its name to the Labour Party in 1906. However, continued splits with the ranks of the SDF weakened them. In 1903, its Scottish members broke off to form the Socialist Labour Party along the lines of the American party of the same name led by Daniel De Leon (1852–1914), who argued for a form of socialism based on socialist, industrial unions taking over industry and running government based on union membership rather than on territorial district representation.[71] In 1905, the SDF split again when some of its members, having completely rejected the reformist policies of the SDF and the Labour Party, split to form the rival Socialist Party of Great Britain, a minor party that still exists in Britain today.[72]

Having been greatly weakened by these splits, the SDF formally reorganized in 1908 and changed its name to the Social Democratic Party.[73] In 1911 this merged with some disaffected members of the Independent Labour Party, a group connected to the publication called the *Clarion*, and others to form the British Socialist Party.[74] The latter party affiliated in 1916 with the British Labour Party.[75]

Hyndman left his own British Socialist Party because of its antiwar stand with regard to World War I and formed the staunchly prowar National Socialist Party, which had very little support.[76] In 1920 this latter group readopted the historic name of the Social Democratic Federation.[77] This group affiliated once again with the Labour Party and was on the latter's right wing, becoming an early critic of Bolshevism.[78]

Hyndman, who had done so much to influence the British socialist movement, died in 1921 of pneumonia.[79] The SDF withered away after Hyndman's death, formally coming to an end at the start of World War II. In summarizing the history of the SDF, E. J. Hobsbawn noted that it was the first of the modern, British, socialist organizations and, even more important, it showed real lasting power, despite numerous splits and crises.[80]

THE FABIAN SOCIETY

A major organization that helped found the British Labour Party was the Fabian Society. Its school of thought helped shape democratic socialism and had a greater impact than Marxism in Britain.

The Founding of the Fabian Society

The Fabian Society was founded in early 1884 in London.[81] It began when Thomas Davidson (1840–1900), a Scottish scholar, returned in 1883 from living in the United States and gathered around him a group of young disciples to whom he had proposed establishing a communal movement to be called the Fellowship of the New Life. Soon after Davidson returned to

America, the group broke into two factions, one of which went forward with its idea of establishing the communal fellowship of the New Life. The second breakaway faction was skeptical of Davidson's utopian ideas and wanted to establish a political organization that would work for socialist reforms in society. This latter group took the name Fabian Society.[82]

The name *Fabian* came from a suggestion of an early member, Frank Podmore (1856–1910). The name was based on the Roman General Quintus Fabius Maximus, known as the Cunctator—"The Delayer."[83] Fabius had successfully used delaying tactics to chip away and eventually to stop Hannibal's army. Like Fabius, the Fabian Society wanted to proceed cautiously and to take the time to formulate the right approach. Later, the idea of gradualism became grafted onto this original conception, apparently coming from Sidney Webb (1859–1947), one of the most influential members of the Fabians.[84]

Among the intellectual influences on the Fabians were Marx, Comte, Coleridge, Emerson, Jevons, Wicksteed, Henry George, and especially John Stuart Mill. Gordon Lewis noted that Mill was the Fabians' intellectual godfather and that such an eminent philosopher should come to call himself a socialist gave the Fabians a feeling of intellectual respectability.[85] To them, socialism seemed a natural outcome of the growth of government. J. H. Steward Reid noted that the Fabians were a middle-class organization in composition and outlook, interested more in dispensing information about socialism than in winning converts by emotional appeals and always focused on achieving specific social reforms.[86]

Shaw and Webb

Among the many intellectuals who were attracted to the Fabians and who built it into an important and highly influential organization was George Bernard Shaw (1856–1950).[87] Led by Webb and Shaw, the Society developed a distinct school of thought—Fabian Socialism.[88] It was, above all, an evolutionary, gradualist form of socialism.[89]

An early document written by Webb, *Facts for Socialists*,[90] represented socialism as the outcome of rational tendencies present in capitalism, not as a revolutionary movement seeking to overthrow society.[91] The Fabians only at the beginning even considered Marxism, only to quickly reject it as impractical and unconvincing.

Shaw, in explaining the change from revolutionary to evolutionary ideas in British socialism in his *Fabian Essays*, "The Transition to Social Democracy," noted that the idea of militant organizing, so attractive at first, proved in time to be impractical and had to be abandoned.[92]

The cautious approach to social change taken by the Fabians was expressed on the title page of *Fabian Tract* No. 1 in a motto attributed to Frank Podmore:

> Wherefore it may not be gainsaid that the fruit of this man's long taking of counsel—and (by the many so deemed) untimeous delays—was the safeholding for all men, his fellow-citizens, of the Common Weal.
> For the right moment you must wait, as Fabius did most patiently, when warring against Hannibal, though many censured his delays; but when the time comes you must strike hard, as Fabius did, or your waiting will be in vain, and fruitless.[93]

It was this belief in "the inevitability of gradualness," in Webb's famous words, that really set the Fabians apart from the revolutionary-inclined Marxists. Marx did not deny the possibility of peacefully bringing socialism about by having it voted in when it came to liberal-democratic nations such as Britain. The Fabians did not insist that peaceful, gradual change was the only policy to follow in all countries. Webb, for example, felt that in autocratic nations lacking democratic traditions, such as Russia, there might be no other choice but for the socialist movement to be revolutionary.[94] However, there is a fundamental difference between the Fabians and the Marxists with respect to their philosophical views of history and the nature of changeover from capitalism to socialism that will allow us to classify the Fabians as "evolutionary socialists" and the Marxists, excluding the revisionists, as "revolutionary socialists."

In *Fabian Tract* No. 70, the Fabians denied that they had any views on "historic evolution."[95] However, if they had not developed an explicit and systematic philosophy of history, there was still a general tendency in their views of history.[96] It was a multiple-causation outlook on history, stressing the growth of ideas such as democracy, as well as economic changes such as the Industrial Revolution, which had some negative consequences—higher unemployment and the concentration of capital into the hands of the few. Their approach might be described as trying to develop a thoroughly pragmatic socialism, married to a strong belief in civil rights and liberties.

Fabian Socialism

There are *Fabian Tracts*, especially the earlier ones before a distinctive Fabian approach had jelled, that do have a strong Marxist influence in them, notably, No. 15, "English Progress Towards Social Democracy," written by Sidney Webb. The sketch of history given there emphasizes the struggle for the surplus product in social evolution; the stages of slavery, serfdom, and the proletariat; and the solution to be found in the political evolution of the working class, which would lead to their abolishing capitalism and establishing socialism.[97] Although neither Marx's nor Engels's name is even mentioned, while numerous other socialists are, it would not be difficult to imagine Marx or Engels writing such a tract.

Later, however, the Fabians distinctly rejected the Marxist materialist conception of history as rigid, crude, and overly simplistic economic determinism and also rejected the implication of a violent class war to come.[98]

Elizabeth Durbin noted that at first the Fabians studied Marx, only to rejected his teachings, and then invited Philip Wicksteed and F. Y. Edgeworth to address them on the new economic theory of marginal utility developed by William Stanley Jevons (1835–1882). She also noted that George Bernard Shaw had been an ardent advocate of Marxism, but after much persuasion he came to agree with Webb's view that the Marxian labor theory of value had to be rejected as incorrect, although Shaw continued to believe that *Das Kapital* was a great work.[99]

It was at the home of Mrs. Charlotte M. Wilson that Shaw's Marxist views were criticized by the Fabians and rejected in favor of the modern economic theories of Jevons.[100] Shaw, himself, came to advise that one should read Jevons and other modern economists for an understanding of economics, but that one should also read Marx for an understanding of history and the present-day class struggle.[101]

The major difference between the Marxists and the Fabians was not over the Marxian labor theory of value versus the neoclassical theories of economics pioneered by Jevons, but rather on the question of how socialism would be brought about. For the Marxists, the breakdown of capitalism and the political revolution were ordained by the laws of history. The process might begin slowly, but political revolution would soon occur at a given "nodal point."[102] Whether the political revolution would be a violent one or a peaceful revolution democratically voted in would depend on specific conditions in given nations. In countries like Britain, with its liberal-democratic traditions, it might be a democratically elected, peaceful revolution. But in autocratic nations such as Germany, it might well be violent revolution that would overthrow the existing state. In either case, peaceful or violent revolution, Marxism is in essence a revolutionary socialism that seeks a rapid and radical change in society, especially in the economy, once the socialists have come to power either by election or overthrow.

For the Fabians, however, socialism would come about as part of an evolutionary, gradual process, already underway, which would continue to advance as the electorate became more and more aware of its ability to run the economy by itself without the need for parasitic capitalists and landlords who had been allowed previously to extract "economic rent" (as the Fabians termed *profits*) as a reward for mere ownership and the means of production, distribution, and exchange.[103]

Geoffrey Foote explained the connection between Fabian economic theory and the political views of the Fabians, noting that once the Fabians came to believe that Marx was fundamentally wrong about the nature of profit and that the capitalists exploited the workers, they adopted the alternative view that the real class struggle was between the idle rich and those that did all the work—be they hardworking employers or employees. Therefore, the aim should not be to expropriate the capitalists but to tax their *unearned* income.[104]

We can see, therefore, that Fabian socialism, unlike Marxism, emphasized action less radical than expropriation and instead emphasized the more moderate methods of taxation of the capitalists. Foote seemed to imply that the Fabians had no interest in social ownership of the economy. This is not entirely the case, although it would be fair to say that the Fabians thought reforms more important.

The Fabians also differed from the Ethical Socialists—a moral-based socialism that developed out of religious socialism, at this time represented chiefly by the Independent Labour Party headed by James Keir Hardie (1856–1915)—over the need for class war and revolution. Beatrice Webb stated that there was some truth in Hardie's statement that the Fabians were the worst enemies of revolution. In the Fabian view, no change in a democratic nation like Britain could possibly occur unless the opinions of all social classes were changed, nor would such socialistic change be desirable without the consent of all.[105]

Whereas Marx tended to view the state as the instrument of the ruling class, the Fabians placed emphasis on gradually having the state serve the interests of the working class by way of having reform legislation passed—including the "sewer socialism" of municipal water and sanitation projects, and so on, which the Fabians were well known for proposing in their *Tracts*. Foote pointed out that the Fabians granted that the state today was controlled by the rich, but they believed that in the future it could be captured by the workers by electing socialist deputies to office. Thus, violent revolution was unnecessary in Britain.[106]

Francis Williams pointed out that the Fabians worked not for proletarian struggle but rather for the masses, including the managers and other professionals, as well as manual workers against the idle capitalists and landed aristocracy.[107]

The Marxist view of history was that it was the story of class wars; the Fabians rejected this theory and instead saw change coming about from an electorate that transcended social classes, informed and aroused by ideas, which played little role in Marx's dialectical materialist views. The voters were becoming more and more insistent on achieving social justice by progressive, gradual reform, and they were coming to the conclusion that only with the socialization of the economy could their aspirations be fully realized.[108]

Gordon Lewis, in comparing the Fabians to the Marxists such as Hyndman, cogently made the point that the Marxists had all the passion for doctrinal argument that Marx himself possessed but without his intellectual capacity. The Fabians' chief virtue, on the other hand, was to substitute reason for the romance of revolutionary posturing.[109]

Fabianism was inherently an evolutionary socialism. The Fabians pointed out that socialism need not be revolutionary, nor did it necessarily mean that industry would be under the control of a centralized state.[110]

Revisionists broke with the orthodox Marxists on this very question of revolution. Eduard Bernstein, strongly influenced by the Fabians during his years of exile in England, became the leader of the evolutionary socialists in the European continent. Hyndman, who argued with Marx over the need for violent revolution, like some revisionists, kept certain Marxist phraseology, including the use of the word *revolution* but meant by it peaceful revolution. Hyndman was critical of the reformism of the Fabian Society and that of the Independent Labour Party and the later Labour Party. J. H. Steward Reid noted that the tactics of the Fabian Society were to use propaganda to convince the voters, to use printed questions and public speeches to influence the candidates, to use personal contacts and persuasive reasoning with the legislators, and to use the marshaling of facts and logical suggestions on the administrators, all with the aim of convincing all of the rightness of socialism.[111]

The evolutionary socialism of the Fabians can be seen in *Fabian Tract* No. 70, entitled, "The Report on Fabian Policy," in which the Fabians declare themselves to be in sympathy with the ordinary citizens' desire for peaceful, gradual change with the aim of voting in socialism.[112]

Even the more Marxist-influenced *Fabian Tract* No. 15, by Sidney Webb, was essentially an evolutionary socialist document rather than one that advocated revolution. The tract spoke of "industrial evolution" of increasing socialization of the means of production along with the increasing impoverishment of the workers, leading to a situation in which "political evolution" would soon make the workers the rulers. The state was growing in power as part of this evolution, the tract argued, and already regulated nearly every industrial enterprise and activity that it had not yet absorbed.[113]

The Fabians' evolutionary views led them to a conception of socialism that was strongly in favor of political democracy. They saw socialism as an extension of democracy from the sphere of politics to the wider sphere of the entire society. *Fabian Tract* No. 15 declared that England already was the most socialist of all the European nations and that socialism would inevitably be democratic. Socialism would not be the violent, revolutionary movement that some imagined, with blood flowing in the streets. The progress of socialism was an evolution that society was destined to make.[114]

What form of social ownership did the Fabians mean in their view of socialism? They thought of it as being government ownership, with control and planning under the auspices of a democratically elected parliament.[115] This was not a worker-owned-and-controlled system of decentralized socialism that some socialists had envisioned, among them the German socialist leader Ferdinand Lassalle, whose party platform called for producers' cooperatives to be established by state aid. Fabian socialism was one of national and local ownership of businesses and industries under bureaucratic control. *Fabian Tract* No. 70 stated that the Fabian Society "energetically repudiates" referendum democracy as opposed to representative government.[116] Furthermore, this tract declared that the socialism advocated by the Fabian Society was strictly state socialism—government ownership and bureaucratic control of the means of production, distribution, and exchange—and they argued that this was practical in England because the state was already democratic. It was not necessary to abolish the state as the Marxists and the anarchists wanted to do in continental Europe, where the states were fundamentally antagonistic to the working class. In England, the workers needed only to use the democratic rights they already possessed to establish socialism. The future economic system—state socialism—was, thus, built on the base of a democratic polity, in the Fabian view of English socialism. Note that this is quite the opposite of the Marxian argument that superstructural systems such as politics are built on the economic base of society—a reflection of the Fabians' rejection of dialectical materialism.

An early Fabian view of anarchism can be seen in *Fabian Tract* No. 4, entitled, "What Socialism Is." No. 4 states that socialism has taken two distinct forms, either collectivist or anarchist, and that English socialism was not yet sufficiently developed to be in either camp. However, in time, the "unconscious Socialists" of England would either become collectivists supporting a strong central administration or anarchists championing individual initiative.[117]

This, of course, was a very early work, written in 1886 before a distinctly Fabian Socialism had emerged. However, the opinions expressed in this tract were essentially correct, even if perhaps a bit exaggerated. British socialism did, in fact, lean toward two schools: the collectivist and the anarchist. However, the split was not as distinct as this tract suggested. Various schools of British socialism ranged between these two poles, somewhat like a spectrum with anarchism and collectivism each at an extreme. At this time, the Fabians had not yet as an organization developed a distinct identity, although shortly they would. When they did, they would lean very much to the collectivist side of the spectrum, whereas the Guild Socialists would lean toward the anarchist side and the Social Democratic Federation and the Independent Labour Party would be more in the center.

Early on in 1886, the issue of whether the Fabians would be anarchist or collectivist came to a head.[118] This is not surprising because it would be extremely difficult for two such differing, ideological viewpoints to coexist in the same organization for long. Annie Besant (1847–1933) moved a resolution, seconded by Hubert Bland (1856–1914), that advised that socialists should organize themselves into a political party. William Morris proposed an amendment, however, that said that it would be a false step for socialists to attempt to take part in parliamentary contests. He proposed this amendment for the sake of compromise and concession, presumably with the anarchists in the Fabian Society. The Morris amendment was defeated and the main motion passed; therefore, the idea of forming a political party with an eye to competing in elections was endorsed, surely an anathema to the anarchists, for this meant that the Fabians were legitimizing the existence of the state. The battles between the anarchists and the state socialists had torn apart the First International and might well have done the same to the Fabian Society. Whereas in the First International the Marxists had expelled the Bakuninists, it is interesting that the leading anarchist among the Fabians, Charlotte Wilson, was not forced nor did she resign from the Fabian Society, which speaks something about the relative liberalism and tolerance prevalent among those democratic socialists. A compromise was worked out: members could join a Fabian Parliamentary League if they so chose, avoiding the split that had so harmed the Social Democratic Federation over this issue.

However, the compromise eventually broke down by 1888, as perhaps was inevitable, given the strong differences between anarchists and collectivists.[119] The Fabians became distinctly collectivist by then, and the Fabian Parliamentary League was turned into the Political Committee of the Society, with the Fabian anarchists either leaving the Society or converting to the collectivist view.[120]

George Bernard Shaw attacked anarchism in his *Fabian Tract* No. 45, entitled, "The Impossibilities of Anarchism," and in his *The Intelligent Woman's Guide to Socialism and Capitalism*. In the latter work, Shaw pointed out that anarchism might work if we were all equally strong and cunning; but in the real world where there are physical inequalities, the strong and the cunning would be able to oppress the weak and the slow-witted in the absence of a government and laws to protect the weak and the slow-witted. Even robber bands and pirates prefer an established division of their spoils to that of the anarchy of having to fight over scraps like the cats of Kilkenny.[121]

Although collectivist state socialism became the principal form of socialism advocated by the Fabians, it would be a mistake to believe, as is often supposed, that they put their main emphasis on nationalization.[122] Rather, their emphasis dealt not with ownership questions as much as it did with the social appropriation of "rent"—profits in all of their forms—and with taxation as the major means of affecting the transfer of these profits from private capitalists to society. This taxation of property owners played a large role in the Fabian plans for nationalizing businesses and industries. The Fabians came in time to believe that the owners of capital should be compensated rather than expropriated without payment whenever their property was nationalized and that the money to pay for this compensation should be raised by the taxation of all property owners.[123] In this way, there would be a real gain to the public, rather than a mere transferring of formal ownership that would leave the public saddled with an interest charge. Compensation would cost the public nothing and would spread the confiscation of "rent" or surplus value over the whole of the upper class.[124] It was an ingenious solution to the objection that nationalization would cost the public more than it could afford.

Carl F. Brand noted that the Fabians believed that evolution of capitalist enterprises into joint-stock corporations managed by professionals had created conditions such that it would be relatively easy to expropriate the functionless stockholders with no more dislocation than would occur by daily stock transactions on the stock market.[125] This was a profoundly nonrevolutionary view, but one with a great deal of practicality. When a company is said to go "public," it is meant that it is no longer owned by a private capitalist or capitalists and that anyone with the money can buy stock in the company. These stockholders were the public when the company went "public." The Fabian approach, in effect, took this idea of going public one step farther. Now the public at large, that of the whole community or even the whole nation, would displace these so-called public (but really private) stockholders and would make the company truly publicly owned; and through the judicious use of taxation of the upper class to raise the funds for buying out the stockholders, the buyout would cost the vast majority of the public nothing, and it would not weigh down the government with debts and interest charges on those debts.

The Fabians saw nationalization as the state merely purchasing the assets of a business or industry and then appointing a minister to oversee the operation of the business, just as in the case of the Post Office.[126] The earliest *Fabian Tract* on nationalization was No. 150 entitled, "State Purchase of Railways: A Practicable Scheme," authored by Emil Davies. This 1910 work outlined a system of management and administration based on the Swiss system, the Port of London Authority, and the Water Board. A minister of Railways would be appointed with responsibility to the House of Commons, which would retain control over the annual budget and would have the power to change conditions of work, terms of employment, and wages.[127] Management would be headed by a committee of five experts—a railway director, a business organizer, a lawyer, a financier, and someone to serve as a connecting link between management and the minister. In turn, the committee of five trained experts were to operate under the supervision of a railway council made up of representatives of county councils and county boroughs served by the railroads, representatives of the Chambers of Commerce and Chambers of Agriculture, and representatives of the Amalgamated Society of Railway Servants. In this way, government control would be balanced by consumer and worker representation.

Fabian Tract No. 171, published in 1913 and entitled "The Nationalization of Mines and Minerals Bill," was the second work by the Fabians on nationalization; it called for the state to buy up the mines from private owners and for the mines to be run under the direct management of a minister of Mines and a staff that the minister would appoint. Details of management were not given, as they were in the tract on railways, and the only discussion of workers' rights dealt only with their rights to take part in political and trade union affairs. Generally, the Fabians opposed worker participation in management.

Sidney and Beatrice Webb's book, *A Constitution for the Socialist Commonwealth of Great Britain*, argued that only about a dozen industries needed to be nationally owned and managed in Britain.[128] Most services could be provided by local governments, which could come to own and control many of the formerly capitalist-owned companies. The national government would own and control only those industries, such as the railroads, that would be natural monopolies,[129] and these would be managed by public boards and commissions similar to the public corporations of today.[130] All the rest would be owned by local governments, with administration by an elected body. These elected members would be paid well enough to attract the most qualified people, to the point of outbidding what the capitalist industries paid.[131]

The Webbs also called on local governments to create jobs for the unemployed by developing public works projects (building roads, bridges, schools, hospitals, housing, and so forth) and by establishing their own farms and factories. Public works projects have long been a key solution of socialists to the problem of unemployment.

The Fabians had a strong belief in democracy and in political and social education.[132] They saw socialism coming about by persuading people to adopt socialist ideas, as well as by historic forces leading to socialization based on developing productive and administrative methods. One might well criticize the Fabians for having bureaucratic, even elitist views. However, the popular belief that the Fabians believed in a centralized, national, government-owned economy is not true, as they placed a good deal of emphasis on ownership by local governments.

The Fabian "Basis," or code, of the Society was drawn up in 1887 and remained remarkably unchanged over the years. The Basis called for the end of private ownership in land and industrial capital by evolutionary, socialist means.[133] In 1905 the Fabian Basis was amended to commit the Society to the pursuit of equality for women and was not amended again until 1919 when the Society formally committed itself to the support of the Labour Party and the Second International.[134]

Unlike revolutionary Marxist statements of principles, the Fabian Basis committed the Society entirely to gradualist change. Working to bring capital and land from private ownership to social ownership would be done by the peaceful dissemination of arguments for socialism. Additionally, as a result of a compromise over language, the Fabian Basis did not dogmatically call for the expropriation of the capitalists; it stated only that if expropriation was to be carried out without compensation, it would be with some relief to the former owners as the community saw fit.[135]

The official Fabian report to the International Socialist and Trade Union Congress held in London in 1896 stated that the Society's aims were to persuade the British people to socialize the economy by entirely democratic means, constitutionally voting in socialism and bringing ownership and administration of economic enterprises under freely national and local governments. More radical ideas of democracy and socialism, such as workers' self-management or the abolition of the wage system, were rejected.

Originally, the Fabians sought to "permeate" their ideas into the Liberal Party.[136] This caused some of their members to defect to the newly formed

Independent Labour Party (ILP), established in 1893 by James Keir Hardie.[137] Of the majority of the Fabians, it can be said that they were not suited to be members or leaders of such a revolutionary party as the ILP. They were, after all, mainly civil servants and business managers.[138] Most of the early Fabians were already part of the democratic left wing of the Liberal Party, demanding an extension of the franchise and other democratic and socialist measures far beyond what the leaders of the Liberal Party of that time were willing to accept.[139] The Liberals did not want an activist government in economic affairs. Their view was rather that state intervention should be kept to a minimum and that governmental action should be used for the protection of life and property and little more. In this respect, their views were closer to the classical liberalism of Locke or to modern conservatism, rather than to present-day liberalism. It was this laissez-faire ideology of the late-nineteenth-century English Liberals that the Fabians sought to fight by permeation of the Liberal party, as well as other parties, with their state-interventionist views.[140] Thus, the Fabians at the time were against the more radical socialist and labor groups as well as against the very idea of an independent labor party.[141] Even their work inside the Liberal Party was fairly minimal. The Fabian Parliamentary League, later called the Political Committee, did little more than issue a single manifesto in 1887, and then only addressed the progress of parliamentary socialism in other countries.[142] Those Fabians who would have none of this and who opposed the idea of permeating the Liberal Party, instead favoring the idea of a labor party, numbered among them Annie Besant, H. G. Wells (1866–1946), and Henry H. Slesser (b. 1883).[143]

No less than Friedrich Engels attacked the Fabians as a clique of "bourgeois socialists" running the gamut from sentimental philanthropists to careerists, united by their fear of the workers and their leaders. Engels also denounced the Fabians as being deeply involved in Liberal Party intrigues.[144]

However, the Fabians became disenchanted with the Liberals when the latter came to office in 1892 and for the next three years did virtually nothing in the field of social reform. This led the Fabians to attack the Liberals in their 1893 pamphlet, *To Your Tents, O Israel!* [145] The Fabians had come to their senses and were ready to consider independent political action. With the issuance of this pamphlet, the Fabians had finally abandoned the idea of permeating the Liberal Party and were ready to join with other socialist groups in Britain that demanded the formation of labor's own political party.[146]

At the same time that the early Fabians were struggling with the Liberals to their political right, they were also fighting the anarchists and the Marxists to their left, who, respectively, sought either the immediate dying or the eventual dying out of the state. For the Fabians, these arguments seemed incomprehensible or at best utopian because, in their view, socialism would be achieved by means of the democratic state. Rather than attack the very institution of the state, the tasks of socialists, Shaw argued, was to use the state's constitutional and democratic machinery for achieving their goals. Because suffrage was being extended, all that was necessary was to persuade the people to use the power they already possessed to vote in socialism.[147]

The Fabians believed that there would be no revolution and that such talk could only hurt the socialist movement.[148] Socialism, in the Fabian view, was to come about by democratic means. Gradually people would be convinced of the need for social ownership; and when enough people were convinced, then it would be enacted by majority rule.

The Fabians constantly put forward the idea that political democracy and socialism were two sides of the same coin and that with the attainment of the former, the latter would gradually, yet inevitably, come.[149] Socialism is the economic side of the democratic ideal, Sidney Webb declared.[150] "The inevitability of gradualness," became the comforting watchwords of the Society.

Sidney Webb offered a "plain definition" of socialism in *Fabian Tract* No. 15, declaring that it was "control by the community" of the economy for public advantage, or, conversely, "the absorption of rent and interest" (*rent* being the Fabian term for profits) collectively by the community. Webb also rejected the charge by some that this was too loose a definition and that a complete plan as worked out by various utopian socialists was needed. In fact, Webb held that there would never come a time when socialism would be established or finished, any more than radicalism could be said to be "established."[151]

There is a certain amount of oversimplification in this early Fabian passage. Socialism has meant democracy to some, but dictatorship to others. Webb complained that anyone saying that they could not understand what socialism meant was simply guilty of intellectual laziness—they need only look up socialism in a modern dictionary or the *Encyclopedia Britannica*. If not that, there were many socialist lectures given weekly in London that one could attend to get an understanding of socialism.

It should be noted that Webb's definition of socialism is reductionist, as well as peculiar to Fabian wording and conception, rather than universal. However, on the positive side, it is a modern definition in that it firmly rejects utopianism and sees socialism as a process in social evolution.

This pragmatism also showed itself in the Fabian attitude toward political parties. As we have seen, originally the Fabians worked within the Liberal Party. When they found that this simply would not work to advance socialism, they quite practically put this idea of permeation aside and joined with the Social Democratic Federation, the Independent Labour Party, and the trade unions in 1900 to form the Labour Representation Committee, which became the Labour Party in 1906. The Fabian Society became a constituent organization within the Labour Party, serving as a think tank, which it remains today. It became an influential center of democratic socialist thought and continues to publish both the *Fabian Tracts* and several volumes of *Fabian Essays*. As a demonstration of the Fabians' pragmatism and openness to new ideas, many of the later writings in these works entertained ideas quite at variance with early Fabian thought, such as advocacy of workers' self-management. In fact, there is no longer today a distinctive Fabian Socialism, advocated by the Fabian Society, characterized by excessive bureaucratism. G. D. H. Cole, a former Guild Socialist who remained an advocate of the idea of workers' self-management, served as the chair of the Fabian Society in 1943 and described the purpose of the Society as one of developing and popularizing new ideas, whether or not they conflicted with past socialist orthodoxy.[152]

A good example of the innovative thinking by the Fabians would be Sidney and Beatrice Webb's *A Constitution for the Socialist Commonwealth of Great Britain*. Published in 1920, it demonstrated rather well the Fabians' commitment to political democracy and to new ways of conceiving the operation of political democracy. A case in point is the proposal that two, parallel parliaments should be created, both democratically elected, one to deal with political matters and the other to deal with social affairs. The "Political Parliament" would deal with foreign and colonial affairs, as well as the judicial system. The "Social Parliament" would deal exclusively with the economic, social, and cultural activities of the nation, including the power to tax and the supervision of the nationalized industries which are one of the three kinds of socialized industries, the other two being local government-owned businesses, and consumers' cooperatives.[153]

The Webbs wrote only of consumers' cooperatives, and not of producers' cooperatives. The latter might imply workers' self-management of industry, to which the Webbs were sternly opposed. They claimed that the advocates of workers' self-management and producers' cooperatives were defining democracy wrongly as "an organ of revolt" rather than as an "organ of government." This was an unsupported assertion on the part of the Webbs. They also referred to workers' self-management as a "primitive" and "obsolete" conception of democracy, again without explaining why.[154] It is a curious thing to say, given the fact that the whole notion of economic democracy is a product of modern times.

The Webbs went on to give several examples of how workers' control would be ludicrous: Just imagine if, instead of the workers that a trade union represents, the clerks, accountants, office-boys, and even the charwomen who work for the trade union bureaucracy could elect the executive council and the General Secretary. Imagine if the postal workers could elect the Postmaster General—someone who ought to be responsible not to them but rather to the public at large. What foolishness would permit the government workers to elect a nation's secretary of state for foreign affairs or even the foreign minister they work for?[155]

The argument made by the Webbs is a good one, even if not wholly convincing. It relates to the problem of defining socialism and especially to the problem of just what is meant by "social" in speaking of social ownership. This can be a trickier problem than the Webbs might have admitted. In all the examples that the Webbs gave, hypothetical situations were set up in which groups smaller than what would appear to be the actual size of the true, social groups involved are given inordinate amounts of power. The true size of a trade union is its national, dues-paying membership of the workers it represents, for example, and no group smaller than this inside the union should have the sole power to determine policy or elect leaders. The same can be said of the other examples given by the Webbs. To give too much power to any small group, just because they happen to work for an organization in some limited capacity, while denying all other members of a social body or nation-state such powers as election of officers, is to deny the majority of their democratic rights.

Determining the actual size of business and industrial concerns can be very difficult, if not arbitrary. The Fabians, for example, argued that most businesses and industries should not be nationalized but, instead, owned and controlled by smaller, local governments. The British Labour Party did not follow this advice, as it turned out, and instead tended to favor nationalization. One could turn the argument made by the Webbs against themselves on this point. The actual or proper size of society, one could well argue, is the nation-state, and, therefore, no group smaller than the nation-state, such as a local government, should be allowed to own and control businesses and industries. To do so would be undemocratic, by this line of reasoning.

However, the Labour Party has also looked very favorably on the development of cooperatives—a decentralized form of ownership and control. At least in some cases, the Labour Party has thought that such smaller societies as cooperatives were the proper ones to own and control businesses and industries. Even the Webbs favored consumers' cooperatives, if not producers' cooperatives.

The kind of arguments the Fabians make for local government ownership can also be applied to cooperatives as well. If local government ownership is more proper than national government ownership for most businesses and industries, because the smaller size of the local government fits the scope of local and regional companies that do business on less than a national scale, then might not even smaller societies—those of the actual workers of companies—also be the proper ones to be the owners and managers?

The Webbs were quite correct in pointing out that such questions are ultimately ones about the meaning of democracy.[156] The argument that the Webbs made would logically follow if we could all agree on what "entire community" was properly involved in owning and managing businesses and industries. Advocates of capitalism might reply that it is the community of stockholders, those who have invested their money in a given enterprise, that ought to be the ones to own and control it. Advocates of socialism, on the other hand, might well reply that it should be the community of workers that should be the owners and managers. Yet different socialists would define such a community quite differently. The Webbs thought in terms of a local, territorial community, except in the cases of the services industries—where, to them, the community was that of the whole nation-state. However, decentralist-minded socialists and social anarchists would think in terms of the community being those working inside a given place of work or perhaps an entire industry that might transcend national boundaries.

For the advocates of capitalism, any group smaller than the group of stockholders having a monopoly of decision making would naturally appear to them as being an improper and undemocratic condition. Any group larger than the community of stockholders having decision-making power would to these advocates of capitalism, seem radically wrong—in fact, that is how they view socialism.

By the same token, advocates of socialism who conceive of social ownership as being nothing less than ownership by the entire nation-state would be expected to condemn anything less than nationalization as "undemocratic," if not petty bourgeois. Arguing that some companies that had only a local or regional trade should, therefore, be owned by local governments would not impress these advocates of socialism—the size of their territory of sales is irrelevant. If it affects the well-being of workers and society in any part or degree, it deserves to be nationally owned, would go their argument. Any argument that the economy should not be nationally owned, but rather internationally owned and controlled, would very likely be considered by such a socialist as utopian or at least impractical at this stage of history, even in the cases of companies selling in international markets.

As did socialists who conceived of socialism solely in terms of nationalization, advocates of local government ownership, such as the Webbs and the other Fabians, would understandably call arguments by decentralist socialists and social anarchists for worker ownership and control "undemocratic," for decentralism would involve power being in the hands of a group smaller than the one they would use to define the proper community that is to socially own businesses and industries. Nationalizing all businesses and industries is a position against which the Webbs argue because they do not usually conceive of the entire nation-state as being the "community."

As for decentralist socialists and social anarchists, because they *do* conceive of the proper size of a community as being the workers themselves at the point of production, distribution, or exchange, any argument that those outside the company walls should be the ones to own and control what goes on inside these confines would seem to be "undemocratic" and an argument for robbery of the workers of their rights. Indeed, decentralist socialists and social anarchists have argued that such statist conceptions of socialism only result in the exchange of a capitalist boss for a "state capitalist" one. Furthermore, they have charged, and not without good reason, that exploitation, repression, and the alienation of workers all continue under such circumstances. Strikes and independent unions, movements, and parties of workers have often been brutally crushed at the hands of government officials in supposedly "worker states" under Communist rule, as well as under social democratic administrations elsewhere. Often viewing all of these misnamed "socialist" societies as being, in reality, state capitalist, it cannot be said that these are much if any improvement over capitalism, and certainly cannot be equated with "true" or democratic socialism. We can see that very much of the arguments about just what does and does not constitute democracy and socialism have to do with how one defines a society.

The final argument that the Webbs made against workers' control was that it simply has never worked.[157] The Webbs pointed out that there have been many experiments in worker ownership and control and that they have all failed miserably. The arguments they made against workers' control, one should note, is one that has been often used against socialism itself, namely, that it cannot work. Indeed, in the opening lines of Sidney Webb's *Fabian Tract* No. 15, entitled "The English Progress towards Social Democracy," Webb wittily stated that there are three stages through which every idea passes in England: (1) It is impossible, (2) it is against the Bible, and (3) we knew it already. Webb argued that socialism was reaching the third stage in his day.[158] Yet, the Webbs' attitude toward workers' control seemed to be in the first stage: it was impossible. That workers' control is not an impossibility can be seen from many recent examples from around the world.[159] To be fair, there was little in the way of successful or long-lasting examples of producers' cooperatives or utopian communities that had practiced workers' self-management in the Webbs' day. This could well lead one to conclude that the idea was not ever going to be viable. However, this was a rash decision on the part of the Webbs and other critics of producers' cooperatives, among them Eduard Bernstein. There had been only limited practice of socialism until that time. England certainly had not yet placed any major industries under social ownership, let alone workers' self-management. Indeed, as the Webbs said, there may have been "innumerable experiments" in workers' control that had so far failed up to that time, but the same can be said of socialism—many utopian socialist experiments had already come and gone. Yet early experimental failure has not prevented eventual successes in scientific experiments, nor in social ones, such as in building stable, political democracies or socialist economies—including those that incorporated elements of workplace democracy.

The Webbs did have a valid point in their argument that a "Democracy of Producers" would have a bias in favor of the workers of a particular company and that this bias may be in conflict with the interests of workers in other companies as well as with the consumers and the public at large. The Webbs admitted that this bias would be a good counterbalance to the biases of consumers and the public, as well as a good defense against the private interests of the capitalist class. However, they pointed out that the biases of the workers in producers' cooperatives or in otherwise worker-self-managed industries that are publicly owned need to be checked. Unchecked, these workers could conceivably restrict production, causing prices for the goods they produce to rise and thus causing their wages to rise. As a result, they would achieve a position of relative economic advantage over other workers and the rest of the community—even if it meant shortages of necessities for others.

There are other ways in which workers' control, if it is unchecked, could harm the public interest. Take the issues of unsafe products and environmental harm. One can imagine workers in control of an industry that produces, as a by-product of the manufacturing process, toxic wastes or pollution. Perhaps the products they make are fundamentally unsafe to the consumer. These workers might resist attempts by the government or consumer groups to ban such hazardous practices and products. Such bans, after all, could well hurt the business and the profits of these offending workers and cause the elimination of their jobs. Just as capitalist managers can be expected to fight or to subvert such attempts at regulation, the worker self-managers might well act with the same callous self-interest. Additionally, a situation may arise in which workplace democracies resist the attempts of government to lower unemployment by inducing them to hire more workers, especially if that is going to mean less of a share of company income for each worker.

However, no economic system is without its problems and conflicts, and the Webbs failed to explain why such problems as these with workers' control could not be dealt with by government regulation and consumer action. For example, the government could attack the problems of industrial pollution or consumer hazards by overcoming the objections of worker-owned companies, the same as it does with capitalist-owned ones, and passing and enforcing environmental- and product-safety legislation. Consumer and public interest groups could play a role in seeing that these laws were carried out—perhaps with voting representatives onto company boards. Although government may not be able to order either worker cooperatives or capitalist-owned companies to hire more workers, they could give them tax inducements and subsidies to do so and they could attack the problem of unemployment with public works projects.

We should not assume that government-owned and bureaucratically managed industries are not in need of the same regulatory measures. Although government-owned, command economies have been better at dealing with unemployment than market economies have, bureaucratic managers appointed by the state might try to avoid safety and environmental regulations at the expense of their employees and the public, just as capitalist-appointed or worker-elected managers might.

As for the problem of unemployment, a command economy, which the Webbs seemed to be suggesting, is not the only solution. Besides the obvious solution of establishing public works projects, the government can attack the problem of unemployment by funding the creation of new cooperatives to employ the unemployed. Such ideas were not new to British socialists of the Webbs' day. Public works projects had already been proposed and established, and the Social Democratic Federation had called for "Home Colonization" in which the unemployed would be settled in cooperative colonies on nationalized land. The latter is a short step away from the idea of the government establishing cooperative enterprises throughout society and turning them over to the workers. This idea had been made famous by Louis Blanc and was the basis of the Lassallean's program.

The criticisms of producers' cooperatives made by the Webbs in this work were not made in a vacuum. They were in large measure meant as an alternative to the ideas of the syndicalists and especially the Guild Socialists, who were campaigning for workers' control of industries and for an Industrial Parliament elected by and representing the trades during this period.[160] Indeed, during the 1920s, the Fabian Society did experience much internal dissension and loss of membership to the Guild Socialist movement.[161] Although the latter would soon fade into oblivion, its ideas would continue to be felt inside the Fabian Society. G. D. H. Cole, who had been one of the principal leaders of the Guild Socialists, went on to become the chairperson of the Fabian Society at a time when Fabian Socialism was being incorporated into the Labour Party when the latter, in 1918, formally adopted socialism.[162]

Author Josephine Fishel Milburn noted that the Fabians put so much emphasis on governmental power because of their faith in the abilities of civil servants.[163] Many of the Fabians were civil servants, not the horny-handed proletariat, and they had the mistrust of the common worker that one might expect of such middle-class professionals.

The strong opposition in some quarters of the Fabian Society in the early years to workers' self-management spoke to the limits of their belief in democracy. Democracy was for government bodies such as parliaments, which would represent the whole of a society's people and not just the workers in their respective industries. The Fabians seemed blind to the ways in which the interests of bureaucrats might well be self-serving, distinct from and even antagonistic to the interests of workers, consumers, and the public. E. J. Hobsbawn pointed out that bureaucratic self-interest is an aspect of Fabianism, and not a surprising one, given that they were largely composed of civil servants. It is these civil servants who would gain the most from a bureaucratic form of socialism.[164] Geoffrey Foote also pointed out that Sidney Webb was fascinated by the philosophy of Positivism and the idea of society being run by an educated elite. Given Webb's background in the Civil Service, this idea only reinforced his belief in collectivism and in the subordination of individuals for the good of all.[165] Webb had the interest of a class at heart, but it was not the working class's interests, as one might suppose from a socialist, but rather his own bureaucratic class's interest.

With such an elitist view, it is little wonder that the Fabians never acquired a mass membership. They did not seek a large membership, in contradiction to their goal of spreading socialist ideas. In fact, the bureaucratic bias was so strong among the early Fabians that it led Shaw to be sympathetic to Benito Mussolini's Fascism and for both he and Webb to be admirers of Stalinist Russia.[166]

Wells

H. G. Wells (1866–1946) had been a member of the Fabians, but he had gone on to attack Shaw and the Webbs as hopelessly bureaucratically minded in his 1911 novel, *The New Machiavelli*.[167] However, Wells's dislike, particularly for Shaw, in part grew out of the fact that the Fabians had rejected his plan to throw out the "Old Gang" (the Society's founders), to get a better-paid staff and larger and nicer headquarters, and to have an active campaign to recruit new members.[168] (We should also note that Shaw moved away from his earlier enthusiasm for democracy and became a critic of it and the supposed stupidity of the working class, as he saw it.[169])

Yet, having noted the limits to their belief in democracy, it is well to keep in mind that the Fabian Society as a whole was committed to democratic electoral methods, to civil liberties, and to gradual change, rather than to the revolutionary seizures of power that have so often led to dictatorships.

The modern-day Fabian Society serves as a think tank for new ideas in democratic socialism, sometimes at odds with the bureaucratic variety of socialism it professed in the past.

THE INDEPENDENT LABOUR PARTY

We come now to the third democratic socialist organization that, along with the Social Democratic Federation and the Fabian Society, as well as the British trade unions, formed the Labour Representation Committee in 1900, renamed the British Labour Party in 1906. This third democratic socialist body was the Independent Labour Party (ILP), founded in 1893 as a predecessor to the Labour Party.

The ILP reflected the ethical socialism of its founder, James Keir Hardie (1856–1915), a Scottish miner and Methodist lay preacher.[170]

The ILP was part of a movement known as the "New Unionism" and reflected the ideology of "New Socialism" or "Ethical Socialism."[171] The origins of the ILP are to be found in the failure of the leaders of the traditional union movement in Britain to get the Liberal Party to adopt a program that could attract working-class support by dealing with the issues and concerns of that class. The left wing of the Liberal Party, the Radical-Liberals lacked the influence in the party enjoyed by the right wing, the Whigs, and thus were incapable of getting the party to significantly help trade unionists. In this situation emerged a growing number of socialists and anarchists who attacked the Liberal Party as hopelessly procapitalist and laissez-faire. Their concern and growing disaffection were fueled by the rapid growth of unemployment in the late 1800s in Britain.[172]

Just as the recession of 1878 and 1888 ended, there was a wave of successful strikes by unskilled workers, which gave strength to the trade union movement. The Old Unionist philosophy of unions providing a "friendly benefit" to workers was pushed aside for the New Unionist belief in strike action. In this environment the ILP was born with the open aim of wooing trade unionists away from the Liberal Party. The death of such strong Liberal leaders as Prime Minister William Gladstone in 1898 helped this process of separation, and reluctantly the British union movement began to strike out on its own course of independent political action.[173]

The New Unionism was born in 1889, determined to break with the Liberal Party and its anti-working-class bias. There was a great influx of new members into the old unions, many of which were socialist inclined; and many new unions formed that year, mostly led by socialists.[174] The socialists, for the first time, gained considerable prestige with the working class, due to their newfound positions of leadership in the New Unionism.[175]

Roger Moore has argued that this view is overly simplistic, and perhaps it is.[176] However, it cannot be denied that the socialist movement in Britain had successfully made the transition from middle-class and sectarian isolation into mainstream working-class politics in those years—no mean feat, and something that American socialists have not accomplished.

The New Unionism, led by these New Socialist trade unionists, believed that their unions had to be based on the interests of the working class as a whole. This was a socialist belief, unlike the narrow interests of the Old Unionists and their craft unions. More important, the New Unionists favored the socialist demand for an independent labor party of their own to be formed, breaking with the Liberals, so as to forthrightly represent their interests in Parliament and in local governments.

Compared to the Fabian Society, who in these years still clung to the idea of permeating the Liberal Party, the New Socialists were politically more advanced, seeing the necessity for bolder action and the formation of a new party.[177] The Fabians would shortly come to the realization that an independent party of labor had to be formed. The Social Democratic Federation, of course, had long argued for an independent party. Unlike the SDF, the New Socialists felt that it was more important to emphasize the idea of creating an independent labor party, rather than of building socialism as an ideological movement.[178] Indeed, New Unionist leader John Burns resigned from the SDF not long after disagreeing with Henry Hyndman, who wanted Burns to display a red flag at demonstrations during a dock strike. Friedrich Engels defended Burns in this dispute.[179] He felt that the immediate task before the British socialist movement was the formation of an independent labor party, which, if it could be successfully launched, would make the SDF and its split-away faction, the Socialist League, fade into the background.[180]

The Old Unionists still continued to send their leaders to Parliament as "Lib-Labs" and supported Liberal candidates. The Old Socialists of the SDF and the Fabian Society were still middle class in composition. However, the

New Socialists were part of a genuinely working-class movement rooted in the trade unions.

However, the New Socialists, and the party they created, the ILP, retained some similarities with the Old Socialists of the SDF and the Fabian Society. All of them viewed basic political government as a legitimate arena for contending political parties and ideologies and thought of Parliament and town councils as bodies representative of the people. All of them agreed with the values of political democracy and procedurally agreed that political democracy meant free political parties and representatives freely elected by the people. None of these groups that had a hand in the formation of the British Labour Party was seeking a violent, revolutionary overthrow of government. On the contrary, they wanted to capture power legally by election and then to use that governmental power to serve the interests of the working class. In sum, the ILP, the SDF, and the Fabian Society were democratic socialists who shared the civil rights and civil liberties traditions of liberal-democracy; they were neither anarchists nor totalitarian communists.

On January 13 and 14, 1893, the founding conference of the Independent Labour Party was held in the Labour Institute in Bradford, England, and was attended by delegates from across England and Scotland. Included among the delegates were members of such socialist organizations as the SDF and the Fabian Society—the latter having only just come around to seeing that socialists needed to break with the Liberals. The SDF and the Fabians chose not to federate with the new party at this time, although some branches of them broke away from their parent organizations and did join the ILP.[181]

The conference had been called the previous September by the annual meeting of the Trade Union Congress (TUC), the federation of British trade unions. Keir Hardie, who had the greatest prestige among British socialists, was a natural choice for chair of the new party.[182]

Hardie

Hardie had been Secretary of the Ayrshire Miners' Union in Scotland and had been elected to Parliament as a Liberal. He was converted to the cause of socialism in 1887 and had helped form a predecessor to the ILP in 1889—the Scottish Labour Party (SLP).[183] However, the SLP had not been a socialist party.[184]

Carl F. Brand pointed out that the Bradford Conference was attended by about 120 delegates, including chairman Keir Hardie and other well-known socialists of the day. Among them were Edward Aveling (1851–1898), Robert

Blatchford (1851–1943), and George Bernard Shaw and other Fabians from the south of England. What was more remarkable was the large number of trade unionists present, particularly from the north of England and from Scotland. The London SDF attended, too, but stood aloof.[185] At the founding conference, some of the delegates wanted to include the word *Socialist* in the name of the new party. This proposal was defeated because tactically the delegates felt that calling themselves the Socialist Labour Party would run the risk of scaring away potential members in the unions who might favor independent representation, but not necessarily socialism.[186] Nevertheless, the ILP was born as a socialist party. At the Bradford Conference, they stated socialism to be the aim of party and defined *socialism* as "the collective ownership" of the means of production, distribution, and exchange.[187] The original resolution had read "collective or communal ownership," but the delegates deleted "or communal," feeling that it smacked too much of anarchism.[188]

The ILP's socialism was flexible rather than rigidly defined and thus could accommodate anything that the trade unionists were likely to demand, from Scottish nationalism to Methodism to Marxism to Fabianism, and even to Burkean conservatism.[189] Always willing to support reform demands, the ILP was in an excellent position to forge links between socialists and trade unionists in a way that the more doctrinally pure socialist organizations could not. This nonsectarian approach, for example, was not shared by the Social Democratic Federation.

The meaning of social ownership, which was not emphasized in the ILP program, was somewhat vague. Hardie, when he had run for a seat in Parliament under the banner of the newly created Scottish Labour Party in 1888, had called for the nationalization of royalties and minerals.[190] The ILP's speakers and publications did call for public ownership of the means of production, distribution, and exchange, and so they did conceive of socialism as taking the form of nationalization.[191]

When Hardie had laid out his proposals for nationalizing the mines to the Scottish Miners' National Federation prior to his run for Parliament in 1888, he had called for the state to nationalize the mines but then to have them leased back to the miners, who would manage them under their own control as cooperatives—a rather imaginative approach.[192] However, in later years, this novel idea was apparently abandoned, and Hardie became more conventional in his ideas about socialist economic organization. When as an ILP candidate he won a seat in Parliament in 1893, he presented a bill that called for the nationalization of the mines; under this bill, however, the mines would be run by a Ministry of Mines, not by the workers.[193]

Because social ownership and control were not the main emphasis in

Hardie's thoughts or of the ILP, not a great amount of time was given to them. Thus, the ILP tended toward the conventional ideas of nationalization and government-appointed management. Clearly, the emphasis for Hardie and the ILP was on reform measures rather than social ownership, and this to a greater degree than was true of the SDF or even the Fabians. The ILP program concentrated on such reforms as achieving the eight-hour workday; abolishing overtime and piecework; abolishing child labor; creating welfare programs for the sick, the disabled, the elderly, and widows and orphans; establishing free and nonsectarian primary and secondary schools, as well as colleges; mandating a minimum-wage law; establishing public measures to reduce unemployment and to give aid to the unemployed; achieving housing reform; and having medical treatment and school feeding programs for children.[194]

This was not the heady stuff of socialist revolution with its romantic appeal; but at a time when none of these elementary social and economic measures yet existed in Britain, such a reform program could achieve what other socialist groups had failed to do—attract a significant working-class following. A program that was disdainful of such mere reforms in favor of the state or the workers seizing control of the government and the capitalist's corporations might appeal to some, but it would have been too radical for the mass of working people that the ILP sought to attract to its ranks.

The program of the ILP was not basically different from that of the SDF or even that of the Fabians.[195] All of them had a mixture of advocating reform measures and calling for social ownership of the economy. However, programs and constitutions can be misleading, or at least not provide the full story.

There were significant differences between the ILP and the SDF and the Fabian Society. Although the latter two were for the most part middle-class organizations, only the ILP among them had a significant working-class composition. The middle-class idealists of the SDF and the Fabian Society had perhaps a greater luxury in being idealistic about achieving socialism and thus tended to emphasize more how they were going to lead the way in transforming capitalism into socialism, as well as how socialism would be organized and run. This was more true of the SDF than of the Fabians, who were somewhat more reform minded; but it was the ILP that was the least idealistic of the three and the most centered on how to achieve real reforms in the near future.

Middle-class people might have the financial means to have some independence from the economic uncertainties of capitalism and, thus, could afford to care less for immediate relief and reform programs in favor of more radical proposals. The poor, having no such luxury and being in dire need of reforms such as the eight-hour workday or minimum-wage legislation, understandably put emphasis on such bread-and-butter issues rather than on revolution. Of course, this might not be the case for all individuals, but in the main, there would likely be such class trends.

It is interesting to note that in the modern-day British Labour Party, the trade unions, which make up the bulk of the party, generally do not support as strongly the left-wing resolutions proposed at the annual conferences as do the constituent parties, which have more of a middle-class composition.[196] For the trade unionists who are in the left wing of the party—and most unionists are not—the commitment to socialism is mainly rhetorical and emotional, while their major goals remain achieving reforms such as wage and pension benefits. One the other hand, the far left minority in today's British Labour Party, mostly made up of people from the academic community and the literary intelligentsia, are largely a middle- to upper-class group and are far more interested in the question of ending capitalism itself and ushering in socialism than they are in reforming the existing system.[197] With a few Marxist trade union leaders in their ranks, this radical minority have been unable to stop the majority of the members from moving the Labour Party rightward toward the political center in recent years.

Given their more working-class composition, which was more directly affected by and thus far more interested in reform measures, the ILP speakers rarely referred to revolution or to class war in their educational and organizational efforts among trade unionists.[198] Where the Hyndmanites tended to denounce trade unions in general as not representing the interests of the working class as a whole, Hardie's followers courted the unionists. Instead of offering doctrinaire Marxism, class-war ideology, and the promised good life after the revolution, the ILP concentrated on a reform program that combined an ethical and pragmatic economic appeal to trade unionists as well as to middle-class sympathizers who supported demands for social justice, but not revolution.[199]

Marx and Engels had commented on the nonrevolutionary nature of the English working class, which they attributed to the English workers sharing in the spoils of British imperialism.[200] Whether this is true or not, the fact remains that the ILP had the program that could begin to win over the British workers. Hardie knew that only the unions had the numbers, organization, and money needed to emancipate the working class. Emancipation from above by middle-class intellectuals such as those in the Fabian Society was either impossible or else would only result in a dictatorship over the proletariat.[201]

The New Socialists got a boost when in 1898 the Trade Union Congress accepted a resolution dropping the provision that only working trade unionists or union officials could belong to the TUC. This had kept Hardie and other socialists out of the TUC, with its large and potentially powerful membership. By 1899, the ILP was able to convince the TUC and the Scottish TUC to call for a special conference attended by their trade union affiliates along with the ILP, SDF, and the Fabians. They met at the Congregationalist Memorial Hall in London on February 27, 1900, to form the Labour Representation Committee (LRC).[202] The original decision to call the conference had passed by a close vote of 546,000 in favor to 434,000 against, with many abstentions. Many trade unionists were suspicious of the socialists' influence in the new party, particularly from the ILP members among the unions and their officers, who had been the most strongly committed to the idea of independent political action. In the beginning, the LRC had little support among the unions, with only 445,450 members out of some 2 million trade unionists by 1902. What changed this situation dramatically was the impact of the Taff Vale decision, which allowed unions to be treated as corporate entities liable for damages. Thus the unions could be sued for taking labor actions against companies. The Taff Vale ruling was nullified in 1906, but the attack on unions spurred them to action. Trade union membership continued to climb, as did the recognition by unions of the need for united political action. In 1906, the LRC was renamed the Labour Party and its membership also was increasing.[203]

Besides the name New Socialism, the philosophy of the Independent Labour Party was also called Ethical Socialism.[204] It had an ethical appeal, rather than one of historical inevitability, as with the SDF's Marxism, or a rationalist one as found in Fabianism. Ethical socialists demanded socialism because it was a system based on ethics, unlike capitalism, which was viewed as based on greed. The need was seen for collective action to abolish human suffering, with a special emphasis on reform measures.[205] Unlike Marxism and Fabianism, Ethical Socialism emphasized moral appeals and religious sentiment, topics of which the former two were devoid or with which they did not often deal.[206]

Although the ILP did not add much to the formal content of socialism, it did infuse it with the traditions of idealism and humanity and brought into the movement a certain moral fervor and integrity, sometimes missing in Marxism and Fabianism, that attracted many that had been left cold by mere economic arguments. It especially appealed to those in the churches and the ethical societies that could not reconcile their moral beliefs with capitalism.[207]

Much of the membership and style of operation of the ILP came from the labor churches of the period—left-wing congregations that combined prayer with socialistic sermons.[208] J. H. Steward Reid aptly noted that the history of the early ILP more resembled that of a Methodist revival than of a socialist movement.[209] Socialism has often been said to be a secular religion. This was doubly so in the case of Ethical Socialism, given Hardie's background as a lay Methodist preacher and the moralistic tone of his political preachings.[210]

As an Ethical Socialist and leader of the ILP and despite being one of the principal leaders of the Labour Party in Parliament between 1906 and 1914,[211] Hardie was at heart a propagandist, not a parliamentary leader.[212] As the best-known propagandist in the ILP, he sought to create an alternative to the Marxian socialism of the SDF, developing a school of socialism that may be viewed as a new form of Christian socialism, strongly emphasizing the immorality and greed of the capitalist system, and the religious-like idealism of socialism.[213]

Hardie thought mainly in ethical terms, despising the cruelty and oppression he saw around him. His Ethical Socialism was a gospel of social justice, of fellowship among men and women, and of a deep belief in the basic goodness of mankind.[214]

Hardie's Christian-based Ethical Socialism, which became the basis of the New Socialist and New Unionist movements, was often directed toward the moral elevation of the lumpenproletariat, the class of people often called "street people" today. Marx and his followers had little hope, interest, or use for these people, seeing them more as possible bribed tools of reactionaries, and likely to be strike breakers and agent provacateurs out to infiltrate and destroy legitimate working-class organizations.[215] Hardie, much like a Salvation Army worker with a radical bent, delivered a sermon in 1893 at the West Ham Congregation Church in which he voiced the opinion that if the people would be righteous and lovers of justice, so would be the laws.[216] Again, on the issue of alcohol and temperance, Hardie preached against drunkenness and expressed a favorable attitude toward prohibition. However, his reasons were different from what one would have expected from an ordinary preacher, for this was a social gospel: It is not original sin or the Devil that is behind drunkenness; rather, it is the evil inherent in the profit system that dehumanizes man and drives him to drink and to moral ruin.[217]

Hardie's writings and speeches are filled with a concern for morality. For what purpose, he asked, has man been endowed with the faculty of reason if not to allow him to rise above the level of the brutes? If the law of the jungle is to be the rule, what becomes of man's claim to be endowed with an immortal soul?[218] For Hardie, capitalism could never be the good or moral life. More important, the whole of his argument against capitalism and for socialism was based on morals and ethics—quite different from the scientific socialism of the atheistic Marxists. Thus, Hardie wrote that socialism is ultimately a question of ethics and morals, dealing with the relationships that ought to exist between people in a society. Furthermore, he stated that socialism challenges the conception of society as a war between all. Although communism is the final goal of socialism, it is very closely akin to the teachings of Jesus in the Sermon on the Mount. Indeed, Hardie wrote that every great religious leader down through the ages had denounced wealth and eulogized poverty.[219] Obviously, Hardie's Ethical Socialism owes much to his Christian beliefs. Similar to Christian Socialism, Ethical Socialism was also based on a criticism of capitalism's immorality and its being the source of poverty.

One difference between Christian Socialism and Ethical Socialism was that the latter saw the working class itself, not religious saviors, as the active agent in creating the moral society. Another difference between the two was that Ethical Socialism did not formally endorse a specific religion, although obviously it could claim inspiration from Christianity. Without making a specific religion its basis, Ethical Socialism could appeal to people of all faiths and denominations. Ethical Socialism was a secular version of the older Christian and Religious socialisms of the past. By envisioning the socialist movement as led by labor, rather than by enlightened philanthropic or religious leaders, Ethical Socialism would be less paternalistic and would thus appeal to a wider audience. Rich sympathizers of labor would no longer be leading the movement, but they would be able to play an important part in helping to finance it.[220]

Hardie often repeated the theme that communism was the final goal of state socialism.[221] A society based on the socialist principal of "from each according to his ability, to each according to his work" would become a society based on the communist credo of "from each according to his ability, to each according to his needs." Again, identifying communism with Christianity, Hardie wrote of the Sermon on the Mount as being full of the spirit of communism.[222] Yet, at least for the time, Hardie found the idea of a communist society based on free distribution and voluntary association in a stateless, moneyless, and classless system to be impractical and anarchistic.[223] Although communism may be equated with Christianity, Ethical Socialism was likened with state socialism as a necessary transition stage.

Hardie was trying to develop a very practical if moralistic form of socialism. Anarchist communism, which attempts to do away with the state immediately, seemed to him to be trying to do the impossible. States are needed instruments of public policy, Hardie believed. Anarchists of various stripes would only end up recreating some statelike organization if they were actually in control.

The question, then, for Hardie was not if there should be a state. For practical reasons, he concluded that there must be a state. The real questions were who will control the state and for what purposes? Shall it continue to be the bourgeoisie and their interests, which Hardie, as an Ethical Socialist, found to be for immoral and unethical purposes such as extracting profits above all else? Shall it be by and for the great majority—the proletariat—and for the needs of the people, such as jobs, decent housing, and so forth? Ethical socialism was in favor of state socialism as a practical way to achieve the good and moral life for humankind. The state would be used to bring about moral ends—the reform program of the ILP—as well as to go deeper and transform the very structure of society by bringing the economy under state ownership and the government under labor's control.

Although Hardie believed that the class struggle did exist, he did not see it, in Marxist terms, as a historical necessity.[224] Whereas Marx saw socialism as a science, Hardie viewed it mainly in ethical terms and desired a socialist society not because it was inevitable, but because, he believed, it would foster human well-being rather than exploitation. Hardie rejected the Liberals, but he did not accept the beliefs of the Marxists either and made clear his opposition to the dry and unemotional nature of Marxism. To him, the Marxist notion of class war reduced socialism from the level of a moral crusade against materialism and greed to that of a mere faction fight.[225] Perhaps Hardie was being unfair in this, for behind Marxist, abstract reasoning there was a powerful, emotional appeal, although not an ethically based one.[226] Certainly the writings of Marx and Engels have been an inspiration to millions, but they did not move Hardie and other Ethical Socialists.

Hardie had a socialist society as his long-range goal; but while working toward that goal, he wanted to do what he could to improve the lives of the worst off in society, especially the unemployed and their families. As an Ethical Socialist, he was deeply moved to fight for reform programs—full employment, the minimum wage, and the eight-hour workday. He was also bitterly critical of the incidence of coal mine accidents, which he blamed directly on the owners' refusal to spend money on safety for the sake of profits.[227]

The Ethical Socialists

Other Ethical Socialists of note were Edward Carpenter (1844–1929), John Bruce Glasion (1859–1920), and Robert Blatchford.[228] The ethical nature of the minimum and maximum programs of the New Socialist movement can be seen particularly well in the writings of Blatchford.[229] He was the editor of *The Clarion*—a weekly, socialist newspaper first appearing in 1891 and lasting until 1935. Blatchford and others had also founded the ILP branch in Manchester. Although the Clarionettes—as the writers and friends of the paper were called—were not all necessarily ILP members, they were in favor of the party and the movement it represented, and they did much to build the membership of each. Blatchford was also an author, and his most famous work, *Merrie England*, demonstrated well the minimum and maximum programs of the Ethical Socialists. He divided socialism into "practical socialism" and "ideal socialism."[230] Practical socialism, he informed us, was so simple that even a child could understand it. In essence, it meant that all the means of production were to be owned and managed by the state. This is elementary socialism, according to Blatchford, whereas ideal or advanced socialism was much like Hardie's vision of the stage of communism to follow that of socialism.[231] Ideal socialism would be a society without compensation for work, and in the place of compensation would be free distribution of goods and services. Chris Cook and Ian Taylor remarked that Blatchford's socialism showed the diversity of thought in the ILP, containing elements of Marxism, Christian Socialism moralism, and William Morris's esthetics, all wrapped up in a revolutionary tone, although antirevolutionary in specifics.[232]

Blatchford's writings were reductionist and overly simplistic, but we must keep in mind that the work was aimed at the uneducated. It was highly successful in bringing to such untutored readers an understanding of the basic principles of socialism.

Hardie wrote many years later in his impressions of the ILP's First Conference that Hyndman and others did not consider the ILP to be socialist at all.[233] Why would this be so when clearly the ILP had been founded on a platform that called for collective and communal ownership of the economy and that had rejected by a landslide a liberal reform program? It is a question that goes to the heart of the problem of defining democratic socialism. To Hyndman and others, a stated belief in the social ownership of the economy was insufficient to define socialism. Thus, because the ILP did not adopt the Marxist beliefs of the SDF, the latter considered the ILP to be not fully socialist, but only a halfway house to socialism. Marxism was a scientific socialism, in the eyes of the SDF leaders, and anything less was a pseudoscience. In this view, Ethical Socialism was to Marxism as alchemy was to chemistry. Hardie, of course, clearly rejected the position that the ILP was not fully socialist, and he based his rebuttal on a reductionist argument that socialism means social ownership of the means of production, distribution, and exchange, and because the ILP voted overwhelmingly for this definition, then the ILP must be socialist. It is the kind of argument that will appear reasonable to many, but it is likely to have little validity with most Marxists, who would not accept such a simple definition of socialism. If the ILP did not accept such Marxian ideas as historical materialism, then it was not fully socialist, according to this view. Different perceptions of what is and is not socialist depend naturally on how socialism is defined. A definition that included certain philosophical ideas as necessary elements is a strict construction, which would declare all other beliefs claiming to be socialist to be false.

Of course, acceptance of a more flexible definition of socialism would not demand adherence to one school's precepts, but it would recognize the legitimacy of all other philosophic schools of socialism. This the Marxists have usually been unwilling to do, however.

The Fabians would also show intolerance toward Hardie's brand of socialism. Hardie gave a speech to the London Fabian Society in which it was reported that Shaw was one of the hecklers.[234] In the speech, Hardie criticized the Fabian Society's policy of permeation of the Liberal Party and stated the reasons why he felt that for socialists to continue to work in the Liberal Party was to play into the hands of the capitalist class.[235] This very same argument is used today in the United States among the members of the Socialist Party, USA, which came out of the Debs Caucus under the leadership of former Milwaukee mayor Frank Zeidler during the early 1970s against the followers of Max Schachtman in the Social Democrats, USA, and against the followers of Michael Harrington in the Democratic Socialist Organizing Committee. The committee was later renamed the Democratic Socialists of America (DSA), after a fusion with the New American Movement. The DSA continued to work inside the Democratic Party in a failed attempt to realign it into a strictly left-liberal party and shunned the idea of a third party. If anything, the Democratic Party moved to the right under the centrist leadership of presidents Jimmy Carter and later Bill Clinton. To the Fabians' credit, they abandoned their idea of permeating the Liberal Party when they came to realize that this simply was not working, and they came around to supporting the idea of a Labour Party.

Francis Williams pointed out that at the meeting in the Memorial Hall, February 27, 1900, which gave birth to the Labour Representation Committee, it was the ILP and the Fabians along with the more moderate trade unionists who united to successfully argue the case for a federated labor party to promote the election of all candidates of affiliated organizations sympathetic to the labor movement. This majority position won out over that of the SDF, which wanted to have the LRC support only candidates pledged to socializing the means of production, distribution, and exchange, and also won out over the position of the older trade unions, which wanted a nonsocialist party that would only run working-class candidates for Parliament.[236]

Although the ILP was generally the most reformist of the three socialist organizations that helped form the Labour Party, its position was radical in the sense that it insisted on the need for an independent socialist party—a more militant stance than that of the early Fabian Society.

Hardie had little interest in socialist history or in attempting to picture the future socialist society in great detail. He remained largely a radical reformist, aloof from the the controversies within the socialist movement, preferring to preach his social gospel as he had long done. In this respect, he was much like his American contemporary Eugene Victor Debs, also someone from a genuine proletarian background turned socialist and long-time presidential candidate of the Socialist Party of America.

Hardie made an exception to his aloofness for the issue of war, an issue on which he felt compelled to speak out, as did Debs. Hardie's foreign policy beliefs were those of a devout internationalist.[237] Unlike many Marxists who dreamed of an international revolution, Hardie thought in terms of international peace and of preventing wars. He was a strong anti-imperialist, attacking the destruction of indigenous economies (as in India) by foreign capitalist competition, taxation, and moneylending. He scorned those who would defend the British Empire as a means to profit off cheap, colonial labor. However, he did not go so far as to call for the breakup of the Empire, calling for Home Rule for India rather than independence.[238] Nevertheless, he expended considerable energy in the House of Commons in criticizing the British government and the army in the Boer War, which he referred to as the "Tory War."[239]

Hardie was heartbroken not only by the vast destruction and death caused by World War I, but also by the failure of most of the Second International parties to live up to their pledge to oppose the war when it came. The British Labour Party, the Fabian Society, and Henry Hyndman all supported Britain's entry into the war, whereas the ILP was in opposition.[240] Even among the ILP supporters there was dissension—again a parallel with Debs and the Socialist Party of America, most of whose members, but not all, opposed the war and U.S. entry into it. In the ILP, Robert Blatchford was a nationalist and a veteran with a soldier's outlook.[241] Before World War I, as a correspondent for the *Daily Mail*, he was sent to Germany and was convinced of Germany's aggressive intentions and Britain's unpreparedness for war. This opinion caused sharp dissension among the left of the labor movement, which was internationalist and pacifist. Additionally, Blatchford had supported Britain in the Boer War. Subsequently, Blatchford and his paper, *The Clarion*, lost their influence.[242]

Hardie, on the other hand, had taken a consistent position against war. He had written of 25,000 men taken from useful work to be set to the job of slaughtering their fellow men in South Africa, all to destroy a self-governing people in the interests of the rich and privileged.[243] Speaking at an antiwar rally in 1914 at the outbreak of World War I, Hardie declared that the workmen of Europe had no quarrel with each other. Therefore why do they allow the ruling classes to make treaties leading them into war?[244] The ILP manifesto was a moving statement of fraternity with the German Socialists.[245] In vain, Hardie demanded a general strike to stop the war. When the war began, the Parliamentary Labour Party and the British unions backed the war effort.[246]

Another difference between Hardie and Hyndman, besides the latter's ardent support for the war effort, was Hyndman's charge that Hardie had sold out because the ILP had openly sought financial contributions from the rich.[247] This accusation was not without hypocrisy, considering that the SDF had accepted campaign funds from a wealthy capitalist in the Tory Gold Scandal. The difference between these two cases was that the ILP openly accepted contributions from all its friends, rich or poor, while the SDF had secretively taken money from a rich benefactor whose real aim was not to help the SDF as much as it was to take votes away from the Liberals. The Ethical Socialists were not rigid on the question of the class struggle to the point where they could not take contributions from anyone wealthy. To the Marxists, however, the class struggle was a fundamental idea, even if they were not above bending their beliefs, taking money from the rich, and, if they could, keeping it quiet.

Hardie supported women's suffrage, looking at the women's rights movement from the point of view that it was a problem of economic oppression—a simplistic position. Although this was not an issue of contention among Hardie, the SDF, and the Fabians, there were individual socialists in all these organizations who, for whatever reasons, did not support women's suffrage.[248] On this as on other issues, however, Hardie's ethical sense of what was just led him to take the most progressive positions with respect to his fellow socialists of the time.

With the victory of the Bolshevik Revolution in November 1917, some ILP members wanted the party to support the Soviets and join the Third International. After 1920 this minority went over to the British Communist Party.[249] The majority of the ILP did not become Marxist but did stay true to their belief in Ethical Socialism. Losing their left wing to the Communists was not the ILP's only problem—they were increasingly losing their more moderate members on the right of their party over to the Labour Party. Although the ILP remained steadfast in their opposition to World War I, even while the British Labour Party supported it, the ILP, nevertheless, did not split with the Labour Party during the war. As the ILP continued to drift to the left, a breakup with the Labour Party was inevitable. After the fall of the Labour government in 1924, the ILP began a campaign for "Socialism in Our Time," urging the Labour Party to make "a living wage for all" its first and foremost objective. However, this issue was shunted aside by the Labour Party in its 1926 Conference.[250]

By 1932 the quarrels between the ILP and the Labour Party over policy and party discipline had reached a point at which the ILP disaffiliated from the British Labour Party.[251]

The ILP Since Hardie

While Hardie was alive, he had prevented this split; but he had died in 1915 and James Maxton (1885–1946) was then the leader of the ILP.[252] After leaving the Labour Party, the ILP's membership drastically declined. The ILP continued to run candidates for Parliament against those of the Labour Party until 1945, winning only a handful of seats. With the death of Maxton in 1946, the few remaining ILP members of Parliament joined the Labour Party. No ILP members were able to win office in the 1950s, and after 1959 the ILP ceased running candidates.[253] Today, *Ulrich's International Periodicals Directory* lists the publication of the *ILP Magazine* since 1987, formerly the *Labour Leader*, published in Leeds, West Yorkshire.

THE BRITISH LABOUR PARTY

By 1906 the Labour Representation Committee was calling itself the Labour Party. That same year, Parliament passed the Trades Disputes Act, granting trade unions the right to picket and boycott, as well as the freedom from collective responsibility should any damages occur during a strike.[254]

Following World War I, the Labour Party adopted in 1918 a new program called "Labour and the New Social Order."[255] With this program, and in Clause 4 of a new party constitution, the Labour Party for the first time officially called for socialism, including the nationalization of mines, railways, and the electric power industry.

In 1924 the Labour Party, led by James Ramsey MacDonald (1866–1937), formed the first Labour government with MacDonald as prime minister. This was a minority government and only lasted nine months. Its reforms were cut short when the British Foreign Office published the so-called "Zinoviev

Letter"—a set of instructions supposedly from the head of The Third International (or Comintern, as it was known), Grigory Zinoviev, to the British Communists on antimilitarist tactics. This letter is now conceded to be a forgery, but it succeeded in getting the British electorate, upset with the entire Left over the idea of foreign communist interference in domestic affairs, to vote Tory and to oust the Labour government in less than a year.

The General Strike of 1926 began with a dispute with the Miner's Federation, and the Trades Union Congress (TUC) General Council called a special Conference of Trade Union Executives, which in turn called for a general strike. The nine-day general strike of May 3 to 12, 1926, however, collapsed, leading to a renewed interest in political activity on the part of labor. The reason for the collapse of the strike was the miners' refusal to accept a memorandum drawn up by Sir Herbert L. Samuel outlining a settlement, which the TUC General Council was going to urge the miners to accept as a basis for negotiation. With this refusal, the General Council declined to call out a "second line" of strikers—mainly engineers and shipbuilders—to join the already striking transport, metal, chemical, building, and printing and newspaper workers and announced to the prime minister that they were calling off the strike. The miners, however, continued to strike until that November.[256]

MacDonald returned to office in 1929 and in 1931 and invited the Liberal and Conservative leaders to join Labour in a "National Government" to provide a united front against the onslaught of the Great Depression. This government reversed Britain's free trade tradition, providing aid to agriculture, to housing, and to the shipbuilding industry. By 1933, conditions began to improve, although MacDonald was repudiated by his own party for his desertion.

Meanwhile, fascism arose in the world, but to a lesser degree in Britain itself in these years. Due to the tradition of reform, democracy, and socialism, fascism never caught on in Britain as it had in Germany, Italy, Spain, Portugal and Japan. How did Britain respond to these states turning fascist and engaging in empire building? When Conservative prime minister (Arthur) Neville Chamberlain (1869–1940) took office in 1937, he tried the policy of appeasement. At the Munich Conference in 1938, Britain, France, and Italy agreed to give in to Hitler's irredentism and to let Germany have the Sudetenland section of Czechoslovakia, which contained ethnic Germans. The hope was that Hitler would be satisfied and demand no more territories. He was not to be appeased; and on September 1, 1939, Germany invaded Poland, causing Britain and France to declare war on Germany, thus beginning World War II. France was defeated in June of 1940, and Holland, Belgium, and Norway soon fell, too. Chamberlain resigned, and Winston

Churchill (1874–1965), a Conservative who had not opposed the appeasement policy, became the new British prime minister. German air raids caused terrific damage, yet the Royal Air Force was strong enough to prevent an invasion.

Fortunately for Britain, Hitler double-crossed Stalin, with whom he had signed a Mutual Nonaggression Pact in 1939, and launched an invasion of the Soviet Union on June 22, 1941. For a time, the Germans would be fighting the Soviets instead of planning an immediate invasion of Britain. An additional stroke of good luck for Britain was the entry of the United States into the war on December 7, 1941, after the Japanese sneak attack on Pearl Harbor in Hawaii. The combined forces of the United States, the Soviet Union, and the British Allies, plus the Free French and other Resistance fighters, were large enough to overpower the Axis powers of Germany, Japan, and Italy.

Churchill had successfully convinced the United States to go along with his plan to attack the "soft-underbelly" of the Nazi empire in Northern Africa and to later fight their way north through Italy. "The soft-underbelly" turned out to be one tough gut, but the strategy did give time for the Allies to prepare for a direct invasion across the English Channel. Landing in Normandy on June 6, 1944, Allied forces on the Western Front and Soviet troops on the Eastern Front crushed the Germany military between them by May 1945.

Before the war, the British Labour Party had attacked Chamberlain's policy of appeasement with Germany and strongly supported the war effort once fighting had commenced, although it denounced war profiteering. When Chamberlain resigned on May 11, 1940, and Winston Churchill had been asked to form a new cabinet, Labour was asked to join it, and they accepted, although the ILP remained in opposition to this deal.

During the war, Britain adopted popular social programs developed by Sir William Henry Beveridge (1879–1963). The Labour Party swept into power on a social democratic platform after the war in July 1945 with a parliamentary majority.[257] Labour parliamentary leader since 1935 and deputy prime minister among other roles in Churchill's coalition cabinet, Lord Clement Richard Attlee (1883–1967) became the new prime minister. His government expanded the social programs begun during the war. Five key social acts were passed: The Family Allowance Act of 1945, the National Insurance Acts of 1946, the National Assistance Act of 1948, and the creation of the National Health Service in 1948—"socialized medicine," in which the majority of health care workers were employed by the state and health services were provided free or at low cost to the public. Thus, the British social security state was created with "cradle to grave" coverage.

The Labour government also nationalized in 1947 and 1948 the Bank of

England, the coal mines, the railroads, the trucking industry, civil aviation, canals, cable and wireless services, the gas utilities, and the iron and steel industries. All of these nationalizations were carried out with fair-market-value compensation paid to the former owners of these companies, not by expropriation, as in Communist countries.

Nationalization of the means of production, distribution, and exchange had been official Labour Party policy since 1918. In the intervening years, Labour and Conservative governments had already nationalized radio broadcasting, electrical utilities, and public transportation in London.

The Attlee government also dissolved the British Empire by granting independence to India and Pakistan in 1947 and to Ceylon, Burma, and Palestine in 1948. In part, the British Empire was broken up because the United Kingdom no longer had the military power to hold it together, having been exhausted in two world wars. Another reason for the breakup was the long-standing opposition of democratic socialists to imperialism, and with Labour in power, the democratic socialists were finally able to act on this ideological principle.

The breakup of the Empire and the high taxes that were needed to run the social democratic state proved to be unpopular enough to cause the Labour Party to lose the election of 1951. The Conservatives returned to power with Winston Churchill again as prime minister. The Tories were intent on reversing the trend toward socialism. The steel industry, which unlike the coal mines and the railroads was not losing money before nationalization, was privatized and sold to capitalist buyers. However, the basic social security programs were left intact, including the National Health Service.

The Conservatives ruled Britain from 1951 until 1964 under prime ministers Churchill, Sir (Robert) Anthony Eden (1897–1977), (Maurice) Harold Macmillan (1894–1896), and Sir Alec Douglas-Home (1903–). Part of the reason the Conservatives ruled for so long was that the Labour opposition found itself divided in these years. The left wing of the Labour Party headed by Aneurin Bevan (1897–1960), the minister of Health under the Attlee government, pressed for the Labour Party to stand for going beyond the stage of social democracy and campaigning for the stage of economic democracy where most of the economy would be socially owned. Bevan had resigned from the shadow cabinet in 1954 because of Labour's failure to oppose West Germany's rearmament. The right wing of the Labour Party was led by Hugh Gaitskell (1906–1963), the chancellor of the exchequer in the Attlee government, who had succeeded Attlee as Labour Party leader upon the latter's retirement in 1955. Gaitskell wanted the Labour Party to drop socialism altogether and become a liberal party. Not successful in this goal because of strong resistance from Labour's left wing, Bevan and Gaitskell reconciled in 1956, but their respective followers have continued this struggle. With the death of Gaitskell in 1963, the leadership of the Labour Party passed to Harold Wilson (1916–), a member from the left wing of the party. Like Gaitskell before him, Wilson was a university-trained economist.

The Conservatives in these years proposed that Britain apply for membership in the European Common Market. Labour split on this issue—the right wing favoring it for the trade opportunities it presented, the left wing opposing it because it might bring foreign control over the economy that could block future nationalizations of industry and force cutbacks in social spending.

The Conservative rule seemed boring to the British people of the sixties era, except for the 1963 sex scandal that helped bring the Conservatives down the following year. The scandal concerned the Secretary of State for War, John Profumo, and a female spy for the Soviets, who was also involved with a Soviet Naval attaché. Profumo at first denied the affair in the House of Commons, but later admitted it and resigned.

The Conservatives were defeated in the 1964 election by Labour, and Harold Wilson became prime minister. Under him, the steel industry was renationalized, but except for that, he disappointed the Labour left wing by not pressing for the nationalizations of remaining British industries.

In foreign policy, Wilson's government abolished the Colonial Office. Rhodesia had declared itself independent in 1965 when Britain insisted that it end apartheid. Wilson's government put an economic embargo on Rhodesia and sought UN help. However, Wilson managed to alienate Labour's left wing in the foreign policy area by not coming out against the U.S. war effort in Vietnam and by reversing himself on Britain's entry into the Common Market, which he had formerly strongly opposed.

Wilson's austerity budgets for social welfare programs and the large number of strikes during the recession under his administration hurt his popularity with the voters. The Conservatives won a thirty-seat majority in the House of Commons in the 1970 election, and Edward Heath (1916–) became the next prime minister.

The Heath government reduced corporate and individual income taxes, reduced welfare payments, maintained a tight money policy that caused unemployment to rise, led the passage of antistrike laws, and, in preparation for Britain's joining the Common Market, revalued the pound and passed higher import duties on meat and dairy products. The result was massive inflation and an industrial slump. Strict wage and price controls were slapped on to put the brakes on inflation. However, coal miners, one of the most underpaid groups of workers in Britain, struck against the wage controls in 1974.

In the 1974 election, Labour won a slight plurality of seats. Heath tried to form a government but failed, and then Harold Wilson returned as prime minister at the head of a minority government. He granted the miners a 35 percent wage increase immediately, ending the highly unpopular strike. He also got the TUC to agree to a "Social Contract" to moderate their wage demands. Wilson's government raised taxes and public payments, and the bad situation in the country eased up. Britain, however, still had problems with inflation and unemployment, and in 1975 taxes were raised again and further cuts were made in spending. Also that year Britain formally joined the Common Market.

Margaret Thatcher (1925–) became the new leader of the Conservative Party in 1975. The following year, Wilson resigned from office, and Labour Party leader James Callaghan (1912–) took his place as prime minister. The unions had tired of waiting for economic relief that never came and broke with the "Social Contract" as a strike wave hit the nation.

Callaghan also proposed devolution—a shift from a unitary state to a federal one by allowing Scotland and Wales to have their own elected assemblies, but this was rejected in a 1979 referendum.

Labour lost support again; and in 1979 the Conservatives returned to power with Margaret Thatcher as prime minister. She cut taxes and was one of the first to adopt monetarism, followed closely by the U.S. Federal Reserve Board's new chairman Paul Volcker. *Monetarism* is the fiscal theory of the Chicago School of Milton Friedman and others that states that inflation, not unemployment, is the root of economic problems and that inflation could be reduced by contracting a nation's money supply. There are two problems with this theory: (1) It does not always work; indeed, in Britain, inflation only rose under Thatcher. (2) Monetarism caused a slowdown in the economy, and the number of unemployed in Britain rapidly rose to a postwar record of 2 million.

It looked as if the Conservatives might soon be out again due to these failures, but two things happened to keep Thatcher in office: First, the left and right wings of the Labour Party began sharply fighting each other again. The left wing won victories in the 1978 Labour Party Annual Conference, getting the party to formally call for a transition to economic democracy to be made once the party came back to power. The right wing of the party could not stand this, and in 1979, led by Roy Jenkins and David Owen, the right wing split from Labour, forming their own party, the Social Democratic Party. They hoped to form an alliance with the British Liberal Party that beat both Labour and the Conservatives, but so far they have failed. The Liberals and the Social Democrats united in January 1988 to form the Social and Liberal Democratic Party (SLD). Because everyone kept calling it the "Salad" Party because of its initials, they changed their name again to the Democrats—a one-word name—at their inaugural Conference in Blackpool in September 1988. The Liberal name was dropped after a 120-year history of use, but this did not sit well with many members. In the 1992 election, they called themselves the Liberal Democratic Party. Although the voter strength of the Liberal Democrats has not been too impressive and they have remained a smaller third party behind Labour and the Conservatives, they were able to take enough votes away from Labour to keep it out of office.

The second happening was the war begun in April 1982 when Argentina seized the Falkland Islands held by Britain. The British people rallied around the Conservative government, giving it new strength; and despite a 13 percent unemployment rate as well as inner city riots in 1981, the Conservatives won a decisive victory at the polls in June 1983. With the economy booming in the 1980s and the standard of living for most British rising as unemployment dropped, the Conservatives again were able to beat Labour in the election of June 1987. Whereas Labour improved its vote in this election, the Liberal-SDP Alliance lost badly.

At the Labour Party's Annual Conference in Blackpool in 1982, the right wing of the party was victorious. Left-wingers Anthony Wedgwood Benn and Eric Heffer were displaced as chairs of important committees, and the Trotskyist "Militant" group was driven out. The 364-day strike by the National Union of Mineworkers in 1984 and 1985 was defeated after the Tory government announced plans to shut down unprofitable mines. The Thatcher government sought to reverse socialism by engaging in the privatization of state-owned industries. Seeking to create a "people's capitalism," the Conservatives denationalized and sold off to private owners such state-owned industries as British Airways and British Telecom in the 1980s.

Government ownership as compared to cooperatives, thus, proved to be an unsustainable form of socialism. The British experience has been that many of the industries that had been nationalized by previous Labour administrations were then privatized by incoming Conservative governments. Only the cooperative sector seemed immune to the changes in government. With the shift toward the right in the Labour Party in the 1980s, the demand for nationalization was largely dropped, although support for cooperatives remained strong. Nationalization had proved increasingly unpopular and hurt the chances of Labour getting back into power. It also did little to achieve the socialist goal of liberating the working class from exploitation and alienation. Evidence of this was to be found in the need to strike against state-appointed management, just as workers had struck against private corporations. A boss was still a boss even if he was a state-appointed one. The 1980s and 1990s were also a rocky time for the Conservatives. West Indians and blacks rebelled in Birmingham, Brixton, and London on several occasions in 1985 over police brutality. Racial attacks against blacks and Asians became more commonplace. The Thatcher government's decision to impose a highly unpopular poll tax to finance elections—the first since a similar bill caused the Peasants' Revolt in 1381—led to a violent protest in London on March 31, 1990. Margaret Thatcher was forced to resign as opposition to the poll tax and her backing of a European monetary union mounted, and John Major (1943–) replaced her as leader of the Conservative Party and as the new prime minister in November 1991. The poll tax was repealed that year. The following year, the Conservatives won again in the Parliamentary elections, and John Major remained as prime minister. Neil Kinnock (1942–) stepped down as Labour Party leader as a result of this defeat and was replaced by John Smith (1938–1994), also from the right wing of the party and pledged to a moderate form of social democracy, continuing the retreat from the demands for nationalization and unilateral disarmament pushed by the left Labourites in the 1970s. In 1992, Labour MP (Member of Parliament) Betty Boothroyd (1929–) was chosen as the first woman Speaker of the House of Commons. Smith died of a heart attack on May 12, 1994, and was succeeded as party leader on July 21 of that year by Tony Blair (1953–). An Oxford-educated lawyer and a political centrist, he sought to rewrite Clause 4 of the Labour Party Constitution adopted in 1918, which had made the party formally socialist by calling for state ownership of the economy over the strenuous objections of the party's left wing. Although some industries such as the National Health Service were kept in state hands and improved, most other industries were not nationalized. Instead a Labour government promoted educational reforms and a youth job-training program. On May 1, 1997, the "New" Labour Party, having moved to the political center, won a landslide victory in the parliamentary elections, capturing 45 percent of the vote and 419 seats. Blair became the youngest British prime minister since 1812.

The new Labour government announced its intention to abolish hereditary peers from the House of Lords. Currently they number over 750, whereas about 550 appointed lords would be left untouched.[258] A breakaway Socialist Labour Party is unhappy with the rightwards direction of Labour Party under Blair.

SCOTLAND AND WALES

The new British Labour government proceeded with plans for devolution upon taking office, allowing for referenda on having parliaments in Scotland and Wales, thus moving the United Kingdom from a unitary state to a federal one. The Scots voted by a 74.2 percent majority for the formation of their own semi-independent parliament in September 1997, their first in nearly 300 years, since the union in 1707 of Scotland with England to form Great Britain.[259] This would allow their 5.5 million people to pass their own decisions on matters such as agriculture, economic development, education, environmental legislation, health, housing, law and order, and sports. A related law granting their parliament limited powers of taxation won by a 63.4 percent majority. These measures had been supported not only by the Scottish Nationalists, but also by the Labour Party. The national government in London will retain powers over constitutional matters as well as over defense, economic policy, and foreign policy. The vote in Wales for their own assembly was closer than in Scotland, but it too passed a week later in September 1997 by a 7,000 vote margin out of 1 million votes cast.[260] The referendum created a Welsh assembly with far more limited powers than the Scottish one. The Scottish and Welsh parliaments opened on July 1, 1999, over Conservatives' objections.[261] A Scottish Socialist Party was formed in 1998, and the Welsh Socialist Alliance seeks to form a Welsh Socialist Party.

IRELAND

Henry Hyndman's Social Democratic Federation in the late 1880s had supported the independence of Ireland from Great Britain, as did the Labour Party early on.[262] This goal was to pass except for the six northern counties of the province of Ulster. The Sinn Fein ("We ourselves") was established in 1900 by Arthur Griffith (1872–1922), a Dublin journalist, to fight for independence from Great Britain. The abortive Easter Rebellion of 1916 led to the execution of many of its leaders, which, in turn, provided martyrs for the cause of independence.[263] At the start of the Irish Revolution (1919–1922) the Sinn Fein members of the Parliament assembled in Dublin as a national assembly and proclaimed the independence of Ireland from Great Britain, with Eamon de Valera (1882–1975) as their president. A guerrilla war ensued by what would later be called the Irish Republican Army (IRA) against government forces reinforcing the Royal Irish Constabulary with volunteers known for their brutality. They were commonly called the Black and Tans. During the war, the British Parliament passed the Government of

Ireland Act of 1920. The Act granted home rule for Ireland, which had a Roman Catholic majority, but also established a separate parliament for the six counties in the province of Ulster in Northern Ireland where pro-British Protestants outnumbered the Roman Catholics who sought union with Ireland. A truce in the Irish Revolution was arranged in 1921, and the war finally ended on January 15, 1922. The Irish Free State was created with Arthur Griffith as its president. Not everyone supported the peace treaty. The Republicans opposed the treaty and the authority of the new Dáil, or parliament, to ratify the treaty. These Republicans, later called Fianna Fail, called for a resumption of the armed struggle with Great Britain. They proclaimed a rival government and fought against the Irish Free State, leading to many casualties on both sides. Numerous Republican leaders were executed. A truce was proclaimed in 1923 before national elections. The border between the Irish Free State and Northern Ireland was fixed in December 1925. In 1937, the Irish Free State was abolished, and Eire was proclaimed as an independent state. On April 18, 1949, the Republic of Ireland was formed and withdrew completely from the Commonwealth of Nations. In the elections of that year, the Nationalist Party, which favored union with Ireland, was defeated by the pro-British Ulster Unionist Party. On May 17, 1949, the British Parliament passed a law retaining Northern Ireland as part of the United Kingdom. The Labour Party represents democratic socialism in Ireland. It was founded in 1912 by James Larkin (1867–1947) and the outstanding revolutionary, socialist, trade unionist leader James Connolly (1968–1916), author of the pamphlet *Socialism Made Easy*.[264]

Northern Ireland

Beginning in December 1955, guerrilla forces of the outlawed IRA started a campaign of armed resistance, fighting for the breaking away of Northern Ireland from the United Kingdom and, instead, its union with the Republic of Ireland. However, the Republic of Ireland denounced all acts of terrorism, and for a time the IRA abandoned its violent campaign.

Fueled by growing resentment over discrimination of Roman Catholics by the Protestant majority in Northern Ireland, a civil rights movement began there. However, a right-wing faction of the Ulster Unionist Party called for active resistance to Roman Catholic opposition. Violence took an upturn after the British abolished the Northern Ireland Parliament in 1972 and imposed direct rule from London. A referendum in March 1973 was boycotted by the Roman Catholics, and so a majority of those voting voted for Northern Ireland to remain within the United Kingdom of Great Britain and Northern Ireland, rather than to join with the Republic of Ireland. The 1974 general strike by Protestants forced the end of a short-lived government in Northern Ireland, and again Britain imposed direct rule. The troubles increased with the Provisional Wing of the IRA engaging in acts of terrorism, matched by those of Protestant paramilitary groups. In August 1979 IRA terrorists ambushed and killed Lord Mountbatten and on the same day eighteen British soldiers. In 1981 the IRA's detained members began a hunger strike to win back sympathy. Several IRA members starved to death during this hunger strike.

Violence continued with the IRA striking British troops and civilians throughout Europe, while British troops continued to patrol the streets of the major Northern Ireland cities of Belfast and Londonderry. In 1985 the British under Prime Minister Margaret Thatcher made an agreement with the Republic of Ireland granting it an advisory role in Northern Irish affairs; but in the main, the British government was unable to quell the sectarian violence in Northern Ireland.

The breakthrough to peace had to wait until the Conservatives were out of power in Britain and Blair's Labour government came into office. On May 22, 1998, twin referenda were held and passed both in Northern Ireland and in the Republic of Ireland on an accord to end the long-running troubles in Northern Ireland between the pro-British Protestant majority and the pro-Irish Catholic minority.[265]

Under the terms of the agreement, Northern Ireland remained part of the United Kingdom, unless majorities in both north and south voted otherwise. The Republic of Ireland amended its constitution to give up its territorial claims to Northern Ireland. A 108-member, Northern Ireland assembly was created with powers to govern over such areas as agriculture, economic development, and finance. Provisions were put in place to ensure that there would be "cross-community" representation for Roman Catholics, who make up 42 percent of the population, as well as the Protestant majority. A North-South council was also created by the terms of the agreement that promoted joint policy making. Its decisions would have to be ratified by both the Northern Ireland assembly and the Irish parliament. An East-West council was formed for Republic of Ireland politicians to meet and discuss issues with their counterparts in the British parliament and the Northern Ireland assembly, the Scottish parliament, and the Welsh assembly, but it had no administrative or legislative powers.

Most importantly, the agreement would try to implement the disarmament of the Irish Republican Army and Protestant paramilitary groups in Northern Ireland, speed up the release of prisoners imprisoned for paramilitary activity, and make progress toward demilitarization of the region.

The major democratic socialist party of Northern Ireland is the Social Democratic and Labour Party, which backed these accords. At least some of the members of the Irish Republican Army and other Northern Irish liberation paramilitary groups also consider themselves to be socialists.

NOTES

1. Harry W. Laidler, *History of Socialism* (New York: Apollo, 1968), p. 679.
2. Ibid., p. 680.
3. Ibid., pp. 680–686.
4. Jerry Voorhis, *Cooperative Enterprise: The Little People's Chance in a World of Bigness* (Danville, IL: Interstate Printers and Publishers, 1975), p. 19.
5. Laidler, *History of Socialism*, pp. 720–728.
6. Ibid., pp. 729–732.
7. Ibid., pp. 179–181.
8. John Stuart Mill, *Principles of Political Economy*, 1848; reprinted in *Collected Works of John Stuart Mill*, 2 vols. (Toronto: University of Toronto Press, 1965), b. 2, ch. 3.
9. Ibid., b. 5; Henry H. Magid, "John Stuart Mill," in *History of Political Philosophy*, 2d ed., ed. Leo Strauss and Joseph Cropsey (Chicago: University of Chicago Press, 1981), p. 753.
10. Laidler, *History of Socialism*, p. 181.
11. G. D. H. Cole, *A History of Socialist Thought*, 5 vols. (New York: St. Martin's, 1953–58), 2:379.
12. Ibid., 2:390; M. Beer, *A History of British Socialism*, 2 vols. (New York: Harcourt, Brace and Howe, 1921), 2:247; Frederick J. Gould, *Hyndman—Prophet of Socialism, 1842–1921* (London: George Allen and Unwin, 1928), p. 70; Chushichi Tsuzuki, *H. M. Hyndman and British Socialism* (Oxford: Oxford University Press, 1961), p. 39; J. H. Steward Reid, *The Origins of the British Labour Party* (Minneapolis: University of Minnesota Press, 1955), p. 48.
13. Roger Moore, *The Emergence of the Labour Party, 1880–1924* (London: Hodder and Stoughton, 1978), pp. 34–35.
14. Francois Bedarida, *A Social History of England 1851–1975* (London: Metheun, 1979), p. 136.
15. Beer, *A History of British Socialism*, 2:227–230; Gould, *Hyndman*, pp. 60–64; Tsuzuki, *H. M. Hyndman and British Socialism*, pp. 32–34.
16. Cole, *A History of Socialist Thought*, 2:394.
17. Geoffrey Foote, *The Labour Party's Political Thought—a History* (London: Croom Helm, 1985), p. 23.
18. Tsuzuki, *H. M. Hyndman and British Socialism*, pp. 33–41.

19. Ibid., p. 34.
20. Gould, *Hyndman*, p. 70; Tsuzuki, *H. M. Hyndman and British Socialism*, p. 21; *The Radical*, July 16, 1881.
21. Morton H. Cowden, "Early Marxist Views on British Labor, 1837–1917," *The Western Political Science Quarterly* 11 (1963): 41.
22. Henry Mayers Hyndman, *The Record of an Adventurous Life* (New York: Macmillan, 1911; reprint New York: Garland, 1984), p. 273; Gould, *Hyndman*, pp. 228–229.
23. Henry Mayers Hyndman, *England For All: The Text-book of Democracy* (London: Gilbert and Rivington, 1881).
24. Cole, *A History of Socialist Thought*, 2:395; Beer, *A History of British Socialism*, 2:229; Gould, *Hyndman*, p. 63; Tsuzuki, *H. M. Hyndman and British Socialism*, p. 141; Philip Poirier, *The Advent of the British Labour Party* (New York: Columbia University Press, 1978), p. 41; Cowden, "Early Marxist Views on British Labor," p. 44.
25. Carl F. Brand, *The British Labour Party—A Short History* (Stanford, CA: Stanford University Press, 1964), p. 4.
26. Beer, *A History of British Socialism*, 2:229; Cole, *A History of Socialist Thought*, 2:395.
27. Beer, *A History of British Socialism*, 2:229.
28. Gould, *Hyndman*, pp. 63–64; Friedrich Albert Sorge, et al., *Briefe und Auszuge as Briefen von Joh. Phil. Becker, Jos. Dietzgen, Friedrich Engels, Karl Marx*, ed., F. A. Sorge (Stuttgart: J. H. W. Dietz, 1906), pp. 180–181.
29. Foote, *The Labour Party's Political Thought*, pp. 21–22.
30. Tsuzuki, *H. M. Hyndman and British Socialism*, p. 47.
31. Hyndman, *England for All*, p. 194.
32. Ibid., p. 31.
33. Poirier, *The Advent of the British Labour Party*, p. 24; *Justice*, September 6, 1884.
34. Gould, *Hyndman*, p. 99.
35. Henry Mayers Hyndman, *Further Reminiscences* (London: Macmillan, 1912), p. 459.
36. Foote, *The Labour Party's Political Thought*, p. 22.
37. Ibid., p. 528; Gould, *Hyndman*, p. 44.
38. Brand, *The British Labour Party*, p. 4.
39. David McLellan, *Karl Marx: Selected Writings* (Oxford: Oxford University Press, 1977), p. 237.
40. Democratic Federation, *Socialism Made Plain* (London: W. Reeves, 1883); Cole, *A History of Socialist Thought*, 2:397; Tsuzuki, *H. M. Hyndman and British Socialism*, p. 50.
41. Cole, *A History of Socialist Thought*, 2:397–398.

42. Tsuzuki, *H. M. Hyndman and British Socialism*, p. 50.
43. Cole, *A History of Socialist Thought*, 2:397–398.
44. Tsuzuki, *H. M. Hyndman and British Socialism*, pp. 50–51.
45. Henry Mayers Hyndman, *The Historical Basis of Socialism in England* (London: K. Paul, Trench & Co. 1883; reprint, New York: Garland, 1984).
46. Tsuzuki, *H. M. Hyndman and British Socialism*, p. 51.
47. Hyndman, *The Historical Basis of Socialism in England*, p. 422.
48. Ibid., pp. 194n.
49. Cole, *A History of Socialist Thought*, 2:398; Beer, *A History of British Socialism*, 2:247–251; Gould, *Hyndman*, pp. 74–76; Tsuzuki, *H. M. Hyndman and British Socialism*, p. 49.
50. Cole, *A History of Socialist Thought*, 2:398; Beer, *A History of British Socialism*, 2:254; Gould, *Hyndman*, p. 94; Tsuzuki, *H. M. Hyndman and British Socialism*, p. 58.
51. Gould, *Hyndman*, pp. 94–95.
52. Hyndman, *England for All*, p. 107; Gould, *Hyndman*, p. 91.
53. Hyndman, *Further Reminiscences*, p. 528.
54. Henry Mayers Hyndman and William Morris, *A Summary of the Principles of Socialism* (London: Modern Press, 1884; reprint, London: Modern Press, 1984); Cole, *A History of Socialist Thought*, 2:398; Gould, *Hyndman*, p. 83; Tsuzuki, *H. M. Hyndman and British Socialism*, p. 61.
55. Cole, *A History of Socialist Thought*, 2:410.
56. Ibid., 2:398–399.
57. Tsuzuki, *H. M. Hyndman and British Socialism*, pp. 82–83.
58. Ibid., p. 58.
59. Cole, *A History of Socialist Thought*, 2:400.
60. Tsuzuki, *H. M. Hyndman and British Socialism*, p. 49.
61. Gould, *Hyndman*, p. 589.
62. Cole, *A History of Socialist Thought*, 2:400.
63. Beer, *A History of British Socialism,* 2:242–245.
64. Cole, *A History of Socialist Thought*, 2:400–401; Beer, *A History of British Socialism*, 2:252–253; Gould, *Hyndman*, pp. 95–96; Tsuzuki, *H. M. Hyndman and British Socialism*, pp. 63–68.
65. Cole, *A History of Socialist Thought*, 2:400–402; Tsuzuki, *H. M. Hyndman and British Socialism*, pp. 66–67; Poirier, *The Advent of the British Labour Party*, p. 25; Reid, *The Origins of the British Labour Party*, p. 49.
66. Beer, *A History of British Socialism*, 2:260.
67. Cole, *A History of Socialist Thought*, 2:403; Tsuzuki, *H. M. Hyndman and British Socialism*, pp. 70–72; Reid, *The Origins of the British Labour Party*, pp. 49–50.

68. Cole, *A History of Socialist Thought*, 2:204; Tsuzuki, *H. M. Hyndman and British Socialism*, pp. 72–73.
69. Cole, *A History of Socialist Thought*, 2:404–405.
70. Beer, *A History of British Socialism*, 2:260–261; Gould, *Hyndman*, pp. 104–105; Tsuzuki, *H. M. Hyndman and British Socialism*, pp. 73–74.
71. Cole, *A History of Socialist Thought*, 3:189; Beer, *A History of British Socialism*, 2:269; Tsuzuki, *H. M. Hyndman and British Socialism*, p. 138.
72. Cole, *A History of Socialist Thought*, 3:190; Beer, *A History of British Socialism*, 2:269; Tsuzuki, *H. M. Hyndman and British Socialism*, p. 139.
73. Cole, *A History of Socialist Thought*, 3:201; Beer, *A History of British Socialism*, 2:385; Tsuzuki, *H. M. Hyndman and British Socialism*, p. 178.
74. Cole, *A History of Socialist Thought*, 3:201; Beer, *A History of British Socialism*, 2:385; Gould, *Hyndman*, p. 147; Tsuzuki, *H. M. Hyndman and British Socialism*, p. 175.
75. Cole, *A History of Socialist Thought*, 4:405; Beer, *A History of British Socialism*, 2:385; Tsuzuki, *H. M. Hyndman and British Socialism*, p. 178.
76. Cole, *A History of Socialist Thought*, 4:405; Beer, *A History of British Socialism*, 2:288–289; Gould, *Hyndman*, pp. 210–212; Tsuzuki, *H. M. Hyndman and British Socialism*, pp. 234–235.
77. Cole, *A History of Socialist Thought*, 2:411–412; Gould, *Hyndman*, p. 272; Tsuzuki, *H. M. Hyndman and British Socialism*, p. 264.
78. Gould, *Hyndman*, p. 285.
79. Ibid., p. 294; Tsuzuki, *H. M. Hyndman and British Socialism*, p. 266.
80. E. J. Hobsbawn, *Labouring Men, Studies in the History of Labour* (London: Weidenfeld Nicolson, 1964), pp. 231–232.
81. Cole, *A History of Socialist Thought*, 3:104–106; Beer, *A History of British Socialism*, 2:274–277; Anne Fremantle, *This Little Band of Prophets: The British Fabians* (New York: Mentor, 1960), pp. 26–29; A. M. McBriar, *Fabian Socialism and English Politics 1884–1918* (Cambridge: Cambridge University Press, 1966), pp. 1–3; Edward R. Pease, *The History of the Fabian Society* (London: Allen and Unwin, 1925), pp. 28–36; Norman MacKenzie and Jeanne MacKenzie, *The First Fabians* (London: Weidenfeld and Nicolson, 1977), pp. 15–19.
82. Josephine Fishel Milburn, "The Fabian Society and the British Labour Party," *The Western Political Quarterly* 11 (1958): 319–320.
83. James D. Forman, *Socialism—Its Theoretical Roots and Present-day Development* (New York: Dell, 1972), p. 28.
84. Cole, *A History of Socialist Thought*, 3:106–107; MacKenzie and MacKenzie, *The First Fabians*, pp. 56–72; Pease, *The History of the Fabian Society*, pp. 46–47.
85. Gordon R. Lewis, "Fabian Socialism; Some Aspects of Theory and Practice," *The Journal of Politics* 14 (August 1950): 444–446.
86. Reid, *The Origins of the British Labour Party*, p. 53.

87. Cole, *A History of Socialist Thought*, 3:107; Pease, *The History of the Fabian Society*, pp. 40–46.
88. Beer, *A History of British Socialism*, 2:275; MacKenzie and MacKenzie, *The First Fabians*, pp. 42–44; Pease, *The History of the Fabian Society*, pp. 66–85.
89. Francis Williams, "The Program of the British Labour Party—an Historical Survey," *The Journal of Politics* 12 (1950): 198.
90. *Fabian Tracts* (reprint, Nendeln, Liechtenstein: Kraus-Thomson, 1969), No. 5.
91. Cole, *A History of Socialist Thought*, 3:109.
92. George Bernard Shaw, ed., *Fabian Essays* (London: Allen and Unwin, 1948), p. 200; *Fabian Tracts* No. 1, p. 1.
93. Cole, *A History of Socialist Thought*, 3:106; Fremantle, *This Little Band of Prophets*, p. 28; MacKenzie and MacKenzie, *The First Fabians*, pp. 41–42; Pease, *The History of the Fabian Society*, pp. 39–40.
94. Sidney Webb, *Socialism in England* (London: Swann Sonnenschein, 1890), p. 8; McBriar, *Fabian Socialism and English Politics 1884–1918*, p. 69.
95. *Fabian Tracts* No. 70, p. 285.
96. McBriar, *Fabian Socialism and English Politics*, pp. 60–68.
97. *Fabian Tracts* No. 15, pp. 205–207.
98. Lewis, "Fabian Socialism," p. 443.
99. Elizabeth Durbin, *New Jerusalem, The Labour Party and the Economics of Democratic Socialism* (London: Routledge & Kegan Paul, 1985), pp. 32–33.
100. Foote, *The Labour Party's Political Thought*, p. 25.
101. George Bernard Shaw, *Bernard Shaw and Karl Marx: A Symposium* (New York: Random House, 1930), pp. 170–171.
102. McBriar, *Fabian Socialism and English Politics*, p. 70.
103. Cole, *A History of Socialist Thought*, 3:112.
104. Foote, *The Labour Party's Political Thought*, pp. 26–27.
105. Beatrice Webb, *Our Partnership* (London: Longmans, Green, 1948), p. 123; Lewis, "Fabian Socialism," p. 447.
106. Foote, *The Labour Party's Political Thought*, p. 28.
107. Williams, "The Program of the British Labour Party," p. 199.
108. Cole, *A History of Socialist Thought*, 3:114.
109. Lewis, "Fabian Socialism," p. 446.
110. Pease, *The History of the Fabian Society*, p. 82.
111. Reid, *The Origins of the British Labour Party*, p. 53.
112. *Fabian Tracts* No. 70, pp. 286–287.
113. *Fabian Tracts* No. 15, pp. 212–215.
114. Ibid., pp. 214–215.
115. Cole, *A History of Socialist Thought*, 3:115; Beer, *A History of British Socialism*, 2:284–285.

116. *Fabian Tracts* No. 70, p. 287.
117. *Fabian Tracts* No. 4, p. 18.
118. McBriar, *Fabian Socialism and English Politics*, pp. 20–21; Fremantle, *This Little Band of Prophets*, p. 56.
119. McBriar, *Fabian Socialism and English Politics*, p. 22.
120. *Fabian Tracts* No. 41.
121. George Bernard Shaw, *The Intelligent Woman's Guide to Socialism and Capitalism*, 2 vols. (London: Pelican, 1937), 1:8.
122. Pease, *The History of the Fabian Society*, p. 82.
123. Cole, *A History of Socialist Thought*, 3:115.
124. McBriar, *Fabian Socialism and English Politics*, pp. 37–38.
125. Brand, *The British Labour Party*, p. 6.
126. McBriar, *Fabian Socialism and English Politics*, p. 114.
127. McBriar, *Fabian Socialism and English Politics*, pp. 115–116.
128. Sidney Webb and Beatrice Webb, *A Constitution for the Socialist Commonwealth of Great Britain* (London: Longmans, Green, 1920), p. 168.
129. Cole, *A History of Socialist Thought*, 3:116.
130. Ibid., 3:118.
131. Ibid., 3:124.
132. Ibid., 3:125–126.
133. *Fabian Tracts* No. 70, p. 297; Beer, *A History of British Socialism*, 2:286–287.
134. Cole, *A History of Socialist Thought*, 3:126–127.
135. McBriar, *Fabian Socialism and English Politics*, pp. 111–113.
136. Ibid., pp. 95–97.
137. Cole, *A History of Socialist Thought*, 3:128; MacKenzie and MacKenzie, *The First Fabians*, pp. 197–198.
138. Pease, *The History of the Fabian Society*, pp. 62–63.
139. McBriar, *Fabian Socialism and English Politics*, pp. 71–73.
140. Poirier, *The Advent of the British Labour Party*, pp. 30–31.
141. Hobsbawn, *Labouring Men*, p. 251.
142. MacKenzie and MacKenzie, *The First Fabians*, pp. 84–85.
143. Milburn, "The Fabian Society and the British Labour Party," p. 325.
144. Friedrich Engels, *On Britain* (Moscow: Foreign Languages Publishing House, 1953), pp. 530–531; Cowden, "Early Marxist Views on British Labor," p. 44.
145. Moore, *The Emergence of the Labour Party*, p. 59; Reid, *The Origins of the British Labour Party*, p. 55; Pease, *The History of the Fabian Society*, pp. 115–116.
146. Poirier, *The Advent of the British Labour Party*, p. 34.
147. McBriar, *Fabian Socialism and English Politics*, pp. 72–73.

148. Pease, *The History of the Fabian Society*, p. 61.
149. Emile B. Ader, *Socialism* (Woodbury, NY: Barron's Educational Series, 1966), pp. 58–59.
150. Shaw, *Fabian Essays*, p. 33.
151. *Fabian Tracts* No. 15, p. 204.
152. Forman, *Socialism*, pp. 29–30.
153. Webb and Webb, *A Constitution for the Socialist Commonwealth of Great Britain*, p. 149; Cole, *A History of Socialist Thought*, 3:217; McBriar, *Fabian Socialism And English Politics 1884–1918*, pp. 93–95.
154. Webb and Webb, *A Constitution for the Socialist Commonwealth of Great Britain*, p. 158.
155. Ibid., p. 159.
156. Ibid., p. 160.
157. Ibid., pp. 161–162.
158. *Fabian Tracts* No. 15, p. 203.
159. Carole Pateman, *Participation and Democratic Theory* (Cambridge: Cambridge University Press, 1970), pp. 85–102; Gerry Hunnius, G. David Garson, and John Case, eds., *Workers' Control—A Reader on Labor and Social Change* (New York: Vintage, 1973), pp. 164–321; John Curl, *History of Work Cooperation in America* (Berkeley, CA: Homeward Press, 1980); Alastair Campbell, *Mondragon 1980* (Los Angeles: CRSP, 1982).
160. Cole, *A History of Socialist Thought*, 3:217.
161. Forman, *Socialism*, p. 29.
162. Milburn, "The Fabian Society and the British Labour Party," p. 328.
163. Ibid., p. 320.
164. Hobsbawn, *Labouring Men*, p. 259.
165. Foote, *The Labour Party's Political Thought*, p. 25.
166. Michael Harrington, *Socialism* (New York: Bantam, 1973), p. 177; Fremantle, *This Little Band of Prophets*, p. 252; Hobsbawn, *Labouring Men*, p. 254.
167. H. G. Wells, *The New Machiavelli* (London: John Lane, the Bodley House, 1911); Cole, *A History of Socialist Thought*, 3:204.
168. Fremantle, *This Little Band of Prophets*, pp. 158–166; MacKenzie and MacKenzie, *The First Fabians*, pp. 228–332; Pease, *The History of the Fabian Society*, pp. 163–184.
169. McBriar, *Fabian Socialism and English Politics*, p. 84.
170. Cole, *A History of Socialist Thought*, 3:129–144.
171. Stanley Pierson, *British Socialism—The Journey from Fantasy to Politics* (Cambridge, MA: Harvard University Press, 1979), p. 34.
172. Cole, *A History of Socialist Thought*, 3:131–132.
173. Cowden, "Early Marxist Views on British Labor," p. 41–42.
174. Cole, *A History of Socialist Thought*, 3:133–134.

175. Henry Pelling, *The Origins of the Labour Party 1880–1924* (London: Macmillan, 1954), pp. 88–89.
176. Moore, *The Emergence of the Labour Party*, pp. 45–46.
177. Cole, *A History of Socialist Thought*, 3:179.
178. Beer, *A History of British Socialism*, 2:298.
179. Friedrich Engels, *Daily Chronicle, I* (July 1893).
180. Cowden, "Early Marxist Views on British Labor," p. 35.
181. Poirier, *The Advent of the British Labour Party*, p. 50.
182. Cole, *A History of Socialist Thought*, 3:227; Beer, *A History of British Socialism*, 2:302; Pelling, *The Origins of the Labour Party*, p. 121; William Stewart, *J. Keir Hardie—a Biography* (London: Independent Labour Party, 1921), p. 73; Fred Reid, *Keir Hardie—the Making of a Socialist* (London: Croom Helm, 1978), p. 143.
183. Robert E. Dowse, *The Left in the Centre, the Independent Labour Party 1893–1940* (Evanston, IL: Northwestern University Press, 1960), pp. 2–3; Pelling, *The Origins of the Labour Party*, pp. 65–81; Poirier, *The Advent of the British Labour Party*, pp. 45–46; Reid, *Keir Hardie*, pp. 72–126; Stewart, *J. Keir Hardie*, pp. 1–37.
184. Reid, *The Origins of the British Labour Party*, p. 61.
185. Brand, *The British Labour Party*, p. 9.
186. Moore, *The Emergence of the Labour Party*, p. 51.
187. Poirier, *The Advent of the British Labour Party*, p. 51.
188. Cole, *A History of Socialist Thought*, 3:157; Pelling, *The Origins Of The Labour Party*, p. 125; Stewart, *J. Keir Hardie*, pp. 73–77.
189. Dowse, *The Left In The Centre*, pp. 6–7.
190. Reid, *Keir Hardie*, p. 113; *Miner* (April 1888).
191. Pierson, *British Socialism*, p. 37.
192. Reid, *Keir Hardie*, p. 133.
193. Ibid., pp. 147–148; *Labour Leader* (December 1893).
194. Cole, *A History of Socialist Thought*, 3:158; Pierson, *British Socialism*, p. 37; Pelling, *The Origins of the Labour Party*, p. 128; Reid, *The Origins of the British Labour Party*, p. 64.
195. Beer, *A History of British Socialism*, 2:304.
196. Stanley Rothman, Howard Scarrow, and Martin Schain, *European Society and Politics: Britain, France and Germany* (St. Paul, MN: West Publishing, 1976), p. 155.
197. Ibid., p. 153.
198. Beer, *A History of British Socialism*, 2:304.
199. Cole, *A History of Socialist Thought*, 3:161; Cowden, "Early Marxist Views on British Labor," pp. 35, 43; Poirier, *The Advent of the British Labour Party*, pp. 52–53.

200. Friedrich Engels, *The Condition of the Working Class in England in 1844* (London: Allen and Unwin, 1892), p. xvii (1892 Preface); Cowden, "Early Marxist Views on British Labor," p. 43.
201. Foote, *The Labour Party's Political Thought*, p. 43.
202. Brand, *The British Labour Party*, pp. 10–12.
203. Kenneth D. Brown, *The First Labour Party 1905–1914* (London: Croom Helm, 1985), pp. 3–4.
204. Pierson, *British Socialism*, p. 34.
205. Cole, *A History of Socialist Thought*, 3:179.
206. Pierson, *British Socialism*, pp. 35–36.
207. Williams, "The Program of the British Labour Party," p. 200.
208. Poirier, *The Advent of the British Labour Party*, pp. 54–55.
209. Reid, *The Origins of the British Labour Party*, p. 65.
210. R. N. Berki, *Socialism* (New York: St. Martin's, 1975), p. 78.
211. Cole, *A History of Socialist Thought*, 3:3:227.
212. Ibid., 3:228.
213. Reid, *Keir Hardie*, p. 146.
214. Cole, *A History of Socialist Thought*, 3:228.
215. Reid, *Keir Hardie*, p. 149.
216. *West Ham Herald* (April 22, 1893).
217. Emrys Hughes, *Keir Hardie's Speeches and Writings—from 1888–1915* (Glasgow: Forward, 1928), pp. 66–68.
218. James Keir Hardie, *From Serfdom to Socialism*, ed. Robert E. Dowse (Rutherford, NJ: Fairleigh Dickinson University Press, 1974), p. 2.
219. Ibid., pp. 35–37.
220. Reid, *Keir Hardie*, p. 150.
221. Hardie, *From Serfdom to Socialism*, p. 89.
222. Ibid., pp. 38–39.
223. Ibid., pp. 5–7.
224. Cole, *A History of Socialist Thought*, 3:228.
225. Foote, *The Labour Party's Political Thought*, p. 42.
226. V. G. Simkhovich, *Marxism vs. Socialism* (New York: Henry Holt, 1913), p. 243.
227. Cole, *A History of Socialist Thought*, 3:229.
228. Foote, *The Labour Party's Political Thought*, pp. 33–36.
229. Cole, *A History of Socialist Thought*, 3:163–178; Beer, *A History of British Socialism*, 2:307–310; Pelling, *The Origins of the Labour Party*, pp. 101–103; Pierson, *British Socialism*, p. 35; Poirier, *The Advent of the British Labour Party*, pp. 56–59.

230. Robert Blatchford, *Merrie England* (New York: Monthly Review Press, 1966), pp. 119–121.
231. Ibid., p. 125.
232. Chris Cook and Ian Taylor, eds., *The Labour Party—an Introduction to Its History, Structure and Politics* (London: Longman, 1980), p. 5.
233. Hughes, *Keir Hardie's Speeches and Writings*, p. 31.
234. Ibid., p. 40.
235. Ibid., pp. 41–42.
236. Williams, "The Program of the British Labour Party," p. 196.
237. Cole, *A History of Socialist Thought*, 3:229.
238. Foote, *The Labour Party's Political Thought*, p. 51.
239. Reid, *The Origins of the British Labour Party*, p. 65.
240. Fremantle, *This Little Band of Prophets*, p. 216.
241. Cole, *A History of Socialist Thought*, pp. 176–177.
242. Ibid., 3:117.
243. Hughes, *Keir Hardie's Speeches and Writings*, p. 96.
244. Ibid., p. 174.
245. Dowse, *The Left in the Centre*, p. 20.
246. Foote, *The Labour Party's Political Thought*, p. 65.
247. Reid, *Keir Hardie*, pp. 150–151.
248. Foote, *The Labour Party's Political Thought*, p. 49–50.
249. Cole, *A History of Socialist Thought*, 4:407–408.
250. Ibid., 4:448–449.
251. Ibid., 5:65; Dowse, *The Left in the Centre*, pp. 152–184.
252. William Knox, *Lives of the Left—James Maxton* (Manchester, UK: Manchester University Press, 1987).
253. Vincent E. Hale and Sharon Skowronski, eds., *The Greenwood Historical Encyclopedia of the World's Political Parties—Political Parties of Europe* (Westport, CT: Greenwood Press, 1983), pp. 959–960.
254. Laidler, *History of Socialism* (New York: Apollo, 1968), p. 318.
255. Ibid., pp. 475–486.
256. Cole, *A History of Socialist Thought*, 4:443–446.
257. Laidler, *History of Socialism* (New York: Apollo, 1968), pp. 785–791.
258. *Philadelphia Inquirer*, November 29, 1998, p. E2.
259. *Philadelphia Inquirer*, September 14, 1997, p. D2.
260. *Philadelphia Inquirer*, September 21, 1997, p. E2.
261. *Philadelphia Inquirer*, July 1, 1999, p. E2.
262. Laidler, *History of Socialism*, pp. 186–187, 318.

263. Richard L. Greaves, Robert Zaller, and Jennifer Tolbert Roberts, *Civilizations of the West—the Human Adventure* (New York: HarperCollins, 1992), pp. 894, 992.
264. James Connolly, *Socialism Made Easy* (Dublin: The Labour Party, 1972).
265. *Philadelphia Inquirer*, April 12, 1998, p. A16.

4

Democratic Socialism in North America

GREENLAND AND CANADA

Under the new Danish constitution adopted in May 1953, Greenland became part of Denmark and gained representation in the Danish parliament. Following a referendum in January 1979, the people of Greenland won the right to home rule. Elections were held that April, which were won by the left-wing Siumut Party.

In a referendum held in February 1982, Greenlanders, by a narrow majority, voted to withdraw from the European Community—a process that was completed by early 1985. In the June 1984 election, the Siumut Party and the moderate opposition Atassut Party each won eleven seats in parliament. The May 1987 election brought a similar division.

CANADA

As early as 1890, branches of the U.S. Socialist Labor Party (SLP) had been established in the Canadian cities of Montreal, Toronto, and Winnipeg.[1] By 1899 a Canadian Socialist League was formed by dissidents opposed to Daniel De Leon's (1852–1914) autocratic style of rule in the SLP—as were U.S. radicals at the time, who would go on to form the Socialist Party of America in 1901.

Other socialist groups were forming as the nineteenth century gave way to the twentieth, and they united in 1905 into the Socialist Party of Canada, paralleling the split from the SLP that was taking place in the United States. Although unable to elect any members to the Federal Parliament in the years before World War I, nevertheless, the Socialist Party of Canada was able to win elections in the provincial legislatures in Alberta and Manitoba.

In 1911 a second democratic socialist group was founded, the Social Democratic Party of Canada, and shortly thereafter it joined the Second International—something the older and more radical Socialist Party of Canada refused to do as long as the decidedly nonradical British and Australian labor parties were members.

During World War I and the period following, the Canadian socialist movement gave much attention to the idea of building One Big Union—a syndicalist idea popularized by the Industrial Workers of the World (IWW), especially in the wake of the general strike in Winnipeg in 1920. Various labor parties also sprang up in parts of Canada during this period and were able to win elections to provincial legislatures. With the support of the United Farmers of Ontario, one such group, the Canadian Labor Party, sent their first candidate to the Federal Parliament in April 1920, Angus McDonald. In 1921 the Labor Party of Winnipeg Center, Manitoba, elected John Shaver Woodsworth (1874–1942) to the Federal Parliament—the leader of the Canadian Labor Party movement in the 1920s and 1930s. In addition to various socialist and labor parties winning elective office in Canada in these years, the Communists began to form their own groups in Canada in 1920 and the following year united to form the Communist Party of Canada, which was soon banned by the government. What was clearly needed was a uniting of the various socialist and labor parties operating in Canada in the interwar years. To this purpose, labor and farm leaders met in Calgary in 1932 to form the Cooperative Commonwealth Federation (CCF). The same had been tried and is still being tried in the United States—so far unsuccessfully—where many labor leaders remained tied to the Democratic Party and the capitalist system. However, the Canadians apparently had no such ties. At the CCF's first convention in Regina, Saskatchewan, it adopted a socialist platform calling for public ownership of industrial monopolies operating against the public interest and for an independent political party. The CCF core was a group of parliamentary members, led by J. S. Woodsworth, already dubbed the "Ginger Group" (another way of calling them the Reds) because of their left-wing stands on social issues.

The CCF grew steadily in the years before World War II, electing eight members to the Federal Parliament by 1940. In 1942, CCF member Joseph Noseworthy was able to defeat the former prime minister and leader of the Conservative Party, Arthur Meighan, for one of Toronto's parliamentary seats. By the following year, the CCF had elected sixty-nine members to various provincial legislatures and were the official opposition in four provinces. Then in 1944, for the first time, the CCF was able to win a majority in a provincial legislature, and Saskatchewan became Canada's first province with a socialist government, electing T. C. Douglas (b. 1904), a former minister and member of the Federal Parliament, as provincial prime minister. Whereas the Socialist Party, USA, was going into decline in these years, the CCF was forging ahead—something perplexing and yet an inspiration to socialists in the United States.

Following the death of Woodsworth, M. J. Coldwell (1888–1974) succeeded him as leader of the CCF members of parliament. Coldwell was active in the British Labour Party in his youth; and after immigrating to Western Canada, he became in turn a teacher, a principal, president of the Canadian Teacher's Association, leader of the Saskatchewan CCF, member of the Federal Parliament, national secretary of the CCF, and later CCF's national chairman.

The Canadian Labor Congress at its 1958 convention voted to have its executive committee meet with the CCF and other interested groups for the purpose of drafting a new constitution for the party. In August 1961 the New Democratic Party (NDP) held its founding convention.[2]

The program of the NDP called for a planned economy, government ownership of some industries, government-guaranteed jobs for the unemployed, greater social security programs, a government-run national health insurance system, public housing, guaranteed parity prices for farmers, the formation of national marketing boards to coordinate provincial boards in helping farmers market their products, public works programs, government aid to small businesses, greater support for the United Nations, and aid to developing countries.

In Saskatchewan, the CCF decided to retain its old name and held office in the provincial government from 1944 to 1964, first under the premiership of T. C. Douglas and then under his successor Woodrow Lloyd (1913–1972). In these years, the CCF in Saskatchewan had established the first government-run health insurance system in North America, as well as provincial-run telephone, bus, forest, fishing, furs, and insurance companies. It also created Canada's first Department of Cooperation and Cooperative Development and a Bureau of Economic Planning, and it signed comprehensive labor union and antidiscrimination laws.[3] The Saskatchewan CCF later changed its name to the New Democratic Party, in line with the national party.

The party increased its delegation to the Federal Parliament in the early 1960s, and its members of parliament (MPs) called for a program of full employment and opposition to nuclear weapons and pushed for negotiations to end the war in Vietnam. The CCF and later the NDP also did well in the provinces of British Columbia and Ontario.

In the election of 1968, the Liberals achieved a majority government under the leadership of Pierre Elliot Trudeau (1919–). His government passed an expansion of social security benefits and attempted to appease nationalist sentiments among French Canadians by passing the Official Languages Act in 1969, which gave English and French equal use in all government activities, as well as championing the idea of multiculturalism and providing aid to restore Indian life and culture.

However, the inferior economic status of French Canadians and Indians compared to English-speaking whites continued to fuel nationalist sentiments that would not be appeased by mere reforms. By the late 1970s, French Canadian separatism was on the rise. In 1976, the Parti Québecois (PQ) had won control in Québec and was seeking independence from the rest of English-speaking Canada. These problems, combined with inflation, resulted in the defeat of the Liberals in May 1979. However, Trudeau's successor, Joseph Clark (1939–) of the Progressive Conservatives (PC), was unable to form a stable majority in parliament, and Trudeau returned to power in February 1980. The government won a victory that May when voters in Québec defeated a referendum urging separation of Québec from the rest of Canada. Trudeau sought to end these problems with Québec, as well as with Alberta and other western provinces that had been protesting the power of the national government and its interference in provincial affairs, by the adoption of a new federal constitution to replace the British North America Act. With the agreement of the English-speaking provinces on the form of the proposed constitution, it was officially proclaimed by Queen Elizabeth II in Ottawa on April 17, 1982, although it had not yet been ratified by Quebec. In June 1984, Trudeau stepped down and was replaced as prime minister by John Napier Turner (1929–), a Liberal. In the parliamentary elections of September 1984, the PC came to power, choosing Brian Mulroney (1939–) as the new prime minister. At a meeting in Meech Lake, Québec, in April 1987, national and provincial leaders approved a series of constitutional amendments designed to satisfy Québec's demand for recognition as a "distinct society" within Canada. By 1990, the deadline for ratification of these amendments had passed without them being ratified, plunging Canada into a constitutional crisis that could pave the way for the breakup of the Canadian confederation.

The year 1990 also saw Canada sliding into a massive economic recession that proved disastrous for the PC and the NDP. Mulroney had resigned in this crisis and was replaced by PC's Kim Campbell (1947–)—Canada's first woman prime minister. In the October 1993 elections, the Progressive Conservatives went from the ruling party with about 160 seats in parliament to a mere 2 seats. The NDP was also a big loser in this election. National NDP leader Audrey McLaughlin (1936–), the first woman to head a major political party in Canada, had replaced Ed Broadbent (1936–) as party leader from 1975 to 1989. She was unable to articulate a clear NDP program for dealing with the recession. Instead, the NDP campaign focused on defending Canada's single-payer, government-run, national health system. This was a strategic mistake and a waste of time, energy, and money because that system was widely popular with the voters, who cared more about the economy and wanted instead to hear about how Canada's staggering unemployment rate of about 15 percent would be dealt with.

Compounding the problem was the NDP government in Ontario, headed by Rob Rae. Pursuing an unpopular, governmental austerity program, Rae's government not only confused the voters in Ontario on how democratic socialists were any different from conservatives, it also hurt the party nationally. The largest union in Canada, the Canadian Union of Public Employees, was so incensed by the layoff of their workers during a time of recession, by imposed rollbacks, and by wage freezes in Ontario that they went so far as to advocate abandoning the NDP altogether, demonstrating again the folly of social democratic parties moving to the political center. In British Columbia, the NDP also managed to alienate the environmentalist movement by allowing logging in the last of the old-growth forest in Clayquott Sound.[4]

As a result, the voters throughout Canada booted out both the PC and the NDP. The latter suffered a loss of thirty-four seats in the Federal Parliament—from forty-three down to a mere nine. Not a single member of the NDP was elected in Ontario, where the party's vote fell to less than 6 percent as a result of its betrayal.

Two winners of the 1993 election were the Liberals, who gained 177 seats out of 295 in the Federal Parliament and brought Jean Chrétien to office as prime minister, and the Bloc Québecois. Running only in Québec on a platform of independence for the province, the Bloc Québecois won fifty-four seats in the Federal Parliament, up from their previous eight seats, with the backing of all three of Québec's labor union federations. In 1995, another referendum on independence for Québec was defeated by the narrowest of margins. Québec may yet achieve its independence, but it is unclear how this will help French Canadians deal with the poverty and unemployment that is the economic basis for their nationalist complaints. Both the PC and the NDP are attempting to regroup and rebuild.

THE UNITED STATES OF AMERICA

In addition to the long history of utopian socialist communities in the United States, there were also attempts to form labor and socialist parties in the nineteenth and twentieth centuries. In the 1820s, the first Workingmen's Parties in the world, commonly called "Workies," were founded in the United States.[5]

In the summer of 1827, some six hundred carpenters in Philadelphia struck for the ten-hour workday. The strike was unsuccessful, but it did lead to the formation of the Mechanic's Union of Trade Associations, uniting all of the city's unionists. This movement spread to other cities, and sixty-one Workingmen's Parties grew out of this between 1828 and 1834, as well as sixty-eight labor newspapers.

Besides the ten-hour workday, the Workies called for the establishment of public schools, the end of fines and imprisonment for not taking party in militias, and the protection of the rights of workers. The most radical of the Workies were in New York City, where George Henry Evans (1805–1855?), Robert Dale Owen (1801–1877), Thomas Skidmore (1790–1832), and Frances "Fanny" Wright (1785–1852) led the movement.

Skidmore, a self-educated man, wrote a book entitled *The Rights of Man to Property! Being a Proposition to Make It Equal among the Adults of the Present Generation; and to Provide for Its Equal Transmission to Every Individual of Each Succeeding Generation, on Arriving at the Age of Maturity.*

Under Skidmore's socialistic plan, every man and unmarried woman twenty-one years old and older would receive 160 acres of land to be held as long as they tilled it. They could not sell or rent the land to others. As for those who presently owned more than 160 acres of land, it would not be redistributed until the death of the owner, at which time an inheritance law would expropriate all land over the 160-acre limit. Skidmore's agrarianism thus focused on equal ownership of land, although he also urged similar schemes for the ownership of other kinds of property, such as factories.

George Henry Evans, Robert Dale Owen, and Fanny Wright criticized Skidmore's agrarianism as "crude communism," and offered an alternative, radical proposal to the Workies. Rather than expropriating property, they proposed to bring about equality and to erase class differences by having "State Guardianship Education." Under this system, the state would adopt all children, rich and poor, two years old and older and raise and educate them together in boarding schools. These "Free Enquirers" would have equal food, clothing, and education in the publicly owned and financed boarding schools. Fanny Wright also demanded women's equality and free love as part of her program.

These two factions agreed on the Workies' reform planks, and for a short time they did well in local elections of the late 1820s. However, by 1830, the movement was sputtering out. Charges in the press that the Workingmen's Parties were guilty of being "Fanny Wrightist," too radical, and antireligious had the effect of turning off many people to the movement. As the depression of 1828 to 1831 came to an end, workers' agitation over the economy quieted down. Many of the Workies joined the Jacksonian wing of the Democratic Party.

To escape the political repression following the failed revolutions of 1830 and 1848, the next wave of radicals to reach U.S. shores came from Germany.[6] Joseph Weydemeyer (1818–1866), who had been associated with Marx and Engels before coming to the United States in the 1850s, was instrumental in organizing the German trade unionists in New York. With them, on March 21, 1853, he founded the American Workingmen's Alliance.[7] The aim of this organization was to build an independent labor party in the United States, and it was able to organize German branches in New Jersey, Ohio, and Pennsylvania, in addition to New York, and an English-speaking branch in Washington, D.C. Weydemeyer's paper, *Die Reform*, lasted less than a year, and the movement itself lasted not much longer, with radical energies going into the antislavery movement as the Civil War approached.

F. A. Sorge (1827–1906), another German immigrant, had organized a Marxist group in the United States around this period. After the Civil War, Sorge's Marxists united with a group of German immigrants of the Lassallean school to form the General German Workingmen's Union in 1867. Two years later, this group affiliated with the First International. During this period, French, Bohemian, and other German sections of the First International were being established in New York, Chicago, and San Francisco. They united in December 1870 to form a provisional committee of the International in the United States, with Sorge elected as the corresponding secretary.

By 1871, the U.S. organization had over thirty sections with several thousand members. However, infighting between the Marxists and the Bakuninists shortly caused the demise of the First International. In 1872 the Marxists at the Hague Congress of the First International were able to get the headquarters of the body transferred to New York to prevent the anarchists from capturing the organization. Sorge was made the secretary of the headquarters following this transfer. But the socialist movement was weak in America and could not sustain the organization. The Marxists would rather have it die out than have it be taken over by the anarchists. After four years of wrangling among the American sections over the course to take, the First International was officially disbanded at a meeting in Philadelphia on July 15, 1876.

Four days later, a unity convention met in Philadelphia, July 19 to 22, 1876, and brought together the defunct North American Federation of the International with the Social Democratic Workingmen's Party of North America, which was founded in May 1874. The latter had been formed by the Illinois Labor Party, previously a Lassallean group called the Universal German Workingmen's Association founded in Chicago in 1869, and later known as the Socio-Political Workingmen's Association and the Socio-Political Labor-Union of Cincinnati. Together they launched the socialist Workingmen's Party of the United States. With a membership of only 3,000, they decided that they would wait until they were larger before entering any political campaigns. Philip Van Patten, a member of the Knights of Labor, was elected as National Secretary. By March 1877, the party had sixty-five sections—thirty-five German, eighteen English, six Bohemian, five Scandinavian, and one French—in forty-four cities. The following year, these sections began running candidates for office and winning elections.

On December 26, 1877, the Workingmen's Party at its convention in Newark, New Jersey, changed its name to the Socialist Labor Party (SLP). It should be noted that the SLP later claimed that the organization was originally called the Socialistic Labor Party and only became the Socialist Labor Party in 1890 when Daniel De Leon (1852–1914) joined the former and organized it into a new party that was a direct opposite of its predecessor in all essential aspects.[8] However, this is in dispute. In any event, the 1877 SLP convention rejected those trade unionists who wanted to devote the party mainly to economic organizing and instead opted for a political campaign strategy. This argument persisted in the new party. There were other disagreements as well: Should the party organize armed struggle? What relationship should they have with anarchists and reform parties?

In 1886, the SLP endorsed Henry George (1839–1897), the advocate of the single tax—all revenue is derived from a single tax on land—who was running for mayor of New York on the United Labor Party ticket. An active supporter of Henry George in this race was Daniel De Leon, the later outstanding leader of the SLP. Born in Curaçao on December 14, 1852, De Leon was educated in Germany and studied law after coming to the United States in the 1870s. A brilliant man, he won a coveted professorship in international law at Columbia University.

After the United Labor Party began to fold following Henry George's loss in the mayoral race in New York, De Leon at first joined the Nationalists—a group of clubs founded on the model of socialism presented in Edward Bellamy's widely popular, utopian socialist novel, *Looking Backward*. Later, De Leon left the Nationalist Clubs because of their refusal to try to organize labor. He applied for membership in the SLP and was admitted in 1890. He rapidly rose to the editorship of the party's official, English-language newspaper, *The People*, in 1892.

De Leon developed a form of socialism that advocated socialist industrial unionism. With the overthrow of capitalism and the state, the system of representation based on territorial districts would be replaced by one based on membership in socialist industrial unions. These unions not only would be the government, but would also own the industries, rather than the state owning them, and would plan the economy to eliminate all the evils of capitalism. The idea has merit, but De Leon tended to be domineering and sectarian. Only this form of socialism, and no other, was considered genuine by De Leon and his followers, despite the fact that there are many other models that socialists have advocated and tried, from government ownership to cooperatives.

De Leon, Hugo Vogt, and party scholar Lucien Sanial (1836–1927) formed the SLP's ruling triumvirate and preached the doctrine of New Unionism, calling for unionists to strive to overthrow the capitalist system and to institute socialism instead of working to achieve a few reforms from their capitalist masters. The De Leonists assailed the union leaders of the time as "labor fakers." After being ousted from the Knights of Labor, which they had tried to capture, the De Leonists formed their own Socialist Trade and Labor Alliance (STLA) at a meeting at Cooper Union in New York on December 13, 1895. The SLP invited all trade unionists to abandon the Knights of Labor and the American Federation of Labor (AFL), which they argued were run by corrupt leaders subservient to the capitalists, and urged them to join the STLA. This created a dilemma for the socialists in the AFL because they were not consulted on this move. Many felt that the existing trade unions in the AFL were viable avenues for working for reform and for educating the workers about the merits of socialism. Some felt that to work for "dual unionism," that is, to establish a second labor federation in competition to the AFL, would be counterproductive in advancing the cause of socialism. At first the STLA succeed in capturing control of the Central Labor Federation of New York, with thousands of members; but in 1898, many of them seceded from the STLA and were followed by some of De Leon's most able lieutenants in the labor movement, who were angered at his attempts to centralize power in his hands.

The STLA, in time, faded away, and the fight over it led to a split in the SLP. There had been splits before in the party, for instance, when anarchist

Revolutionary Clubs held a convention in Chicago in October 1881 to form the Revolutionary Socialist Labor Party, urging violent revolution to overthrow capitalism, rather than the electoral methods of the reformist SLP.[9] But now another split was brewing that would displace the SLP as the leading American socialist body. This fight was between the De Leonists and those within the SLP who had been resisting De Leon's control. The argument came to a head at the meeting of the General Committee of SLP Section Greater New York on July 8, 1899. The De Leonists were in charge of this meeting; and as soon as it began, a fight broke out for control, with each side claiming victory. The De Leonists retained control over the National Office and the party's paper, *The People*. The "kangaroo socialists," as the anti-De Leonists who had jumped from the party were known, attempted at first to also claim that they were the SLP, reminiscent of a conflict in the Students for a Democratic Society (SDS) seventy years later. Now that there were two SLPs, with the membership split in half, De Leon was free to drop from his party's faction any mention of reform demands, which he proceeded to do at the SLP convention on June 28, 1900. Indeed, any party member who even accepted an office in the reformist trade unions would be expelled from the party, and any officer in such a union would be barred from membership in the SLP.[10]

There are other nineteenth-century American socialists that deserve mention. Among them are William H. Sylvis (1828–1869), a labor leader who issued a call in 1866 for a labor convention, which resulted in the founding of the National Labor Union that year in Baltimore.[11] A key strategy of this union was the establishment of producers' cooperatives as an alternative to strikes, as a way to free workers from wage slavery. Sylvis raised funds to start a cooperative foundry in Troy, New York, after employers in the Albany-Troy area had announced that they were no longer going to recognize the union. Other cooperatives soon followed. By 1868 eleven cooperatives had been established, and twenty more were being formed in several industries in U.S. cities. Although they did well at first, they were unable to raise enough capital for new and improved equipment; so in time, they all foundered. Sylvis concluded that in order for the cooperatives to succeed they need state aid, for which the National Labor Union had been calling since 1867. Before he died in 1869, Sylvis was also working for the establishment of a labor party, and the National Labor Union was one of the first to affiliate with the newly established First International.

The first American group to actually join the First International in January 1868 was the Social Party of New York and Vicinity.[12] A poor showing in its electoral campaign that year forced the group out of business, and its place was taken by the General German Workingmen's Association, known in the International as Section 1 of New York, as well as being an affiliate of Sylvis's National Labor Union. Shortly afterward, some thirty other sections were organized in the United States along ethnic lines. One of the more interesting ones was English-speaking Section 12, which was led by two sisters, Victoria Claflin Woodhull (1838–1929) and Tennessee Claflin (1845?–1923). The sisters had been born in Homer, Ohio, and had traveled the country as part of their father's wagon show, telling fortunes, giving exhibitions of spiritualism, and later posing as clairvoyants in Cincinnati, before coming to New York in 1868. Both sisters had been married young and were later remarried. Along the way, they had become advocates of free love.

In New York, Tennessee Claflin became the mistress of railroad magnate Cornelius "Commodore" Vanderbilt (1794–1877); and with his backing, the sisters set themselves up as successful "lady brokers" in the male-dominated stock market. Victoria Woodhull met Stephen Pearl Andrews (1812–1886), a linguist reputed to be able to speak thirty-two languages, who was also interested in spiritualism and who was an associate of anarchist Josiah Warren's Time Store. He was also a sympathizer with the First International. With Andrews and Victoria Claflin's lover, one Colonel Blood, the sisters launched a newspaper called the *Woodhull and Claflin Weekly*, which carried articles on free love, prostitution, abortion, and exposés of illicit love affairs of prominent citizens, such as that of minister Henry Ward Beecher (1813–1887). Their paper was also the first to publish an English translation of *The Communist Manifesto*.

Along with their mentor, Andrews, the sisters joined the First International and became leaders in its Section 12 in New York. Scandalizing the German workers with their doctrines of free love, they were booted out of the International, whereupon Woodhull called for a convention to establish the Equal Rights Party and ran as its candidate for president with Frederick Douglass (1817–1895), the famed Negro abolitionist, as the vice-presidential running mate.[13]

Eugene Victor Debs (1855–1926) was the most outstanding of all the early American socialists.[14] Born in Terre Haute, Indiana, on November 5, 1855, he became the secretary-treasurer of the National Brotherhood of Locomotive Firemen in 1880. Serving in this position until 1892, he also became the city clerk of Terre Haute (1879–1883), and was elected to the Indiana state legislature as a Democrat in 1885. In 1892, he resigned from the secretaryship of the Brotherhood of Locomotive Firemen, a craft union, to accept a position with the American Railway Union (ARU), an industrial union that sought to organize all railway workers regardless of skill.

In 1894 the ARU voted to support the strike at the Pullman Company, refusing to handle Pullman cars until the company agreed to negotiate with its workers. This brought the ARU into confrontation not only with U.S. railroads but also with the government, with President Grover Cleveland (1837–1908) sending federal troops to Chicago to break the strike.

Debs was arrested and sentenced to six months in Woodstock jail in Illinois for contempt of court. He spent his time reading the socialist books and pamphlets of Edward Bellamy (1850–1898), Robert Blatchford (1851–1943), Laurence Gronlund (1846–1899), and Karl Kautsky (1854–1938). Debs was also visited in jail by Milwaukee socialist leader Victor Berger, who delivered an impassioned plea for socialism. By the time Debs left prison, he was moving toward socialism.

Although Debs supported the populist Democratic candidate William Jennings Bryan (1860–1925) in the 1896 election, by the following year, he was ready to break with the Democrats. In the January 1, 1897, edition of ARU's *Railway Times*, Debs declared, "The issue is Socialism versus Capitalism. I am for Socialism because I am for humanity."

Later that year the ARU met in convention in Chicago and voted to dissolve itself and to merge with other socialist groups to form the Social Democracy of America (SDA). This new organization called for public ownership of monopolies and utilities, public works projects to employ the unemployed, a shorter workday, and a utopian plan for colonization of a western state where socialists could concentrate, win elective office, and, thus, establish a model cooperative commonwealth. With the success of socialism in one state, they reasoned, the movement would eventually fan out and bring a national cooperative commonwealth to the entire country.

Other socialists joining the SDA were some fifty-eight Jewish Socialist delegates who met in convention in New York claiming to represent 1,200 former SLP members at odds with De Leon. That August, Victor L. Berger (1860–1929) and his mainly German Milwaukee "Independents" also joined the new party, breaking with De Leon and his autocratic style and hostility to the established trade unions. Berger, an Austrian immigrant and former secondary school teacher, had built the Milwaukee socialists into the largest local machine in the American socialist movement. Tending to be on the right of the movement, he was an evolutionary socialist who thought of himself as the "American Bernstein." A third group to join the new party was led by Morris Hillquit (1869–1933), a Jewish immigrant born in Riga, Latvia, who had risen to the position of secretary of the United Hebrew Trades and subsequently became a prominent attorney. Originally a member of the SLP, Hillquit led the "kangaroos" that bolted from the party over De Leon's purist attack on reformist demands, which were removed from the platform at its convention of 1900. In February of that year, fifty-nine of the kangaroo faction met in Rochester, New York, and voted to join with Debs's party.

Meanwhile, the SDA underwent a split over the issue of colonization. At its second convention in 1898, the colonizers had captured a short-lived majority. Thereupon, Debs, Berger, and their followers walked out and established a rival Social Democratic Party of America, dropping the utopian colonization plank. In the election of 1900, Debs was their presidential candidate, with Job Harriman (1861–1925) of the kangaroo faction as the running mate.

Negotiations between the Debs and Berger faction and the kangaroos went on for a new name for the party. The unity convention between the two was held in Indianapolis on July 29, 1901, and chose the Socialist Party of America (SPA) as its new name, with headquarters in St. Louis. In later years, it came called the Socialist Party, USA (SPUSA).

In the years before World War I, the Socialist Party of America steadily grew in size, reaching a peak of 118,045 members in 1912. That year, the party had elected 1,039 dues-paying members to public office, including one congressman, Victor Berger, fifty-six mayors, and numerous state legislators and local councilmen. The Socialists were strongest in the city of Milwaukee, the only U.S. city to have three Socialist mayors: Emil Seidel from 1910 to 1916, Daniel W. Hoan from 1916 to 1938, and Frank P. Zeidler from 1946 to 1960.

In 1904 and again in 1908, the party ran Debs for president and Ben Hanford (1861–1910) for vice president, receiving over 400,000 votes. In 1912, the party ran Debs and Seidel, with their vote doubling to the highest they have ever received, 897,011, or about 6 percent of the vote.

The American socialist movement in these years was publishing scores of newspapers and magazines, notably the *Appeal to Reason*, from Girard, Kansas, with a half million subscribers. There were several labor colleges and other left-wing schools being established at this time, such as the Rand School of Social Science in New York. Among the student wings of the movement was the Intercollegiate Socialist Society (ISS), founded in 1905, a direct predecessor of the League for Industrial Democracy, whose student group became the Students for a Democratic Society in 1960. The SPA's own youth group was the Young People's Socialist League (YPSL), pronounced "Yip-sel."

Also founded in 1905 with the participation of many of the Socialists was the radical trade union, the Industrial Workers of the World (IWW), led by William D. "Big Bill" Haywood (1869–1928). A fight developed in the party over the IWW's syndicalist tactics of sabotage and violence, which led to Haywood's expulsion for the Socialist Party's Executive Committee in 1913 and SPA's rejection of violent tactics as counterproductive.

The steady growth of the party was interrupted by events far from American shores. With the outbreak of World War I in 1914, the SPA urged the United States to remain neutral. In the 1916 election, the party used a referendum vote for the first and only time in its history to nominate writer Allan L. Benson (1871–1940) for president and lecturer and former college teacher George R. Kirkpatrick (1867–1937) as the running mate, campaigning on a prosocialist and antiwar ticket. Opposition to the war was divisive both within and without the world socialist movement. Most of the Second International parties supported their governments when they declared war. Many, like the German Social Democrats, suffered defections and splits over this stance. In the SPA, its antiwar position cost it members and votes. In the 1916 election, the party's vote dropped by a third over its previous 1912 high.

The crisis intensified shortly after the United States entered World War I in 1917. In that year, the party's emergency St. Louis convention rejected a prowar resolution offered by John Spargo (1876–1966) and instead adopted a resolution proposed by Morris Hillquit, pledging the party's unalterable opposition to the war and calling upon the workers of all countries to refuse to support their governments in making war. A more moderate proposal was offered by Louis B. Boudin (1874–1952), declaring that although the party had opposed the war, now that war was a fact, the party should work for the advancement of democratic collectivism to protect the rights of the people and should establish communications with socialists in enemy countries, which was the surest way to bring peace about by democratic means at its earliest. This proposal would have, in effect, kept the SPA out of direct involvement with the antiwar movement, but without adopting a prowar stand. It, too, was defeated. Following the convention, a number of influential prowar socialists quit the party, including Spargo, Robert Hunter (1874–1942), Charles Edward Russell (1860–1941), J. G. Phelps Stokes (1872–1960), Rose Pastor Stokes (1879–1933), and William English Walling (1873–1936), to form the short-lived Social Democratic League of America, which conducted educational campaigns on behalf of the war effort.

In June of 1917, the U.S. Congress passed the Espionage Act, amended in 1918 to include a Sedition Act that made several nonmilitary offenses illegal, including using profane, scurrilous, or abusive language about the government. SPA headquarters around the country were raided, and the Attorney General withdrew second-class-mailing privileges for the party's paper, the *American Socialist*, for the crime of advertising a pamphlet that claimed that the plutocrat John Pierpont (J. P.) Morgan Jr. (1867–1943) had loaned the Allies $1.9 billion before U.S. entry into the war, and that the U.S. government was protecting this loan that was behind U.S. involvement in the war.[15] As the war continued, other Socialist newspapers also were denied mailing rights.

The October Revolution and Russia's withdrawal from the war brought another wave of mass arrests and censorship in direct violation of the U.S. First Amendment guarantees of freedom of speech, press, and peaceable assembly. The editors of *The Masses*, one of the most innovative radical magazines of all time, were hauled into court. Thousands of Socialists were arrested, including Debs for the crime of giving an antiwar speech in Canton, Ohio, on June 30, 1918. Debs was convicted, and the U.S. Supreme Court upheld the decision in *Debs v. United States* (1919). He was sentenced to eight years and served four in Atlanta prison before being pardoned by postwar president Warren G. Harding (1865–1923) in 1922. Debs was the first man to run for president from a prison cell, receiving nearly over 900,000 votes in 1920. He also wrote a valuable and still timely work on prison conditions, *Walls and Bars*.

General Secretary of the Socialist Party, Charles T. Schenck, was also convicted under the Espionage Act for mailing antiwar leaflets to men drafted into the U.S. Army. Like the Debs case, *Schenck v. United States* (1919) was upheld by the U.S. Supreme Court. Justice Oliver Wendell Holmes (1841–1935), writing the opinion for the case, stated that "the most stringent protection of free speech would not protect a man to falsely shout fire in a theatre and cause a panic." With twisted logic, Holmes compared this to criticizing the government, despite the fact that the First Amendment to the U.S. Constitution explicitly protects this very kind of political free speech and press.

Of course, this had not been the first time that the First Amendment had been violated. The Alien and Sedition Acts of 1798 resulted in jailing persons who had published statements critical of the Federalist administration of President John Adams (1735–1826). This had involved relatively few people—only about twenty-five were sent to trial, and only ten were actually convicted. However, during World War I and the Red Scare period following it in 1919 and 1920, thousands of Communists and anarchists were jailed or deported, in some cases for merely making a critical comment in the privacy of their own homes. The SPA and the socialist press never fully recovered from this blow of massive, government repression.

Another case worthy of mention was *Gitlow v. New York* (1925). Benjamin Gitlow was a member of the Left Wing Section of the SPA, which in 1919 had begun agitating for the party to affiliate with the Third International in the wake of the Bolshevik Revolution. He was charged with publishing "The Left Wing Manifesto," stating this section's beliefs and criticisms of moderate socialism in the movement's newspaper, the *Revolutionary Age*. Calling for mass political strikes and revolutionary action, Gitlow was convicted in a New York court for violating that state's criminal anarchy statute. He appealed the conviction all the way to the U.S. Supreme Court. The "clear and present danger" test of the earlier Espionage Act cases was now replaced with the "bad tendency" test. Justice Edward T. Sanford (1865–1930), delivering the opinion of the High Court, argued that all that needed to be shown was that a speech had a tendency, no matter how remote, to advocate and advance prohibited actions for it to be declared unlawful. Because "The Left Wing Manifesto" called for proletarian revolution and because the state had outlawed utterances advocating the overthrow of the government, the Gitlow conviction was upheld.

The Left Wing Section of the SPA held a conference in New York on June 21, 1919. At this meeting, one faction, dominated by the foreign language federations that had grown in membership that year, declared for an immediate break with the Socialist Party and for the formation of the Communist Party of America. The leader of this group was Italian-born immigrant Louis C. Fraina (1892?–1953).[16] The other faction at the conference wanted to continue the policy of working within the Socialist Party to convert it to Communism. This faction was dominated by American-born members of the party, who were led by John Reed (1887–1920). Those calling for immediate withdrawal from the party lost at this conference and, upon doing so, withdrew from it and issued a call for a convention to launch the new Communist Party of America. The remaining left-wingers, who had hoped to capture the Socialist Party for their own, also issued a convention call. Both of these conventions were to be held in Chicago, to coincide with an emergency convention called by the SPA for that city on August 30, 1919. The left-wingers who had wanted to capture the SPA had a strong case. In previous elections for the National Executive Committee of the party, they had won twelve out of fifteen seats. The leading vote getters were all left-wingers: Fraina, Reed, Charles E. Ruthenberg (1882–1927), and Kate Richards O'Hare (1876–1948). The Old Guard, right-wing leader in the party, Morris Hillquit, ran a distant fifth. By any fair procedure, the left-wingers, both foreign and native born, were entitled to leadership of the Socialist Party. However, the Old Guard, still in control of the party machinery, declared the election to be invalid on the questionable grounds that only a minority of party members had voted. This had not stopped party elections before or since. Now they refused to certify the results of the vote on this excuse. The Old Guard then proceeded to expel the left-wingers from the party, even though the latter constituted a majority of the party. First, the 6,000-member-strong Michigan state organization was expelled, followed by seven foreign language federations with a total of over 20,000 members. From 110,000 members in 1919, the party declined to 40,000 in six months, and then down to a mere 13,000 by 1921—barely above its strength when the Socialist Party had been launched in 1901. Hillquit and the other Old Guard leaders were willing to have the Socialist Party, which they had long labored to build, divided and weakened rather than to succumb to Communism.[17]

The American-born left-wingers locked out of the 1919 Chicago convention then immediately met separately to form the Communist Labor Party. Bad blood between them and the foreign language federations that had just founded their own Communist Party prevented them from uniting at this time.

In its weakened state, the Socialist Party now saw its salvation in an attempt to form an American labor party. This was an old dream, going back at least to 1828 and the formation of the Workingmen's Party in Philadelphia. Periodically, American socialists and radicals had called for a labor party, as they continue to do to this day. This had been done successfully in several European countries, and some American trade unions were also calling for the formation of a U.S. labor party in 1919, among them the United Mine Workers at its convention that year.[18] At a national convention held on November 22, 1919, the Labor Party was launched, later to be called the Farmer-Labor Party. In 1920, they ran Parley Parker Christensen (1869–1954) for president with Max Hayes (1866–1945) as his running mate, receiving over 265,000 votes. Other local labor parties were also being formed at this time, as was the Nonpartisan League in North Dakota, founded in 1915 by former socialist Arthur C. Townley (1880–1959) and later spreading to other western states to advance candidates of any party friendly to farmer interests. Although no national labor party was to emerge, out of these efforts came the Farmer-Labor Party of Minnesota, which had considerable power in that state for many years.

Meanwhile, on February 20, 1922, the Conference for Progressive Political Action (CPPA) was formed at a meeting in Chicago. It had been called by William H. Johnston, president of the International Association of Machinists, and by the presidents of five of the railway unions. Leading members of the Socialist Party, including Hillquit and Berger, attended. In February 1924, the CPPA called for a nationwide conference to be held on July 4 of that year for the purpose of nominating candidates for president and vice president of the United States. Hillquit, a member of the CPPA permanent committee of fifteen, and other Socialists present urged the formation of a permanent third party. The Railroad Brotherhoods, which dominated the meeting, opposed this radical step. Instead, the convention nominated Wisconsin Senator Robert M. LaFollette (1855–1925) for president and Senator Burton Wheeler (1882–1975) as his running mate. Now for the first time in its history, the SPA would deviate from its practice of only supporting Socialist candidates for office. The LaFollette-Wheeler campaign received nearly 5 million votes in the 1924 election, running on the Progressive Party ticket. [19]

The 1924 convention of the CPPA had instructed its national committee to call for a special convention to address the issue of whether a permanent third party ought to be formed. That convention was held in Chicago, February 21 to 25, 1925.

Of course, the Socialists at the convention urged that this party be formed; but the Railroad Brotherhoods opposed this idea, maintaining that they had no mandate for this and, instead, sought only to continue the CPPA as a nonpartisan body. A vote was not taken on either motion because there was a lack of unity on this issue. Instead, a motion was passed to adjourn, with the proviso that those wishing to organize a new party might reconvene and do so. Without the support of unions, there was little chance that a viable third party could be formed, and the Socialists refused to take part in the reconvened convention, citing the fact that this would be an entirely different body from the one making up the original convention and that, without the unions, it was likely to be only a middle-class, liberal group. Thus the CPPA folded, and a chance was missed to build a major third-party challenge to the Democrats and the Republicans. Without the solid support of the unions, no attempts to build a permanent labor party in the United States have been successful.

Eugene Debs died on October 20, 1926, in Elmhurst, Illinois. Norman Thomas (1884–1968) became the next leader of the Socialist Party, USA.[20] Born on November 20, 1884, in Marion, Ohio, Thomas, the son of a Presbyterian minister, graduated from Princeton University and was the valedictorian of his 1905 class. He graduated from the Union Theological Seminary in 1911. While at the seminary, he served as the assistant pastor of the Brick Presbyterian Church in New York City; after graduation, until 1918, he served as the pastor of the East Harlem Church and chairman of the American Parish, a New York settlement.

Opposed to U.S. entry into World War I on pacifist grounds, Thomas joined Morris Hillquit's antiwar Socialist campaign for major of New York in 1917 and also joined the Socialist Party, USA. Resigning as pastor, he went on to served as editor of The *World Tomorrow*, and as secretary of the pacifist Fellowship of Reconciliation.

Thomas had initially been uncertain about the merits of the Bolshevik Revolution, although he soon came to support it, even to the point of offering his East 17th Street home in New York as a meeting place to visiting Soviet government representatives when they could find no other. Thomas was also critical of the Old Guard's expulsion of the Communists from the Socialist Party, but he had little taste for factionalism and so did not quit the party to join either of the two Communist factions that formed in 1919. Though he sympathized with the aims of the Communists, he found their centralist tactics to be alienating and was put off by the sectarian bombast of the left-wingers in his branch, such as Jay Lovestone (b. 1898).

As a brilliant orator and writer, Thomas soon rose within the ranks of the Socialist Party and was their candidate for governor of New York in 1924, candidate for mayor of New York City in 1925 and 1929, and the presidential candidate six times.

Thomas's running mate in 1928 and 1932 was James H. Maurer (1864–1944), president of the Pennsylvania Federation of Labor (1912–1928), and Socialist member of the Pennsylvania House of Representatives in 1910, 1914, and 1916, where he introduced workmen's compensation and other important labor legislation. In the 1936, election Thomas ran with farm leader from Wisconsin, George Nelson; in 1940, with assistant professor of economics at the University of Chicago, Maynard Krueger (b. 1906); in 1944, with attorney and former Socialist member of the Pennsylvania House of Representatives from the city of Reading, Darlington Hoopes; and in 1948, with Olivett College Economics Department chair, Tucker Smith.

During the Great Depression, the party's membership increased somewhat, although by now they were outdistanced in size by the Communist Party, USA. The Depression had brought into the Socialist Party a new group of young "Militants" who challenged the Old Guard, whom they felt were not doing enough to build the party with the opportunities to do so presented by the extraordinary economic crisis in which American capitalism found itself in the 1930s. Victor Berger had died in 1929, and so the leadership of the Old Guard fell to Morris Hillquit, whom the Militants tried unsuccessfully to unseat as chairman of the SPUSA's National Committee at the 1932 party convention, backing instead Daniel Hoan (1881–1951), one of the three Socialist mayors of Milwaukee.

By the 1934 convention, the Militants had gotten the party to adopt a new statement of principles declaring that should the capitalist system collapse, the Socialist Party would not shrink from the duty of organizing a workers' government. It was all wishful thinking, of course, but it annoyed many of the Old Guard who thought this declaration smacked of Communism.

By 1936 one of the many splits that have so often hurt the American Socialist and radical movements occurred, with many of the Old Guard members leaving the party to form a rival Social Democratic Federation (SDF). Among the leaders were Socialist mayor of Bridgeport, Connecticut, Jasper McLevy (1878–1962); president of the Rand School of Social Science, Algernon Lee (1873–1954); editor of the *Jewish Daily Forward*, Abraham Cahan (1860–1951); former editor of the *New Leader*, James Oneal; former state representative August Claessens; and attorney Louis P. Goldberg. At their 1937 convention, the SDF permitted its members to support candidates of state labor parties. In New York State, the SDF first supported the American Labor Party and then, in 1944, the newly formed Liberal Party. However, for the most part, the SDF supported Democrat Franklin D. Roosevelt over Socialist Norman Thomas in the presidential races from 1936 onward.[21]

In 1936 the Socialist Party allowed several hundred Trotskyists to join, only to expel them the following year for disloyalty and disruptive tactics. It was found in the years since that time, that when the Socialist Party allowed Marxist-Leninists to join, they would attempt a takeover in the party, resulting in expulsions or forced resignations in order to save the democratic socialist characteristic of the party. It became necessary to ban Marxist-Leninists of all stripes from joining the party and to expel them if they sneaked in, as would happen again in 1978.

Attempts were made to reunify the SPUSA and the SDF in 1939, but they failed over the issue of U.S. entry into World War II. As in World War I, the majority of the Socialist Party opposed U.S. involvement in World War II. However, the SDF favored it under certain circumstances as the war approached.

Following the Japanese surprise attack on Pearl Harbor and U.S. entry into the war, the Socialist Party somewhat shifted its position. Unlike World War I, the U.S. had been attacked, and there was the added dimension of fighting the new and terrible ideologies of fascism and national socialism. The Socialist Party would not oppose U.S. entry into World War II as it had World War I. Instead, it would campaign for the preservation of civil liberties and the social programs of the New Deal, as well as for the establishment of democratic control over the war and a permanent peace.

After the war, with the Socialist vote still declining in the 1948 election, Thomas circulated a pamphlet among party members urging them to stop wasting energy on campaigns for political office that were only winning a handful of votes, and instead to work with liberals and unionists in the primary and general elections of various political parties, while continuing efforts at socialist education. In practice this meant no longer running Socialist Party candidates and instead backing candidates in the Democratic Party, who may even be opposed to Socialism. The change in policy, Thomas noted, was in part a response to state election laws which enacted high signature requirements, that increasingly made it difficult for Socialists to even get on the ballot.[22]

Although a majority of the National Executive Committee backed Thomas on this retreat from running Socialist candidates, the 1950 SPUSA National Convention meeting in Detroit did not. The party continued to run its own local candidates for office and, in 1956, ran Darlington Hoopes and Samuel H. Friedman for president and vice president. However, they received a mere 2,000 votes that year.[23]

By 1957 a majority of what was left of the SPUSA was ready to abandon independent, political campaigning and to work to support Democratic candidates. This cleared the way that year for the SPUSA to merge with its former split, the SDF, under pressure from the Socialist International. A rightwing group within the SDF refused to go along with this reunification and broke away to form their own group called the Democratic Socialist Federation (DSF), which retained control of the Rand School, the socialist journal *The New Leader*, the Taminent Institute, and radio station WEVD named after Eugene V. Debs.[24]

The merger was complete by 1958, and the party was renamed the Socialist Party-Social Democratic Federation (SP-SDF), with Frank P. Zeidler (1912–), the third of the Socialist mayors of Milwaukee, elected as its co-National Chairperson. Also in 1958, a group of ex-Trotskyists led by Max Schachtman (1903–1972) and called the Independent Socialist League (ISL), entered the SP-SDF.

The Schachtmanites, as they were called, including socialist author (Edward) Michael Harrington (1928–1989), began pushing the idea of "realignment." Their Realignment Caucus in the SP-SDF argued that American labor had gone over to the Democrats, and because labor was the motor of all social change, that is properly where all progressive forces belonged. What needed to be done was to have a political realignment, with the Democrats becoming a party of the left and the conservatives leaving the Democratic Party to join the Republicans as a party of the right. The other faction within the SP-SDF was the Debs Caucus, which held to "Debs's" principle to have and to keep the party as an independent political organization that ran its own candidates.

There were other issues that divided the two caucuses. Schachtman had become increasingly conservative over the years, and he and his followers came out in favor of the war in Vietnam as a way to check Communist expansion. The Debs Caucus, however, opposed the war and called for an immediate withdrawal of U.S. forces. Harrington broke with the Realignment Caucus on this issue and took a middle stance. Even though his smaller Coalition Caucus agreed with the idea of working in the Democratic Party, they called for peace negotiations, although not an immediate pull-out of U.S. forces from Vietnam.

The Debs Caucus on the left of the party complained that its views were being prevented from appearing in the party's paper, *New America*, and began working outside the Socialist Party with such antiwar groups as the Students for a Democratic Society.

As a result of the prowar stand that the majority of the Socialists had taken, it was the only left-wing group on the U.S. left not to experience an upsurge in membership in the 1960s as a result of the war. By the 1970 convention, both the Debs Caucus and the Coalition Caucus were headed for a split with the party.

In the 1972 presidential election the Realignment Caucus supported the candidacy of Henry Jackson (1912–1983) in the Democratic presidential primaries. He was the most prowar and uncritical of Israel among the candidates. When Jackson failed to win the Democratic nomination, the Schachtmanites joined the leadership of the anticommunist AFL-CIO in taking a neutral stand in the race between Republican nominee Richard Nixon and the antiwar Democratic candidate George McGovern (1922–). This was becoming too much for Harrington's Coalition Caucus, who had strongly backed McGovern in both the primaries and the general election. The Debs Caucus for their part, because the Socialists had given up running their own candidates for president, supported Benjamin Spock, the famed pediatrician running as the antiwar candidate of the People's Party, with the Debs Caucus leader Frank Zeidler (as part of Spock's "shadow cabinet") nominee for Secretary of Health, Education, and Welfare.

The SP-SDF had moved far enough to the right by 1968 that it was able to merge with the DSF to form the Socialist Party-Democratic Socialist Federation (SP-DSF). In December 1972 the Realignment Caucus was able to get the National Convention to drop altogether the historic name of Socialist Party and to change the name of the SP-DSF to the Social Democrats, USA (SDUSA), pronounced "Seduce-sa" by its critics. This was the final straw. Several Debs Caucus–controlled state organizations and locals of what was to become known as "the old Socialist Party" began to disaffiliate with the parent group, among them the Wisconsin and California bodies. In May 1973 the Debs Caucus and an outgrowth of it called the Union for Democratic Socialism, along with the state organizations and locals that had bolted from the party, called "A Conference on the Future of Democratic Socialism in America" to be held over the Memorial Day week-end in Milwaukee. That conference voted to "reconstitute" the Socialist Party, USA, under that name. Unofficially and for the purposes of distinguishing it from the pre-1973 old Socialist Party, the group born that year is sometimes called "the new Socialist Party." The party adopted the Debs Caucus paper, the *Socialist Tribune*, as its own official organ, later shortened to the *Socialist*. The Socialist Party, USA, through most of its history was a member of the Second International and the post–World War II Socialist International. When the old Socialist Party, USA, became SDUSA, the latter retained its membership in the Socialist International.

In October 1973 Harrington's Coalition Caucus also quit the SDUSA to form the Democratic Socialist Organizing Committee (DSOC). It, too, joined the Socialist International. Not wanting to have more than two member organizations in its ranks from any one country, the new Socialist Party, USA, has not been admitted to the Socialist International. Functioning as a socialist group within the Democratic Party, DSOC almost never ran any of their own candidates for office, although some previously elected Democrats were DSOC members. Both DSOC and SDUSA supported the victorious, moderate Democrat candidate Jimmy Carter in the American presidential election of 1976, whereas the SPUSA opted to resume running a Socialist candidate for president for the first time since 1956 in the person of Frank Zeidler, with J. Quinn Brisben (1934–), a Chicago public school history teacher and civil rights activist, as his running mate.

Because of restrictive state-ballot-access laws, the party has been unable to get on the ballot in more than a handful of states, but it continued to run national and local candidates for office in the 1980s and 1990s. SPUSA today has only about a thousand members. For the 2000 campaign, the party nominated David McReynolds (1919–) for president.

During this time, DSOC went on to become the largest group on the American left, with perhaps as many as ten thousand members. In 1982 it merged with the New American Movement (NAM), an antiwar group that emerged from the student New Left of the 1960s, to form the Democratic Socialists of America (DSA).

The dream of realigning the American party system has been frustrated in recent years by the Democratic Party moving increasingly to the right and becoming a largely centrist party under presidents Jimmy Carter and later Bill Clinton. SDUSA has continued to move to the right as well, with some of its members working in the Republican Reagan administration in support of its anti-Communist goals, especially in Central America.

Why there is no major socialist party in the United States as there are in other countries is a question that has perplexed theorists for many years.[25] Some theorists look to the factionalism in the American socialist movement as its undoing. Splits upon splits have divided and weakened the entire socialist movement. It can be argued that even if there had been no splits in the American socialist movement, the lack of class consciousness on the part of U.S. workers, their high degree of social mobility, the public's identification of socialism with feared totalitarian Communism, and the capitalist system's ability to accommodate all combine to prevent socialism from becoming popular in the United States.[26]

Another argument is that the Socialist Party of America faced such brutal, government repression during and after World War I that it was never able to recover.[27] By 1918 the party had won 1,200 political offices, including electing seventy-nine mayors, thirty-two state representatives, and one Congressman. From 1917 to 1920, the Socialists, the Communists, and the IWW faced the combined attacks of federal, state, and local authorities.[28] Their headquarters in a number of cities were raided and sacked, their members were jailed or deported, their funds were confiscated, their newspapers were denied mailing privileges, and their elected representatives were denied their seats in the House of Representatives and in several state legislatures. The problem with this repression argument, as with the factionalism argument, is that some European socialist parties faced even worse repression, yet they managed to grow in spite of it. The German Socialists were repressed under Bismarck's Anti-Socialist Laws, and under the Nazis they were outright banned. Yet they emerged from both of these setbacks stronger than ever. The anticommunist hysteria of the 1940s and 1950s poisoned the minds of many Americans against all schools of socialism.

Another explanation for the lack of a major socialist party in the United States is the existence of a two-party system that prevents any third party, including the Socialists, from becoming large.[29] It has been argued that the United States has a two-party system out of sheer habit and inertia, out of the relative egalitarianism of the United States that has translated into an electorate not clamoring for radical alternatives, and out of the political maturity of the American people that has manifested itself in compromise, accommodation, and thus a stable two-party system.[30] However, why would the United States be so tradition bound as this explanation implies, as compared to other, older countries with multiparty systems and mass socialist parties such as Britain?

Other explanations as to why there is no mass Socialist party in the United States is that the institutional structure of the U.S. government and the party system precludes the development of third parties. The United States has a presidential system, whereas most countries are parliamentary. With a parliamentary system, it is usually necessary for several parties to form a coalition in order to form a government, and this tends to give each party importance. With a presidential system, there is no such bargaining behavior. It is a winner-take-all system, where only the largest of parties can win the presidency and choose an administration. Furthermore, the United States has an indirect system of electing its presidents in the form of the Electoral College. By its very nature, it is an extreme winner-take-all system. The candidate's slate in a state that wins most of the popular votes is elected to the Electoral College. Voting for a minor candidate would be wasting a citizen's vote because none of the losing candidate's slate is elected. Only in the states of Maine since 1969 and Nebraska since 1992 are there district elections.

Another institutional feature of American politics that mitigates against the rise of third parties is the federal system. Most countries are unitary—they have a central government but no state governments in which a Socialist party has to worry about trying to win power. In a federal system like that of the United States, there are state governments, and a Socialist party would have to spend considerable effort in capturing and holding on to power in these state governments. This tends to dilute the Socialists' efforts and to divert their funds away from capturing the national government. Without winning the central government, the Socialists would find that although they might succeed in winning elective office in some of the states, the decentralized nature of federal systems would tend to isolate and contain their victory to just those states and would have only limited impact on the national economy and society. Recognition of this containment of radical action can be seen in the words of American Founding Father James Madison (1751–1836), who in arguing for the federal system stated in *Federalist Paper*, No. 10, "The influence of factious leaders may kindle a flame within their particular States, but will be unable to spread a general conflagration through the states." And he named the ideas of *levelling*, a term commonly used in his time before the coinage of the word *socialism*, that he thinks federalism will limit: "A rage for paper money, for an abolition of debts, for an equal division of property, or for any other improper or wicked project, will be less apt to pervade the whole body of the Union than a particular member of it, in the same proportion as such a malady is more likely to taint a particular county or district than an entire State."[31]

Another feature of the U.S. system that acts as a brake on all third parties, including radical ones, is the single-member district system of elections for local, state, and national representatives and senators. This system tends to cause people to vote only for the moderate parties that can pick up the most votes. Michael Parenti, in quoting Maurice Duverger, noted that the proportional representation more commonly used in other countries would eliminate the disparity between political parties caused by the single-member district system.³² Proportional representation tends to favor smaller parties, including radical ones, because in having people vote for a slate of candidates put up by a party in a multimember district, such smaller, radical parties only need to win a small percentage of the vote to win some representation—the lifeblood of a party. Parenti gave the example of Communists Benjamin Davis and Peter Cacchione—both were elected to city council seats in New York and then lost them in 1947 as a result of a shift made from proportional representation to single-member district elections. He also cited the case of local elections in Cambridge, Massachusetts, where in 1972, after the victory of a few, radical candidates, proposals were introduced to end proportional representation.³³

Yet one must wonder about the importance of the institutional reasons for preventing the rise of a mass Socialist party in the United States when other countries without proportional representation, without unitary states, or without parliamentary systems nonetheless manage to have more than two major parties, at least one of which is at least social democratic. One suspects that there must be more to the failure of the American Socialist Party than mere political structural reasons.

Looking to economic reasons, Werner Sombart argued that in the United States socialism had foundered upon the shoals of "roast beef and apple pie." In other words, the United States is just too wealthy a nation and has such a high standard of living that socialism does not have much appeal for its people. It is interesting to note that Sombart felt that this was only a temporary condition and that in time the United States would develop a Socialist movement like the rest of the world.³⁴

Michael Harrington argued that Sombart's premise was overly simplistic. American workers were not all that rich and in point of fact, never have been. The United States is such an egalitarian society in other ways, argued Harrington, so much so that it is too socialistic for a Socialist party to be needed or wanted.³⁵ He cited Friedrich Engels's view that the existence of cheap land and the huge number of immigrants are important factors in the United States.³⁶ The availability of cheap land is a powerful, deradicalizing force in American politics. If things were bad in the cities of the East, the American worker always had the option of going west and getting cheap land to live on and farm and to start over. This ability to escape hardship helped develop the famed "rugged individualism" of Americans. Instead of dealing with social problems, the American could find a personal solution in moving away from them.

Even more important is the immigration factor. The United States is more a nation of immigrants than any other. Most of these immigrants came from places that are much worse off than the United States economically and politically. Coming to a more prosperous and freer country tended to put these immigrants into a frame of mind to be highly supportive of the United States and its political and economic institutions, and this too has had a deradicalizing influence on the immigrants and their descendants. Harrington also pointed out that the heterogeneous nature of the American working class made them extremely difficult to organize around a single cause such as socialism or any other *ism*. Ethnic rivalry, religious hatred, and racism were much more likely to flourish than socialism. These factors helped to divide the American working class, rather than to bring it together, as socialism requires. Competition for jobs from arriving immigrants, and later from blacks coming to northern cities from the South, as well as displacement by the introduction of automation, has led to mass unemployment. However, instead of blaming the capitalist system for not providing enough jobs for all those who needed them, the white, native-born American always found it easier to blame the foreign worker or the African American for "taking away our jobs." Meanwhile, this process of displacement in the unskilled jobs has led to the white, native-born workers rising to the positions of skilled blue-collar and educated white-collar workers and becoming something of a "labor aristocracy" with corresponding conservative views.

Do these aforementioned reasons forever preclude socialism or some other radical movement from taking hold in the United States? The rapid rise of the New Left that came in the 1960s and early 1970s, after the deadest of decades for interest in left-wing ideas in the 1950s, should give us pause in concluding that nothing will ever change. The Next Left could be waiting another unpopular war, another economic depression, or some other source of discontent to call it into existence. Although the political structure of the U.S. government and its party system have not changed, there is little in the way of cheap land left to run away from urban problems to, nor is the United States the nation of immigrants it once was. As income inequality and unemployment increase in an era of corporate downsizing, it is not impossible that a mass socialist or labor party might come into existence. Indeed, in the 1990s, a social democratic New Party and a Green Party were founded as well as an American Labor Party in 1996.[37] Some theorists have postulated a political cycle in the United States. Typically, a left-wing decade is followed by an era of conservative rollback that partially reverses the gains in equality of the preceding period.[38] If this process continues, the United States over the long haul of history should continue to move toward greater political and economic equality.

One way in which the Socialist Party, USA, shoots itself in the foot in gaining and keeping new members is the charging of membership dues that discriminates against the poor, especially racial minorities and women who have less income on average than white men. It also causes a steady drain of members who fail to renew their dues each year because they cannot afford the cost. In the Pennsylvania state organization, for example, inability or unwillingness to continue to pay dues has cost half the party membership in recent years. Having people ask to have their dues waived for reasons of poverty or for being a prisoner, as is the current practice, is demeaning to them, and not many will ask. The Socialist Party, USA, cannot effectively compete with the Democrats and the Republicans who charge no dues as long as it continues this practice. By rarely sending out direct-mail fundraising letters and even more infrequently engaging in advertising of any sort, the reconstituted Socialist Party, USA, will likely remain the small, mostly middle-class, white, men's organization that it is. Its local, the Socialist Party of Greater Philadelphia, and its state organization, the Socialist Party of Pennsylvania, in contrast, have always published a free newsletter and engaged in advertising and have never felt the need to charge state or local dues in their history.

Instead of a maximum program of advocating immediate, total nationalization of the means of production, distribution, and exchange, as small socialist sects have tended to do and which has often proved to be too radical for the majority of people to accept in many countries, American Socialists would do well to advance a minimum program calling for the creation of a national health plan—which all other developed nations except for the United States already have. It can be argued that just as the United States has a system of both public and private and parochial schools and of public libraries and private bookstores, it needs a system of national health insurance and private health insurance for those who want it. Another program would be to abolish unemployment by having the government hire all those who want and need to work but whom the capitalist system is unwilling or unable to hire. Still another program would be to abolish poverty by the creation of a guaranteed annual income by means of a negative income tax. If a person's or a family's income fell below the poverty line, then the Internal Revenue Service would give them enough money to bring them to some point above the poverty line as defined by the U.S. Census Bureau. In the context of American politics, any one of these reforms would likely to be considered revolutionary. As for a maximum program of nationalizing companies, this would likely be more acceptable and less likely to be reversed in time if it was understood that ownership and management would be turned over to their workers, and not retained by the state.

MEXICO

Socialist groups connected to the newspaper *El Obrero Socialista* with headquarters in Guadalajara and in Yucatan appeared in the early twentieth century to offer resistance to the dictatorship of Porfirio Díaz (1830–1915).[39] The Díaz regime had run Mexico since 1877. Díaz had favored the wealthy owners of landed estates and had assisted in their seizing of communal Indian lands to add to their holdings. When the people revolted, they were brutally suppressed and sold into peonage. The education of the people was also severely neglected. Aware of rising discontent, Díaz announced in 1908 that he would welcome opposition candidates. When liberal candidate Francisco Madero (1873–1933) actually gained a following, Díaz had him imprisoned.

Díaz was reelected in 1910 but was forced from office the following year by a rebellion, and Madero became president. However, some of the rebel leaders, notably Emiliano Zapata (1877?–1919) and Francisco "Pancho" Villa (1877–1923), refused to acknowledge Madero's authority. Gen. Victoriano Huerta (1854–1916), head of the Madero army, conspiring with the rebels, seized control of Mexico City in 1913, and had Madero murdered.

New armed revolts led by Zapata, Villa, and Venustiano Carranza (1859–1920) broke out, forcing Huerta to resign in 1914. A commission representing Latin American countries and the United States recognized Carranza as president of Mexico in 1915, and all the rebel leaders except Villa submitted to his rule. Villa waged war against the Mexican government; and when the U.S. government sided with Carranza, Villa launched raids against U.S. territory at Columbus, New Mexico, in 1916. This lead to a punitive U.S. expedition under the command of General John J. Pershing (1860–1948), which was unable to capture Villa, who continued his raids until 1920.

Meanwhile, one of those rare military men with leftist sympathies, General Salvador Alvarado, seized control of Yucatan in 1915, organized a large Socialist Party, and engaged in extensive land reform. The large landed estates were confiscated, and the land was redistributed to the freed peasants. The party gained the overwhelming support of the people, backed by a large propaganda campaign paid for by the government, which also paid the membership dues of its 100,000 Socialist Party members.

A new constitution for Mexico was adopted in 1917, limiting the president to one term in office, establishing a labor code, expropriating all properties belonging to churches, establishing a relatively advanced social welfare system, and returning communal lands to the Indians. Carranza was elected president under this new constitution in 1917, but unrest continued. In 1920, three generals, Plutarco Elías Calles (1877–1945), Álvaro Obregón (1880–1928), and Adolfo de La Huerta (1877–1955) revolted, killing Carranza and seizing power, with Obregón being elected president that year. When Obregón consented to arbitrate claims by U.S. oil companies that had been taxed by the Carranza government, the U.S. government decided to recognize him. Alvarado and his socialist followers in Yucatan had joined in forming the army that had toppled Carranza, and they established Obregón's regime as a "labor government."

During the 1920s, the Mexican Labor Party, led by Luis Morones, secretary of the Mexican Confederation of Labor (CROM), the parent body of the Labor Party, was the leading party representing the workers. In the 1924 election, Calles was elected president. His administration was more prolabor than the previous one, and Morones became minister of labor. But Calles's attempts to secularize Mexican society led to strong opposition from the Church. Calles declined to run again in 1928 and called for the formation of a new party, the National Revolutionary Party.

Returning as president, Obregón was elected on July 1, 1928, but was assassinated on July 17 by a religious fanatic. That September, the Mexican Congress chose Portes Gil as the provisional president. Morones and CROM, however, opposed Gil for his threats to suppress the trade union movement and for his imposing censorship in his administration. The outcome of this fight was a loss for labor, which lost control of the municipal government of Mexico City and several of the state governorships.

After a period of movement to the right in the late 1920s and early 1930s, Mexican society again shifted to the left. An associate of Calles, Abelardo L. Rodríguez (1889–1967), was elected provisional president in 1932. The National Revolutionary Party became the official government party that year and announced a six-year plan to achieve a cooperative economic system, which was heading toward the goal of eventually establishing socialism. The party platform called for a new labor code, a large public works program, land reform, and the nationalization of foreign-owned oil fields.

In the 1934 election, Calles's protege, Lázaro Cárdenas, was elected president, and the National Revolutionary Party program was then put into effect. The more-moderate Calles and his followers opposed some of these ideas; this led to a labor conference that resulted in Calles being forced to resign from politics, and he soon left the country. His followers in the cabinet were also forced to resign. Labor was given a large role in the administration of the government and was permitted to participate in the management of the railroads, which were nationalized in 1937. Foreign-owned oil companies were soon nationalized under a 1936 law that permitted nationalizations whenever necessary for public welfare. The government also pursued land reform, social welfare programs and educational reforms. In 1938 a broader-based political party was founded. It included not just the workers but also farmers and soldiers and was called the Party of the Mexican Revolution. CROM had also previously reorganized at the Confederacion de Trabajadores Mexicanas (CTM).

The Mexican Communist Party, founded in 1919 and reorganized in 1924 and 1925 by American Bertram Wolfe (1896–1977) of the Communist Party of America, was legalized under the Cárdenas government and soon increased from about 2,000 members in 1936 to 17,000 the following year. With the assassination of Leon Trotsky (1879–1940) in Mexico in 1940, President Cárdenas accused the Mexican Communists of complicity in the murder, leading to charge and countercharge that resulted in the expulsion of the secretary of the Communist Party from the CTM.

In the 1940 election, Manuel Ávila Camacho (1897–1955) was chosen as president with the backing of labor. This began a period of more conservative rule in the Mexican government and in the CTM. The unions were less combative, and control of the railroads was taken from them and given over to the state. With Franklin D. Roosevelt's Good Neighbor Policy in the United States coming into being, Camacho's government was inclined to cooperate more with the United States in commercial and military matters, and this trend accelerated with the advent of World War II. Mexico agreed to allow the United States to use its airfields and to export critical goods and strategic minerals only to the Allies. Mexico also severed diplomatic relations with Japan and Germany; and with the sinking of two Mexican ships by submarine, Mexico declared war on Germany, Italy, and Japan on May 22, 1942. In 1944 the Mexican government agreed to pay U.S. oil companies $24 million plus 3 percent interest for the oil fields it had expropriated in 1938 when the government agency Petróleos Mexicanos (PEMEX) was established. That year, PEMEX and U.S. officials agreed to a twenty-year plan to expand production of the Mexican oil industry.

A system of land-owning cooperative villages, or *ejidos*, had been established in Mexico along with other cooperatives in forestry, fishing, and transportation. In 1944 the Mexican National Bank for Development of Cooperative was established to extend credit to them.[40]

After the war, Miguel Alemán Valdés was elected president on a platform calling for further industrialization of Mexico; public works, especially in the building of irrigation systems; and a more equal distribution of wealth. U.S. oil companies in 1949, for the first time since the expropriation of their properties in 1938, were allowed back into Mexico to drill under the supervision of PEMEX. The governing party was also renamed in 1949 the Partido

Revolucionario Institucional (Institutional Revolutionary Party, or PRI), which dominated the elections and the Chamber of Deputies. In 1962 a controversial constitutional amendment was passed that gave the government the power to force businesses to share their profits with their workers.

The PRI continued to win election after election in Mexico, but over the years the party has moved to the right. In 1968 the Mexican government was confronted with student demonstrations that threatened to prevent the Olympic Games from being held that year in Mexico City. The government responded with a brutal crackdown that led to the death of hundreds of students.

In 1976 José López Portillo (1920–) was elected president and shortly thereafter embarked on a campaign of economic austerity. His successor, Miguel de la Madrid Hurtado (1934–), elected in 1982, was faced with increasing foreign debt and falling oil prices. As the Mexican financial situation worsened, the challenges from the left and the right to PRI domination, electoral fraud, and government corruption became ever stronger.

PRI had long tolerated so-called "official" opposition parties, as long as they continued to back PRI's presidential candidates. The "official left" party is the Popular Socialist Party (PPS), and the "official right" party is the Authentic Party of the Mexican Revolution (PARM). Attempts were made to form genuine opposition parties that would run against PRI's presidential candidates. On the right, the National Action Party (PAN) has become a genuine opposition party to PRI. On the left, there has been a process of uniting large and small socialist groups, which was led by the Mexican Communist Party, legalized in 1979. An earlier attempt was made in the 1960s with the formation of the National Liberation Movement, but this proved abortive. In 1981 the Communists united with the Popular Action Movement, the Mexican People's Party, the Movement for Socialist Action and Unity, and the Revolutionary Socialist Party, to form the Unified Socialist Party of Mexico (PSUM). In 1987 PSUM merged with the Mexican Workers' Party, the Patriotic Revolutionary Party, the People's Revolutionary Movement, and Left Communist Union to form the Mexican Socialist Party (PSM).

In 1988 Cuauhetmoc Cárdenas Solorzano, the leader of a dissident faction of PRI, the Democratic Current founded in 1986, broke with the parent body to form his own Democratic Revolutionary Party (PRD). Cárdenas had earlier run for president on a leftist coalition ticket called the National Democratic Front. Many leftist groups, including the Mexican Socialist Party, now joined the PRD. In a rejection of sectarianism rare in the world, most of the Mexican left was able to come together into a single party.

Cárdenas was the son of the popular, former president Lázaro Cárdenas.

When Cárdenas Solorzano ran for president in 1988 against Carlos Salinas de Gortori (1948–) of PRI and Manuel Clouthier of PAN, there were widespread charges of election fraud that many people believe robbed Cárdenas of the victory and handed it over to Salinas de Gortori.

The PRD's loss in 1989 to PRI in the gubernatorial races in the state of Michocan intensified the charges of electoral fraud and led many PRD members to occupy municipal buildings and to seize control of public roads, which resulted in clashes with PRI supporters and government troops. The PRD has been denied legalization on the national level and has had some sixty of its members killed in alleged political assassinations, one of its most prominent members, Leonel Godoy, being kidnapped. In November 1991 the PRD defied a new law making it criminal to make false accusations of electoral fraud by claiming that the PRI had used all known forms of violating the elections in the states of Mexico and Hidalgo.

An armed rebellion calling for the overthrow of the regime of Carlos de Gortori and the establishment of a socialist government erupted in 1994 in the southern Mexican state of Chiapas, which borders Guatemala. Shortly after midnight on January 1, 1994, guerrillas of the heretofore unknown Zapatista National Liberation Army seized four towns, including San Cristobal de las Casas, and a dozen villages. Fighting the social injustices and vast inequalities between the poor Indians of the region and the wealthy, the Liberation Army battled the Mexican army in the lush, mountainous land of Chiapas. After four days of fighting and using one-fifth of the Mexican armed forces, government troops backed by warplanes were able to push back into the hills the estimated 2,500 rebels from the towns and villages they had seized, leaving over a hundred people dead—perhaps as high as four hundred according to some reports from local church officials.

This was the first armed rebellion in Mexico since the 1970s. Chiapas is Mexico's poorest state, and it has frequently been the scene of clashes between the descendants of the Maya Indians and government troops over land rights.

The Zapatistas, named after the famed revolutionist Emiliano Zapata, launched their rebellion the same day that the North American Free Trade Agreement (NAFTA) took effect. The rebels believe that NAFTA would make the lives of the Indian people even more miserable than they already are.

With malnutrition and infant mortality rates in Chiapas being some of the highest in Mexico and with corn prices on which many families depend already low, NAFTA could push corn prices even lower as U.S. corn hits the duty-free Mexican market. Fighting between the Indians and the powerful ranchers in the area seeking more land for their grazing cattle is another bone of contention. (There had not been a major, regional rebellion in Mexico since the late 1920s. Anarchist author B. Traven wrote about the oppression and rise of rebellion in the mahogany forests of Chiapas in his series of six jungle novels. Of these, *The Rebellion of the Hanged* and *General from the Jungle* stand out.)

The Mexican military at first bombed villages and killed rebels they captured to try to crush the movement. When that didn't work, the Mexican government abruptly changed tactics and decided to negotiate a cease-fire on January 12, 1994. Peace talks led to an interim agreement in which government promised reforms. According to the masked rebel leader known only as subcommandante Marcos, it will be up to the Indians to decide whether to accept the peace accords.

The assassination of the hand-picked PRI candidate for president, Luis Donaldo Colosio, by Mario Aburto Martinez on March 23, 1994, threw the entire peace process into question. The Zapatistas announced that they had suspended consideration of the peace treaty for fear that the Mexican government would use the assassination as a pretext for attacking them.

On August 21, 1994, Colosio's successor, Ernesto Zedillo (1951–), won the presidential election, beating the PAN candidate Diego Fernandez de Cevallos, and PRD's Cárdenas. Shorty after Zedillo took office, Mexico was plunged into a severe economic downturn.

NOTES

1. Harry W. Laidler, *History of Socialism* (New York: Apollo, 1968), pp. 601–604.
2. Ibid., pp. 820–821.
3. T. C. Douglas, *Canadians Find Security* (New York: League for Industrial Democracy, 1949).
4. Joe Flexer, "Canadians' Unions Face Political Crisis—Labor-Backed NDP Nearly Wiped Out in Federal Elections," *Labor Notes* (December 1983): 16 and 14.
5. Sidney Lens, *Radicalism in America,* rev. ed. (Cambridge, MA: Schenkman, 1982), pp. 73–81.
6. Laidler, *History of Socialism*, pp. 577–601.
7. John R. Commons and Associates, *History of Labor in the United States*, 2 vols. (New York: Macmillan, 1918), 1:618.
8. Arnold Petersen, *Bourgeois Socialism: Its Rise and Collapse in America* (New York: New York Labor News Co., 1963), pp. 20–21.
9. Lens, *Radicalism in America*, pp. 163–164.
10. Laidler, *History of Socialism*, pp. 579–583.
11. Lens, *Radicalism in America*, pp. 133–139.

12. Ibid., p. 160.
13. Ibid., pp. 160–162.
14. Ibid., pp. 195–215; Laidler, *History of Socialism*, pp. 583–599; Ray Ginger, *Eugene V. Debs: A Biography*, originally published as *The Bending Cross, A Biography of Eugene Victor Debs* (New York: Collier, 1962; [New Brunswick, NJ: Rutgers University Press, 1949]).
15. Lens, *Radicalism in America*, p. 251.
16. Ibid., pp. 266–274.
17. Laidler, *History of Socialism*, pp. 591–592.
18. Ibid., pp. 593–594.
19. Ibid., pp. 594–595; Lens, *Radicalism in America*, pp. 293–295.
20. Lens, *Radicalism in America*, pp. 298–300; Laidler, *History of Socialism*, 596–597.
21. Laidler, *History of Socialism*, p. 598.
22. Ibid., p. 817.
23. Ibid., p. 818.
24. Ibid., p. 819; Robert W. Tucker, *The Debs Caucus: A Party within a Party* (Milwaukee: Socialist Party of Wisconsin, 1970); updated as the pamphlet *The Socialist Party—Bibliography and History* (New York: Socialist Party, USA, 1988); Frank P. Zeidler, *Ninety Years of Democratic Socialism: A Brief History of the Socialist Party, USA* (New York: Socialist Party, USA, 1991); R. W. Tucker, *Rise and Decline among the Reds* (Philadelphia: Privately published by the author, limited edition, 1991).
25. Milton Cantor, *The Divided Left—American Radicalism, 1900–1975* (New York: Hill and Wang, 1978), pp. 4–5.
26. Ibid., p. 108.
27. Michael Parenti, *Democracy for the Few*, 5th ed. (New York: St. Martin's, 1988), p. 182.
28. James Weinstein, *The Decline of American Socialism* (New York: Monthly Review Press, 1967).
29. David V. Edwards, *The American Political Experience—An Introduction to Government*, 4th ed. (Englewood Cliffs, NJ: Prentice Hall, 1988), pp. 139–141.
30. V. O. Key, *Politics, Parties, and Pressure Groups*, 5th ed. (New York: Crowell, 1964), pp. 229ff.
31. James Madison in *The Federalist Papers*, No. 10, edited by Clinton Rossiter (New York: Mentor, 1961), p. 84.
32. Maurice Duverger, *Political Parties* (New York: Wiley, 1955), p. 248.
33. Parenti, *Democracy for the Few*, p. 180.
34. Werner Sombart, *Warum gibt es in den Vereinigten Staaten keiner Sozialismus?* (Tubingen: Mohr, 1906); Werner Sombart, *Socialism and the Social Movement* (London: J. M. Dent, 1909), p. 276.
35. Michael Harrington, *Socialism* (New York: Bantam, 1973), pp. 131–161.

36. Friedrich Engels in *Marx-Engels Werke* (Berlin: Dietz Verlag, 1957–1967), XXI: 253.
37. *Labor Party Advocate,* vol. 2, no. 8 (Washington, DC: Labor Party Advocates, December 1995), p. 1.
38. Arthur M. Schlesinger Jr., *The Cycles of American History* (Boston: Houghton Mifflin, 1986), pp. 23–31.
39. Laidler, *History of Socialism*, pp. 605–608.
40. Ibid., p. 706.

5

Democratic Socialism in Central America, the Caribbean, and South America

GUATEMALA

In 1954 a nonviolent revolt by Guatemalan students and middle-class people overthrew the regime of General Jorge Ubico Casteñada (1878–1946), Guatemala's dictator since 1931. In the first democratic election in Guatemala, Juan José Arévalo (1904–1990), a university professor and democratic socialist, was elected president with the support of the National Renovation Party and the Popular Liberation Front Party.[1] Arévalo pursued a policy of establishing social security, ending forced labor, encouraging labor unions, legalizing the small Communist Party, and refusing to allow U.S. oil companies to enter and exploit the nation.

In the 1951 election, Colonel Jacobo Arbenz Gúzman (1913–1971), the minister of defense in the Arévalo government, was elected president. There were some Communists in the government coalition, but they were not in control. The Arbenz government engaged in making further reforms, including what is often the greatest demand in Third World nations—land reform. Arbenz wanted to give land to poor, landless peasants. In 1953 the government approved the nationalization of 225,000 acres of uncultivated land owned by the giant and politically powerful fruit company very well known in Central America—the United Fruit Company, today known as United Brands. By the middle of June of that year, more than 162,000 acres of land had been redistributed to landless peasants. The Arbenz government offered to pay United Fruit $609,572 for the land—the dollar amount based on the company's own valuation for tax purposes. However, the company insisted that the land was worth considerably more—$16 million.

United Fruit's attorney in Washington asked the U.S. government for help. U.S. Secretary of State John Foster Dulles (1888–1959) began a campaign to label the Arbenz government as Communist. It was not coincidental that Dulles's law firm had prepared United Fruit's 1930 and 1936 contracts with Guatemala. His brother, Allen Dulles (1893–1969), who had been president of United Fruit, was now the director of the Central Intelligence Agency (CIA). There were still other connections between the company and the U.S. government. The assistant Secretary of State for Inter-American Affairs, John Moors Cabot, was a major stockholder in United Fruit. Henry Cabot Lodge (1902–1985), the U.S. ambassador to the United Nations, was on the board of directors of United Fruit. The CIA director before Dulles was shortly to become the president of United Fruit.

It is little wonder that with these vested interests, the U.S. government set about to overthrow Arbenz. The CIA organized Operation SUCCESS, putting together an invasion force in Honduras. Strategic support was also given to the rebel army by Nicaraguan dictator Anastasio Somoza García (1896–1956). The rebel army attacked on June 18, 1954. The day that the invasion began, an urgent message was sent by the Guatemalan government requesting that the UN Security Council be called into session, but it was turned down by the president of the Security Council, who happened to be Henry Cabot Lodge.

Arbenz was forced to step down on June 27 by a group of Guatemalan army officers. The leader of this army group, Colonel Carlos Enrique Dias, became the temporary president. Two days later, the Guatemala legislature was disbanded, and prominent Communist leaders were arrested. With the help of the U.S. ambassador to Guatemala, John E. Peurifoy, a dispute over who would be the leader of the junta was settled, and Colonel Carlos Castillo Armas (1914–1957), the leader of the invading rebel forces, was named president. The land reform program was suspended, and United Fruit Company received its land back. The junta also abolished all taxes on profits and dividends payable to foreign investors, and as a result, the United Fruit Company had an $11 million windfall.

Guatemalans since the overthrow of Arbenz have lived under a number of military dictatorships and frequent coups. The government has been fighting left-wing guerrillas since that time, at last signing a final peace accord with the Guatemalan National Revolutionary Unity to end the civil war on December 29, 1996.

EL SALVADOR

El Salvador has experienced numerous peasant revolts against the coffee growers' oligarchy known as the "Fourteen Families."[2] These are the descendants of the original Spanish plantation owners, who have been joined by plantation owners from other nations and who now number about 250 families. One of the most important of these peasant revolts occurred in 1932. That year, hundreds of poor peasants rose up in rebellion against the government and the near feudal conditions on the coffee plantations. The leader of this rebellion was Agustín Farabundo Martí (d. 1932), a college-educated radical, and one of the founders in 1925 of the Central American Socialist Party. After years of activism and organizing, he, as a representative of the International Red Aid, along with the Communist Party of El Salvador, planned an insurrection for January 22, 1932. However, word somehow leaked out, and Farabundo Martí was arrested on January 18 and executed February 1. A hoped-for army barracks revolt never materialized, and mass arrest began. The Communist Party tried to call off the revolt, but it was too late. The rebels captured several small towns in the western coffee region, but ultimately the army was prepared for them and crushed the rebels.

Then came the *matanza* (Spanish for "massacre"). Outraged, the oligarchy wanted to teach the peasants a lesson they would never forget. The National Guard, formed in 1912 exclusively to maintain order in the countryside on behalf of the coffee oligarchy, was sent out to kill everyone they encountered. Their victims were forced to dig their mass graves before being cut down by machine gun fire. It is estimated that about 30,000 people—some 2 percent of the population—were killed in the matanza.

From 1932 onward, the military ran the government of El Salvador until very recently. Originally, the military had been a mere servant of the oligarchy, but they rose in importance. For the next several decades, all of the presidents of the nation would be generals or colonels.

The vice president under Alberto Araujo, General Maximiliano Hernández Martínez (1882-1969), had seized power in a coup a few days before the outbreak of the 1932 rebellion and had made himself president and dictator. During the next dozen years of his rule, he would flirt with Fascist leaders Franco, Mussolini, and Hitler. Everyone was required to carry an identification card. Industrialization was discouraged because it might produce a radicalized proletariat. He even refused international aid and modern methods of controlling a measles epidemic and simply ordered that the street lights be wrapped in colored cellophane so that the colored lights could purify the air.

After years of repression, another rebellion broke out in El Salvador in 1944. Workers went on a general strike, and students closed down the schools. After several weeks with the economy paralyzed and the police forces unable to break the strike, Maximiliano Hernández Martínez resigned and fled the country.

The new president "elected" in 1945 was General Salvador Casteñeda Castro. He in turn was toppled in 1948 by Colonel Oscar Osario, who represented the interests of that part of the oligarchy that wanted to diversify their wealth into other industries besides coffee growing. These modernizers had Osario repeal the anti-industrialization laws passed under the regime of Hernández Martínez. This may be thought of as a bourgeois ascendancy over the feudalists, or "agro-front," that sought to keep the nation predominantly agricultural and feudal in its social relations. However, it was not a revolution because the agro-front was not, by any means, destroyed. The modernizers were not free to pursue industrialization of the economy; they largely left the land holdings of the agro-front alone. Both wings of the oligarchy agreed on the fundamental use of repression to control the population, and the Osario government and its successor in 1960, that of Colonel José Maria Lemus (1911–), packed the jails with political prisoners every time a protest occurred.

In 1962 Colonel Julio Alberto Rivera won the presidency with his new political party, the Party of National Conciliation (PCN). Another of the bourgeois modernizers, he was successful in attracting U.S. multinational corporations to locate in El Salvador, among them ESSO, Westinghouse, Procter and Gamble, and Kimberly-Clark. He also led the way to the formation of the Central American Common Market to free up trade in the region. The economy prospered in the 1960s, and the manufacturing sector grew. His government also built more roads and schools and was considered a model of the John F. Kennedy (1917–1963) administration's Alliance for Progress aid program in Central America. Rivera also engaged in a measure of political modernization, allowing some opposition parties, such as the Christian Democratic Party and the democratic socialist National Revolutionary Movement (MNR).

In the 1967 election, Rivera was replaced by Colonel Fidel Sánchez Hernández (1917–) of the PCN. Under this new government, a war broke out between El Salvador and Honduras, partially over a soccer game. The Salvadoran soccer team was to play the Honduran team in the semifinals of the World Cup. General José Alberto "Chele" Medrano, director of the Salvador National Guard, tried to create disturbances in the street in front of the hotel where the Honduran team was staying to try to keep them awake so that they would be too tired to play well the next day. In July 1969 Salvadoran and Honduran forces clashed in the short "Futbol War" over this incident.

Actually this was the culmination of long-simmering hostilities between the two nations. Honduras had never liked the fact that destitute Salvadorans were immigrating illegally to Honduras. The Hondurans had forcibly evicted these Salvadorans in 1959, and this treatment had also been a major cause of the war. The war lasted only 100 hours, and was indecisive. Its major effect was to put an end to the Central American Common Market. This hurt the local economy at the time when much of the rest of the world's economy would soon be entering a recession.

In 1972 the Christian Democrats, the MNR, and the Communist Party formed an electoral alliance to run against the PCN. The alliance was called the National Opposition Union (UNO—Spanish for "one.") The Christian Democratic mayor of San Salvador, José Napoleón Duarte (1925–1990), a moderate, was the presidential candidate, and Guillermo Ungo of the MNR was his running mate. The PCN put up Arturo Armando Molina (1927–). Duarte campaigned vigorously, despite harassment by the National Guard and a paramilitary group of ex-guardsmen called the Democratic Nationalist Organization, but better known by their initials ORDEN ("order" in Spanish). The best-known of the death squads that came to operate in El Salvador, ORDEN was founded by General Medrano. General Medrano in later years admitted that he had been on the payroll of the CIA and that it was they who instructed him in setting up El Salvador's infamous death squads.[3] This effort dates back to the Declaration of San Jose, March 19, 1963, and involved not only the CIA but also the U.S. State Department and the Green Berets. Medrano had also founded his own political party in 1971, the Independent Democratic United Front, and ran as the agro-front candidate for president.

On February 22, 1972, the Central Election board announced that the PCN had beaten UNO by several thousand votes. Then that day, the Election Board in the capital announced that the Central Election Board had made a mistake in counting San Salvador's returns. The new totals were reported to give UNO the lead. A news blackout was imposed. No word was heard for two days. Then the Central Board published new figures handing the victory back to the PCN. The cry of fraud went up throughout the land. In a month, Colonel Benjamin Mejía, a maverick liberal military officer, arrested President Sánchez Hernández on charges of violating the constitution. The National Guard and most of the Salvadoran Air Force units remained loyal to the president and counterattacked. Some two hundred people died in the fighting, and Duarte was dragged out of the Venezuelan embassy, where he had taken asylum, by Salvadoran soldiers, who broke his cheekbones with rifle butts and cut off three of his fingers. Duarte went into exile, first in Guatemala and then in Venezuela, lucky to have escaped from the ordeal with his life. Then Sánchez Hernández was released from arrest, and Molina became the next president. His regime continued the heavy repression.

Some UNO people concluded that peaceful change was impossible in El Salvador. Even the democratic socialists in the nation, who usually favor peaceful change, supported violent revolution because there was no other way to make changes under these conditions. Guerrilla groups like the Popular Liberation Forces and the People's Revolutionary Army began to appear. They were soon joined by other groups making armed attacks on the government and building support among the people for demonstrations and strikes. The more the government killed demonstrators and strikers, the more the guerrilla forces grew in size and boldness. The government, for its part, encouraged ORDEN to likewise step up its efforts to crush these rebel forces.

In the 1977 election, the agro-front was able to recapture power from the modernizers in the PCN and chose General Carlos Humberto Romero (1924–) as the PCN candidate. UNO ran Colonel Ernesto Claramount. The official vote count was three to one in favor of the PCN. Popular reaction perceiving this as a fraudulent result was so strong that 50,000 people held a sit-in at the Plaza Libertad in downtown San Salvador that lasted five days. The army, the National Guard, and other police forces arrived at the end of these five days, sealed off the plaza, opened fire into the crowd, and spent the rest of the day beating and shooting people.

During the last six months of Molina's presidency and the first two years of the Romero regime, it seemed if a madness had seized the land. Killings reached a new high. The U.S. administration of Jimmy Carter delayed economic aid to El Salvador, fulfilling a promise to base U.S. foreign policy on human rights. However, as soon as Romero lifted an eight-month state of siege in 1977, Washington immediately approved of a stalled $90 million loan and named a new ambassador to El Salvador. However, the repression did not stop. The Salvadoran legislature passed the Law of Order in 1977—a sedition act—which was used to prevent information about the repression from reaching the outside world. Things only appeared quieter in El Salvador. Meanwhile, the killing continued.

On October 14, 1979, General Romero was overthrown in a coup led by young military officers and was sent into exile. The young officers detested the greed and corruption of the Romero regime and feared that if it did not stop, there would be another popular rebellion. Beyond this immediate goal, they had no program. A five-man junta was formed to rule the nation. The junta consisted of representatives from both junior and senior military officers, a representative of the business community, and Guillermo Ungo of the MNR to represent the left.

Popular organizations such as the People's Revolutionary Bloc and the United People's Action Front demonstrated for reforms in hopes that the new government would grant them. However, the police forces continued to visit brutal repression on them, despite the efforts of junta member Colonel Adolfo Majano, a moderate social democrat, to stop them. The junta did raise wages, considered land reform, and officially outlawed ORDEN, although it only changed its name to the Broad National Front and continued as the same old oppressive apparatus.

A confrontation was building in the government between the reformers and the reactionaries. As repression continued, the reformers began resigning from the government.

In early 1980 a second junta was formed, this time between the reactionaries and the moderates in the Christian Democratic Party. More killings caused a number of the latter to quit, especially after the assassination of Mario Zamora, the moderate attorney general. A third junta was formed later in 1980, with Duarte as president of the junta.

The long-awaited land reform, socialist in principle, was carried out with only slight reforms. Phase I was to nationalize large estates, with compensation paid to former owners, so that the land could be turned over to cooperative peasant associations. However, little of the land actually redistributed was suitable for cultivation, and most of it was grabbed by the death squads. Phase II, which would have distributed even more land, was canceled; and Phase III, the "Land to the Tenants" program for tenant farmers, gave only pitifully small amounts of land away to each tenant, too little to be of much use to anyone.

While the government was carrying on this ineffective land reform scheme, it at the same time launched a new state of siege, sending the army on a rampage in the countryside—a classic carrot and stick strategy. Those that could be bought off with a small amount of reform would be, and those that could not would be eliminated. Killings averaged ten a day.

The radio sermons of Archbishop Oscar Arnulfo Romero (1917–1980) had been an important source of information and inspiration to the protest movement in this period. For this, he was assassinated during a mass on March 18, 1980, in the metropolitan cathedral in San Salvador, the capital of El Salvador.

On April 18, 1980, some five thousand people met in the auditorium of the National University to witness the coming together of popular organizations and the opposition parties from the Democratic Revolutionary Front (FDR). The same year, the guerrilla groups united to form the Farabundo Martí National Liberation Front (FMLN). The FDR and the FMLN recognized each other as the political arm and the military arm, respectively, of the revolution. For the first time in Salvadoran history, the FMLN-FDR united virtually all opposition groups into a broad united front.

On May 8, 1980, Colonel Majano had retired Major Roberto D'Aubuisson Arrieta, the leader of ORDEN, arrested on his estate on charges of plotting a right-wing coup. D'Aubuisson, by his own admission, was a Fascist and an admirer of Adolf Hitler. The planned coup sought to stop the regime from making even token reforms. The following day, the entire officer corps of the army met in a national assembly and demanded D'Aubuisson's release. Majano was demoted as commander-in-chief, and D'Aubuisson was shortly released. Evidence was found at the time of D'Aubuisson's arrest that he had had a hand in the assassination of Archbishop Romero. In fact, Colonel Roberto Santivanez, former head of ANSESAL, the Salvadoran intelligence agency, was later to say that two Nicaraguan National Guardsmen were the triggermen in the assassination, acting under the orders of Colonel Richardo Lau, who, in turn, was under the orders of D'Aubuisson.[4]

One of the worst massacres in Salvadoran history occurred at this time. Salvadoran troops and ORDEN members slaughtered some six hundred men, women, and children trying to flee across the Sumpul River into Honduras, with their path blocked by the Honduran army. In 1993, a forensic team from El Salvador's Legal Medicine Institute began to exhume the bodies from the massacre.[5]

General strikes in 1980 failed to topple the government. The FMLN struck time and time again, capturing about a third of the countryside, while the FDR attempted to gain international support for the revolution. While the United States turned a deaf ear to their pleas, they were able to gain support from Mexico, European nations, and the Socialist International.

On November 27, 1980, five top leaders of the FDR were kidnapped, tortured, and killed, including its president, Enrique Córdova Alvarez. On December 2, Catholic sisters Ita Ford, Maura Clarke, Dorothy Kazel, and lay missionary Jean Donovan, all Americans doing relief work in El Salvador, were raped and murdered for trying to help the poor. Colonel Roberto Santivanez, former head of ANSESAL, the Salvadoran security agency, has claimed that General Vides Casanova, defense minister under Duarte, was responsible for the murders. Only after intense U.S. pressure were five Salvadoran National Guardsmen brought to trial and convicted on May 24, 1984. One of the worst atrocities of the war was the killing of six Jesuit priests in San Salvador on November 11, 1989. Colonel Guillermo A. Benavides Moreno, the commander of the Salvadoran military academy, was convicted of the murders in September 1991.

Throughout the 1980s and up to 1992, the war between the FMLN guerrillas and the Salvadoran government raged, killing an estimated 75,000 people. The U.S. government poured billions of dollars into the government's war effort. Duarte had beaten D'Aubuisson and his newly formed Republican Nationalist Alliance (ARENA) party in the presidential elections of 1984. D'Aubuisson was succeeded as head of ARENA by wealthy coffee grower, Alfredo Cristiani (1948–), who went on to win the presidency on March 19, 1989. Weary of the war, both sides agreed to end the war on December 15, 1992. For the FMLN's part, they agreed to disband as a military force and instead to become a political party that would contest elections. As for the government, it promised there would be political and social reforms that had been demanded by the rebels.

In the first election since the end of the war, the ARENA candidate for president, Armando Calderón Sol, beat Ruben Zamora Rivas, the candidate of the leftist alliance including the FMLN, on March 24, 1994.

NICARAGUA

In 1821 Nicaragua achieved its independence from Spain.[6] An American adventurer from Tennessee, William Walker (1824–1860, seized control of the nation in 1856 and became dictator. Slavery was legalized under his presidency, but he was eventually ousted from power.

Over the years, the U.S. government would militarily intervene in Nicaragua eleven times. The U.S. Marines occupied the country from 1912 to 1933, except for a brief respite in 1925, to stop the fighting between the Conservative and Liberal parties and to protect U.S. property and lives, as well as the Panama Canal. Augusto César Sandino (1895–1934) fought the U.S. occupation from 1927 to 1933. With the election of the Liberal president Dr. Juan Bautista Sacasa in 1932 and the U.S. Marine withdrawal from Nicaragua on February 2, 1933, Sandino agreed to a cease-fire with the Nicaraguan government. However, he was machine-gunned to death after leaving a farewell dinner at the presidential palace on February 21, 1934, by the Nicaraguan National Guard; and his body was buried under an airport runway, on the orders of the commander Anastasio "Tacho" Somoza

García (1896–1956). Hundreds of his followers, the original Sandinistas, were also murdered by the National Guard, which had been created by the U.S. government. With his control over the National Guard, plus his own fascist "Blue Shirts," Somoza seized the presidency in a fraudulent election in 1936.

Because Somoza was in favor of American business interests, the U.S. government did not to interfere with his dictatorial regime. He was forced to resign as president in 1947 by a revolt of the Nicaraguan people that began in 1944. Roman Reyes served as president until his death in 1950, at which time Somoza served out the unexpired term in 1951. In 1956 Anastasio Somoza was shot by a young poet, Rigobetto López Pérez, who was immediately gunned down by Somoza's bodyguards. Somoza died shortly afterward, and his older son, Luis Somoza Debayle (1922–1967), took over as president in 1957. When Luis Somoza died of a heart attack in 1967, his young brother, Anastasio "Tachito" Somoza Debayle (1925–1980), a West Point graduate and commander of Nicaragua's National Guard, used the guard to win the presidency, in a brutal campaign of repression, so as to keep the Somoza dictatorship alive. Although he systematically looted the country, he was the last of the Somoza dictators.

In 1961 a new generation of rebels calling themselves the Sandinista National Liberation Front (FSLN) rose up to challenge the Somoza regime. Rapidly gaining in strength, the FSLN overthrew the last of the tyrants on July 19, 1979.

The U.S. government was extremely hostile to this revolutionary government, considering the Sandinistas to be Communists. Soon the CIA was organizing ex-Nicaraguan National Guardsmen in exile in Honduras into a contra army to overthrow the Sandinista government, much as the CIA had done years before in Guatemala.

The U.S. administration of Ronald Reagan cut off aid to the Sandinista regime in 1981, accusing them of siding with the rebellion in neighboring El Salvador. In 1982 the Sandinistas signed an aid pact with the Soviet Union. The Sandinista presidential candidate, Daniel Ortega Saavedra (1946–), won the election in November 1984 by a wide margin. With the civil war raging with the U.S.-backed contras, Ortega in October 1985 declared a state of emergency, suspending civil rights. Military aid to the contras was defeated in the U.S. Congress in 1985, but it resumed in 1986. A major scandal erupted when it was learned that the contras had gotten funds diverted from payments made for secret arms to Iran during the time that U.S. military aid to the contras had been suspended. A truce was signed between the contras and the Sandinista government at peace talks held in March 1988. Elections were held in February 1990, and the anti-Sandinista coalition, called the

National Opposition Union (UNO), won a majority in the National Assembly. Their candidate Violetta Barrios de Chamorro (1929–) was also elected president over Ortega. She launched a program to demobilize the contra army and reduce the government's own troop strength, but much tension remains between the FSLN, now in opposition, and the contra forces. Ortega, running as a moderate social democrat, lost the presidential election again in 1996 to ARENA's Arnoldo Alemán.

COSTA RICA

Liberal-minded Colonel José Figueres Ferrer (1906–1990) led a successful revolt on March 12, 1948, in Costa Rica, and was chosen provisional president.[7] He resigned in 1949 when constitutional government was restored. His National Liberation Party (PLN) ran him successfully for president in the 1950s and again in the early 1970s. His government raised income and inheritance taxes and embarked on a low-cost housing program. The PLN candidate Francisco Orlick won in 1962 and did much to expand the nation's industry. The PLN won the presidency in 1974 with Daniel Oduber Quiros (1921–), and the party returned to power in 1982 under Luis Alberto Monge Alvarez (1925–), and again in 1986 under Oscar Arias Sánchez (1942–), who would do much to promote peace in the civil wars convulsing Central America. This plan was accepted by five governments in Central America in 1987, and Arias was awarded the Nobel Peace Prize that year for his efforts. The PLN obtained observer status in the Socialist International in the early 1960s. Its main opponent is the conservative Social Christian Unity Party, which has won several elections.

JAMAICA AND PUERTO RICO

In 1962 Jamaica gained its independence from Great Britain.[8] In its first democratic election, the Jamaica Labor Party (JLP), which supports private enterprise, won the first election, and its leader Sir Alexander Bustamante (1884–1977) became the prime minister. He was succeeded in office after retiring by JLP member Hugh Lawson Shearer (1923–) in 1967. The democratic socialist party, the People's National Party (PNP), won power in 1972, and its leader, Michael N. Manley (1923–1997), became prime minister. His left-wing policies and his friendship with Cuban Communist leader Fidel Castro proved to be highly controversial. Unable to revitalize the Jamaican economy, Manley was voted out of office in 1980. The JLP leader, Edward

Seaga ((1930–), came into office, pledging to reverse socialism and to sever ties with Cuba. Seaga attempted to improve the economy by attracting foreign capital, especially from the United States. Low prices for Jamaica's mineral exports, especially bauxite and alumina, prevented economic recovery. Additionally, Hurricane Gilbert in September 1988 caused an estimated $8 billion in property damages and left a half-million Jamaicans homeless. Under these failures and setbacks, the PNP swept back to power in 1989 with a large parliamentary majority, with Manley returning as prime minister. However, Manley resigned from office in March 1992 for reasons of health and was succeeded by Percival J. Patterson (1935–) as PNP leader and prime minister. In recent years, Manley has repudiated much of the socialist policies in which he had believed and has become an advocate of free markets.

Puerto Rico has socialist parties favoring independence.

HAITI, THE DOMINICAN REPUBLIC, AND GRENADA

In Haiti, the long-standing Duvalier regime was finally overthrown in 1986. Right-wing military juntas and coups followed Jean Claude Duvalier's (1951–) departure, until internationally supervised democratic elections could be held in 1990, bringing leftist Roman Catholic priest Jean-Bertrand Aristide (1953–) to office as president as the candidate of the poor. However, his presidency was short-lived, being toppled in 1991. Haiti was then ruled by a military junta until the United States, moved to act by a wave of Haitian boat people trying to reach the United States to escape the poverty and oppression in Haiti, used the threat of a military invasion to force the Haitian military from office and to restore Aristide to power on October 16, 1994. He finished out the rest of his term, much of it spent in exile, as U.S. and other multinational troops began to end their peacekeeping role. He was succeeded by Rene Preval, elected on December 17, 1995. Preval has promised to cut the number of state workers, as demanded by the International Monetary Fund (IMF), in order to receive loans—an unpopular move given the high unemployment in Haiti.

In the neighboring Dominican Republic, General Rafael Leonidas Trujillo Molina, the dictator for thirty-two years, was assassinated on May 26, 1961. The following year, Juan Bosch (1909–), a democratic socialist, was elected president on a reform platform calling for land reform, higher wages, public works, projects and cooperatives.[9] He was subsequently overthrown by the rightist military. Bosch and armed forces loyal to him launched a coup on

April 24, 1965. To prevent Bosch from returning from exile and assuming power, the U.S. administration of President Lyndon Johnson led a multinational force in invading the Dominican Republic.

Achieving its independence from Britain in 1974, Grenada's first prime minister was Eric M. Gairy (1922–). A conservative, Gairy was overthrown in a leftist coup headed by Maurice Bishop (1944–1983) in 1979. The New Jewel Movement government earned the enmity of the Reagan administration for its advocacy of socialism. A second coup in 1983 that resulted in Bishop's murder was conducted by Communists. At that time, the United States and the Organization of East Caribbean States sent troops to invade Grenada on October 25, 1983. The U.S. government used the safety of American students in Grenada as a pretext for its invasion. The coup was quickly crushed. An Interim Advisory Council ruled Grenada until December 1984, at which time a parliamentary election was held bringing Herbert A. Blaize (1918–1989) to office as prime minister at the head of a conservative coalition National Party. After Blaize's death, Nicholas Brathwaite (1925–) became prime minister in 1990.

Aruba, Cuba in exile in the United States, Curacao, Dominica, St. Kitts-Nevis, St. Lucia, and St. Vincent and the Grenadines have social democratic parties.

VENEZUELA AND GUYANA

In 1945 the democratic socialist Democratic Action party (AD) leader Dr. Rómulo Betancourt (1908–1981) had taken power as Venezuela's provisional president after the overthrow of the dictator, General Isaías Medina Angarita (1897–1953).[10] The AD was founded by Betancourt, Raúl Leoni, and novelist Dr. Rómulo Gallegos Freire, who had taken office as the democratically elected president in 1948 and who was overthrown the same year by an army coup. The subsequent junta forced leaders of the opposition parties to leave the country in the early 1950s. A general strike in 1958 led to another army coup and Betancourt's subsequent reelection as president later that year, followed by Raúl Leoni (1905–1972) in 1963, both of the AD. The opposition Social Christian party (COPEI) narrowly won the presidential election of 1968 with its leader Rafael Caldera Rodríguez (1916–) over Leoni. AD and COPEI were the two main parties in Venezuela, alternating in winning the presidency as the nation entered the 1990s, with several attempted coups throughout this period by both military leaders and leftists. Both parties also favored nationalizing Venezuela's oil industry, which was accomplished in 1976 by AD president Carlos Andrés Pérez (1922–). A drop in world oil prices in 1989 led to austerity measures and, along with anger over corruption, produced an attempted but failed coup in 1992.

Smaller parties in Venezuela were the Movement Toward Socialism and the Communist Party. The leftist Patriotic Pole coalition of Venezuelan President Hugo Chavez won 92 percent of the constitutional assembly's seats in the elections on July 25, 1999. Chavez took office in February 1999 and has been consolidating his power in the armed forces by appointing officers loyal to him. He has called for the constitutional assembly to undertake a "social revolution" and to break the stranglehold of the traditional political parties, COPEI and the center-left AD, which he claims has corrupted Venezuela's government and impoverished the nation. The assembly is charged with the power to rewrite the Venezuelan constitution, a highly controversial move, especially since Chavez led an unsuccessful 1992 coup attempt in Venezuela that landed him a two-year prison term. The leftist majority in the constitutional assembly is planning to replace the Venezuelan Supreme Court and to fire about half of the judges in the country on charges of corruption, a move opposed by the Venezuelan Supreme Court.[11]

The socialistic and anti-imperialist People's Progressive Party (PPP), founded in 1950, was organized by British Guiana's Cheddi Jagan (1918–), an East Indian, and Forbes Burnham (1923–1985), an African. The PPP won a majority of the seats in the parliamentary elections of 1953, and Britain suspended British Guiana's constitution fearing a Communist takeover by the PPP. Forbes Burnham split from the PPP to form his own political party, the People's National Congress (PNC), founded in 1957. In 1964, Burnham replaced Marxist Jagan as prime minister by forming a coalition with the minority conservatives. British Guiana became the independent nation of Guyana on May 26, 1966, with Burnham as prime minister. Guyana had a socialist constitution go into effect in 1980, establishing a presidential system. Burnham was elected president and was given wide state powers. He died in 1985 and was succeeded as president by PNC's Desmond Hoyte (1929–). In 1992, the PPP won a majority in the National Assembly, and Jagan was elected president.

The constitution of Guyana gives the president the power to veto the bills passed by the unicameral National Assembly. The government has provided for, among other things, a social security system. The nation was the scene of the tragic 1978 Jonestown mass murder of over nine hundred followers of leftist U.S. religious cult leader Jim Jones (1931–1978), who ordered the massacre.

BRAZIL AND BOLIVIA

After years of socialists being banned in Brazil, in 1966, a Socialist party was founded in the nation.[12] The Social Democratic Party and the Communist Party (renamed in 1992 the Popular Socialist Party) are among several opposition parties today in the nation. The Communists were legalized by President José Sarney (1930–) in the mid-1960s. High inflation led President Fernando Collor de Mello (1949–) in the 1990s to introduce shock plans to restructure Brazil's statist economy. Inflation was wrung out of the economy. The current government of President Fernando Henrique Cardoso, also a free-marketer, is addressing fundamental problems of recession, while continuing to privatize state-owned industries. Brazil also has a Democratic Labor Party and a Workers' Party.

"Cerro Rico" (Rich Hill) is a mountain of silver in Potosí, Bolivia, discovered in 1544. A great city arose to mine that wealth, reaching a population high of 160,000 before the mines gave out and consumed the lives of an estimated 8 million Indians working in brutal conditions.[13] The wealth went to Spain where it was squandered or wasted in religious wars, eventually ending up in the banks of Europe. It is said that this fortune fueled the birth of modern capitalism, although that may be an oversimplification because antecedents of capitalism existed in earlier times. In time, other metals became important in Potosí, especially tin. Although the government mines are now closed, Potosí mines still exist and are now run by miner-owned cooperatives.

Bolivia's National Revolutionary Movement (MNR) overthrew the military men who ruled the nation in 1952, and MNR exiled leader Victor Paz Estenssoro (1907–) became president. His administration nationalized Bolivia's tin mines, redistributed land, and was prolabor but anti-Communist. The MNR came under fire from its former supporters for being oppressive, and Paz was overthrown. A military junta came to power. Civilian government was eventually restored.

ECUADOR AND PERU

Among Ecuador's leftist parties are the Democratic Left and the Socialist Party of Ecuador, founded in 1924. The latter is a party of intellectuals and workers often working in coalition with the Radical Liberal Party, one of the two largest parties in the nation and somewhat to the left of the other major party, the Conservative Party. The nation has frequently been beset by political turmoil and military seizures of power. Civilian rule was restored in 1979.

One of the best known of the South American democratic socialist parties is found in Peru, the American Popular Revolutionary Alliance (APRA).[14] Founded in 1924, APRA was led for more than forty years by Victor Raúl Haya de la Torre (1895–1979). APRA called for basic social democratic reforms and for the improvement in the living conditions of the Indian population of Peru. The nation has long been ruled by a series of dictators since its independence from Spain was formally proclaimed on July 28, 1821, and finally realized with the defeat of the Spanish armies in 1824 by the forces of the great Venezuelan revolutionary, Simon Bolívar (1783–1830). However, Spain would not recognize the independence of Peru until its defeat in another war in 1886 over Spanish attempts to seize the guano-rich Chinicha Islands, owned by Peru.

Soon after APRA was founded, it was banned by President Augusto Leguía y Salcedo (1863–1932), one of Peru's many dictators. Despite this, APRA continued to become one of the most influential parties in Peruvian politics. In 1945 APRA, in coalition with other liberal and leftist parties, managed to elect José Luis Bustamante y Rivero (1894–1989) as president. He instituted numerous reform measures, including press freedom and the abolishing of some of the dictatorial powers of the president by constitutional amendment. All of this was too much for the Peruvian right, which toppled Bustamante in a coup in October 1948 and again banned APRA. The leader of the coup, Manuel A. Odria (1897–1974), was elected president in 1950 in an election in which his chief opponent was not allowed to be placed on the ballot.

Peru continued this pattern of rigged elections, which was followed by more military coups throughout the 1950s, 1960s, and 1970s. APRA finally was able to elect one of its own as president in 1985 in the person of Alan García Pérez (1949–). He became president at a time when Peru's economy was rapidly declining, and he was unable to stop this slide. Peru is beset with serious violence by the Maoist guerrilla army known as the Sendero Luminoso—"the Shining Path"—which the government was unable to crush. As a result of the failures of the Garcia government, Alberto Keinya Fujimori (1938–) was elected president in 1990 of the Chance '90 party. He imposed an economy austerity program upon taking office, but rising economic hardships led to an upsurge of Shining Path violence. In April 1992, Fujimori, a former agricultural economist of Japanese descent, suspended the constitution, claiming that the corrupt Peruvian congress and judiciary had blocked his efforts to crush the Shining Path and the drug trade in his nation. Shining Path's leader, Abimael Guzmán Renoso, was captured in September 1992, but this did not halt Shining Path's attacks. On December 17, 1996, members of another guerrilla group, the Tupac Amaru Revolutionary Movement, seized the Japanese embassy in Lima, Peru, taking hostages to win reforms from Fujimori's government.

URUGUAY

In 1910 the Uruguayan Socialist Party was founded.[15] A 1921 split took most of its membership away to form the Communist Party of Uruguay. With a small representation in the National Congress, the Socialist Party supported the leftist front known as the Unión Popular in the 1962 election. The dominant parties are the conservative National (the White, or Blanco) Party and the generally more liberal Colorado Party. In 1971 the Broad Front was formed to oppose these two major parties and was made up of the Socialists, the Communists, and the Christian Democrats, along with mavericks from the Colorado and Blanco parties. The leftist National Liberation Movement, better known as the Tupamaros, battled the government with armed force in the late 1960s. They were brutally murdered and suppressed by the military in the early 1970s, and the nation became a military dictatorship. Civilian rule returned in 1985. Paraguay's socialist party is the Revolutionary Febrerista Party (PRF).

CHILE

The Chilean Socialist Labor Party was formed in 1912, and it participated in the 1920 coalition government of Arturo Alessandri Palma, who was overthrown in a rightist, military coup in 1924. Another coup the following year returned Alessandri to power. However, this was shortly followed by a rightist government that was headed by Colonel Carlos Ibáñez del Campo (1877–1960), president from 1927 to 1931. Following a leftist revolt in 1932, a socialist republic was proclaimed, with Alessandri again serving as president until 1938. During the Popular Front era in the Great Depression and in the post-World War II era, the Radical Party formed governments. In 1952 General Ibáñez was again elected president, and a series of Christian Democratic governments followed.[16]

Dr. Salvador Allende Gossens (1908–1973) and his leftist Popular Unity coalition won the 1970 presidential elections.[17] Allende was a moderate democratic socialist. Both U.S. corporations and government were afraid that Allende would nationalize American-owned businesses in Chile. When Allende had run in the 1958, 1964, and 1970 elections, the CIA had spent several million dollars to defeat his bid for the presidency, organizing scare campaigns and covertly paying over half the costs of the opposition Christian Democratic campaign. The CIA also helped multinational corporations in Chile to contribute hundreds of thousands of dollars to anti-Allende candidates. Allende was considered to be a dangerous communist by U.S. government officials, none more so than Henry Kissinger, National Security Adviser to President Richard Nixon and later the Secretary of State. Kissinger told the supersecret 40 Committee (40 of the top national security experts advising Nixon, chaired by Kissinger) that he saw no reason why the United States had to stand by and do nothing while another country went Communist due to the irresponsibility of its voters.

Despite the unleashing of the CIA on Allende's campaign, he won a narrow plurality in the presidential election of September 4, 1970. Because no one obtained a majority, the Chilean Congress was scheduled to meet October 24 to select a president. The 40 Committee met in September and advised Nixon to prevent Allende's election at any cost. CIA Director Richard Helms met with Nixon on September 15 and came out of the meeting with a two-track program to stop Allende.

Track I called for a variety of political and economic tactics to be used. The CIA launched a coordinated attack on the Chilean economy, including asking multinational corporations to cut off credit and to halt the shipment of spare parts. A major financial panic resulted. The Track II program involved efforts to foment a military coup in Chile. Unlike Track I, neither the 40 Committee nor the State Department were told about the existence of this program. The CIA proceeded to make twenty-one contacts with key Chilean military personnel over the next two weeks to encourage them to revolt.

A major obstacle to this plan was in the person of Chilean Chief of Staff, General Rene Schneider, a strong supporter of the Chilean military's tradition of staying out of politics. The CIA's reaction was to propose removing General Schneider by force. After two unsuccessful attempts to kidnap him, General Schneider was killed in the third kidnap attempt. Despite the best efforts of the CIA, Allende was elected president by the Chilean Congress on October 24, 1970. The CIA then stepped up Track I and Track II. Economic sanctions were further tightened, right-wing terrorist groups were funded, truckers' strikes were encouraged, and the military was urged to act.

Allende's government nationalized copper mines, and social welfare programs were augmented. However popular these programs were, they were not enough to offset the economic depression that Chileans were experiencing due to CIA-inspired actions against their country. On September 11, 1973, a group of Chilean military officers rose up and overthrew Allende, who died in the presidential palace.

The military dictatorship of General Augusto Pinochet Ugarte (1915–) unleashed a state of siege, imprisoning, torturing, killing, and exiling thousands of Allende's supporters. The constitution was suspended, the congress dissolved, political parties were banned, and strict censorship was imposed. Economically, the Pinochet regime adopted an open-door policy that encouraged multinational corporations to come to Chile. A plebiscite was finally held in 1988 on whether the Chilean people wanted Pinochet's presidency to be extended to 1997. A resounding *no* vote led to Pinochet's stepping down. In 1990 Christian Democrat Patricio Aylwin (1918–) was elected president, and he initiated a reform program and a commission to investigate human rights abuses under the Pinochet dictatorship. Pinochet was subsequently arrested in England and was facing extradition to Spain on charges of murdering its citizens in Chile. As of this writing, he will probably be returned to Chile because of his advanced age and ill health.

In January 2000 socialist Ricardo Lagos was elected president of Chile, the first socialist president there since Allende. This is an amazing comeback for the Socialists in Chile.

ARGENTINA

In Argentina, the Socialist Party was founded in 1896 and drew its support from the working class. During the 1940s, the Socialists opposed the dictatorship of General Juan Perón (1895–1974).[18] Most of the Socialist leaders were arrested, and its headquarters and press were destroyed. Perón and his wife, Eva (1919–1952), created a Labor Party commonly known as the Peronistas. They found backing in the working class, the *descamisados* ("shirtless ones"), with their promises of higher wages, social security, and land reform. The Peronistas also created a puppet party, the Movimiento Socialista, in place of the Socialist Party and manned it with many people whom the Socialist Party had expelled. With the end of the Perón dictatorship in 1955 by military overthrow, the Socialist Party rebounded and became the third-largest party. The largest of the Argentine parties is the Unión Cívica Radical (the Radical Party), which was founded in the 1890s and which became split into factions. One faction, the Intransigent Radicals, itself split into factions, whereas the other main faction, the People's Radicals, today goes under the old name of Unión Cívica Radical. Democratic government was not to last long; a military junta took control in 1966 and abolished all political parties. The Socialists, now split into many factions, have virtually disappeared from national politics. What remains of them is in coalition with other parties and factions, the Frepaso coalition. In 1973, Perón returned from exile and was again elected president. He died on July 1, 1974, and was succeeded by his third wife, Isabel (1931–), the vice president. By the mid-1970s, terror by rightist and leftist groups resulted in the deaths of hundreds of people, and a military junta seized power in 1976. The Argentine Commission for Human Rights blamed the regime for the arrest, death, and disappearances of many thousands of people. The failed attempt to seize the Falkland Islands from the United Kingdom in 1982 discredited the regime of General Leopoldo Galteri (1926–), who was soon replaced. Argentina's presidential election brought the Radical Party's Raúl Alfonsín (1927–) to office. Some military and political officials were charged with human rights abuses, and the armed forces and government were reformed. In 1989, the Peronist candidate, Carlos Saúl Menem (1930–), won the presidency and imposed an austerity program; he also moved the nation toward free-market economics.

NOTES

1. John M. Swomley, Jr., *The American Empire—The Political Ethics of Twentieth-Century Conquest* (New York: Macmillan, 1970), pp. 153–157; Felix Greene, *The Enemy—What Every American Should Know about Imperialism* (New York: Vintage, 1971), pp. 196–199.
2. Robert Armstrong and Janet Shenk, *El Salvador—the Face of Revolution* (Boston: South End Press, 1982).
3. Allan Nairn, "Behind the Death Squads," *The Progressive*, May 1984, pp. 20–29.
4. *The Guardian* (New York), April 3, 1985, p. 15.
5. *Philadelphia Inquirer*, May 19, 1993, p. A7.
6. Karl Bermann, *Under the Big Stick—Nicaragua and the United States since 1848* (Boston: South End Press, 1986).
7. Harry W. Laidler, *History of Socialism* (New York: Apollo, 1968), pp. 829–830.
8. Ibid., pp. 830–832.
9. Swomley, *The American Empire*, pp. 157–167.

10. Laidler, *History of Socialism*, pp. 827–829.
11. *Philadelphia Inquirer*, July 26, 1999, p. A6; ibid., August 20, 1999, p. A10; ibid., September 1, 1999, p. A16.
12. Laidler, *History of Socialism*, p. 823.
13. Richard L. Greaves, Robert Zaller, and Jennifer Tobert Roberts, *Civilizations of the West—the Human Adventure* (New York: HarperCollins, 1992), p. 538.
14. Laidler, *History of Socialism*, pp. 824–826.
15. Ibid., pp. 826–827.
16. Ibid., pp. 611–616, 823–824.
17. Morton H. Halperin, Jerry J. Berman, Robert L. Borosage, and Christine M. Marwick, *The Lawless State, the Crimes of the U.S. Intelligence Agencies* (New York: Penguin, 1976), pp. 15–29.
18. Laidler, *History of Socialism*, pp. 822–823.

6

Democratic Socialism in Asia, Australia, Africa, and the Middle East

JAPAN

The Japan Socialist Party, founded in 1945, changed its name in 1996 to the Social Democratic Party of Japan. However, it still remains behind the procapitalist Liberal Democrat Party in size.[1] After many years in power, the Liberal Democrats lost control of the government in the 1990s, as a result of corruption scandals, to newer reform parties that have included the Socialists as coalition partners. On June 29, 1994, Tomiichi Murayama became the first Socialist prime minister since 1948 in a new coalition with the Liberal Democrats. In a convention in 1994, the Socialists moved to remove some of the radical positions of their traditional program that they felt were holding them back. Dropped was their opposition to Japan having a military, a flag, a national anthem, nuclear power, and a security treaty with the United States. The party moved toward the political center to reinvent itself as a party for social democrats and liberals to widen its electoral base. This change did not sit well with all the Socialists, some of whom broke off to form the New Socialist Party in 1996. Among other issues, they are opposed to U.S. military bases being allowed to remain in Okinawa. There had been another split from the Japan Socialist Party in 1960 called the Democratic Socialist Party, but it had merged with eight other parties in 1994 to form the New Frontier Party, which later merged into the Democratic Party of Japan. In 1996 Murayama stepped down, and the Liberal

Democrats regained the prime ministership of Japan. However, Japan in the late 1990s has been thrown into its worst economic recession since the end of World War II.

SOUTH KOREA

With the proclaiming of Republic of Korea on August 15, 1948, Syngman Rhee (1875–1965), a strong anti-Communist, was elected its first president by the national legislature.

These elections were boycotted by almost all of the left-wing groups and parties in the nation, who were subsequently suppressed by the new government. It was this suppression that contributed to the North Korean attack in June 1950 and the commencement of the Korean War and U.S. entry into the fighting. Rhee was reelected in 1956 and 1960; however, in the later election, the electoral fraud on the part of Rhee was so great as to provoke national protests that forced him to resign April 27, 1960. A more moderate government under John M. Chang (1899–1966) briefly took power, but on May 16, 1961, the South Korean military staged a coup. The junta was led by Park Chung Hee. His government was willing to send troops into the Vietnam conflict on the side of the United States. His Democratic Republican Party completely dominated South Korean politics in those years, and the Korea Central Intelligence Agency (KCIA) spied on and did their best to intimidate opposition groups in South Korea. On September 20, 1966, the United Socialist Party of South Korea was founded and became an observer member of the Socialist International.[2] Its founding congress called for the end of the suppression of freedom by the government and for reunification with North Korea and opposed sending South Korean troops into the Vietnam War. In 1972, the Park regime declared martial law. Mass demonstrations broke out in 1979 and were violently suppressed. The Director of the KCIA, Kim Jae Kyu (1926–1980), assassinated Park on October 27, 1979. General Chun Doo Hwan (1931–) was to emerge as the leader of a junta that followed. The Democratic Justice Party dominated the South Korean legislature in those years. More years of political repression followed under Chun and his successors, but in time a multiparty democracy emerged.

CHINA AND VIETNAM

In pre-Communist China, Sun Yat-sen had developed the *San Min Chu I* (Three People's Principles). These were nationalism, democracy, and people's livelihood—a vague conception of socialism. Sun and his Kuomintang (Nationalist) party argued for popular suffrage, the initiative, referendum, and recall, but he also insisted that China still needed "political tutelage" and, thus, restrictions on what he saw as excessive liberties for the people.[3] Eight so-called "democratic parties" continued to exist after the 1949 Communist revolution and participated in the Chinese People's Political Consultative Conference that formally established the People's Republic of China in 1949. They serve as vehicles for the socialist reform of their own membership, and they must follow the lead of the Communist Party and play only a minor role.[4] A Chinese Socialist Party had been organized about the time of the 1911 Chinese Revolution, but it did not survive.[5] The Democratic League was organized in 1941. From it emerged the National Socialist Party in 1946, later renamed the China Democratic Socialist Party, but it also faded away with the coming of the 1949 Chinese Communist Revolution.[6]

Vietnamese socialists joined the Saigon Federation of the French Socialist Party in 1931 and participated in the resistance against the Japanese occupation of their country in World War II.[7] On September 12, 1952, a secret congress was held to found the Vietnamese Socialist Party. However, its activities were curtailed during the 1960s.

Post-Communist Mongolia has a social democratic party.

BURMA, AUSTRALIA, AND NEW ZEALAND

Peasant revolts in Burma in the 1930s led to the formation of the Burma Socialist Party.[8] Another movement was the *Dobama Assi-a-yong,* or *Thakin,* Party that emerged as a peasant- and worker-based socialist and anti-imperialist party after a ruthless suppression of a revolt over economic conditions in the Tharrawaddy district in the 1930s. During World War II, this party reorganized itself as the Burmese Revolutionary Party. It participated, along with the Communist Party and the Burmese Independence Army, in the formation of a broader front, the Anti-Fascist People's Freedom League (AFPFL). After the war, U Aung San (1915–1947), a Socialist, became the leader of the nation. The Communists were expelled from the front, leaving the Burma Socialist Party as the leading group in it. The Socialists were active in organizing the Asian Socialist Conference that met in Rangoon in January 1953. In May 1958 a faction fight developed in the Burma Socialist Party. General Ne Win took control of the government, dissolved the parliament, abolished the constitution, and formed the new Burmese Socialist Program Party as the sole political party in the nation. It has no ties to the Socialist International and moved to suppress all opposition, so it cannot be considered to be democratic socialist. Antigovernment protests in 1988 forced Ne Win to resign as party chairman, but they did not restore democracy. In

1989, the name of the nation was officially changed to the Union of Myanmar. The opposition National League for Democracy won an overwhelming victory in the legislative elections of 1990; however, the ruling council refused to allow the People's Assembly to convene. In 1991, the Nobel Peace Prize was given to Daw Aung San Suu Kyi (1945–), the daughter of U Aung San. As an opposition leader, she has been under house arrest since July 1989.

Malaysia has a Democratic Action Party on the left.

Australia has had numerous, moderately social democratic Labour governments—from 1915 to 1923 under William M. "Billy" Hughes, from 1929 to 1931 under James H. Scullin (1876–1953), from 1941 to 1945 under John Curtin (1885–1945), from 1945 to 1949 under Joseph B. Chiefley (1885–1951), from 1972 to 1975 under Gough Whitlam (1916–), from 1983 to 1991 under Bob Hawke, and from 1991 to 1996 under Paul Keating (1924–), who was defeated by a conservative coalition headed by John Howard.

The New Zealand Labour Party, founded in 1910, at first backed the Liberal governments; but from 1935 to 1949, it was able to form its own government under Michael Joseph Savage (1872–1940). At that time, the Labour government nationalized several key industries and expanded the social welfare system. Defeated by the National Party, Labour did not return to power until 1957. Out of power again in 1960, Labour returned again in 1972 with party leader Norman Eric Kirk (1923–1974) becoming prime minister. When Kirk died in office in 1974, he was succeeded by Wallace Edward Rowling (1927–), but the Nationalists returned to office the following year. The elections of July 1984 gave control of the parliament to Labourite David Lange (1942–), who won reelection in 1987. Among the more controversial policies of the Lange government was the banning of nuclear vessels from New Zealand ports, leading the United States to end its defense commitments to New Zealand. Lange resigned in 1979 due to poor health and was replaced by Geoffrey Palmer (1942–). Infighting in the party and a decline in Palmer's popularity caused him to resign in September 1990 to be succeeded by Michael Moore (1949–). In the election of that October, the Labour Party was ousted from office by the National Party, headed by James Bolger (1935–).

The Philippines Democratic Socialist Party and the Fiji Labor Party are both consultative members of the Socialist International.

INDIA AND PAKISTAN

Since its independence in 1947, India has followed a nonaligned policy in foreign affairs, friendly to both the West and to the Soviet Bloc. India has a mixed economy, mainly privately owned; but since 1956, the official policy is that certain sectors of the economy would be entirely nationalized and others placed under public control and planning. The Indian National Congress was founded in 1885. From within its ranks came the oldest of the Socialist parties in India, the Praja Socialist Party.[9] As mass civil disobedience began to emerge in the nation in the 1930s, Socialist groups within the Indian National Congress founded the Congress Socialist Party in 1934. It played an important role in spreading the ideas of socialism within the Indian National Congress. They worked in the independence movement to free India from British colonialism. India's independence from Great Britain was achieved by 1947, the movement led by its great leader Mohandas K. Gandhi (1869–1948), the great proponent of nonviolent civil disobedience to colonialism and social equality. By 1952, the Socialists were disenchanted with the conservative direction they saw in the Indian National Congress and broke away from it to form the Socialist Party of India, calling for a democratic and decentralized form of socialism based around the idea of cooperatives. Another group of Socialists to split from the Indian National Congress in 1951 established the Kisan Mazdoor Praja Party. These two groups united in 1952 to form the Praja Socialist Party (PSP). Dr. Rammanohar Lohia also formed a Socialist party in 1955. That year, the Indian National Congress (or Congress Party) was to declare its socialistic aims at its Madras meeting under Prime Minister Jawaharlal Nehru (1889–1964), as it did under his successors, including his daughter Indira Gandhi (1917–1984). What they had in mind was a mixed economy in which large sections of the economy would remain privately owned. The Praja Socialist Party merged in 1964 with the Lohia Socialist Party to form the Samyukta Socialist Party (SSP). Some of the Praja Socialists reformed their own party, whereas many followed Ashok Mehta into the Indian National Congress. Mehta became a member of Indira Gandhi's cabinet as minister of planning. After 1957 the PSP declined. Today, the Praja Socialist Party and the Samyukta Socialist Party are strong only in the Hindi-speaking areas. The SSP is more militant than the PSP and is noted for its criticism of the use of English as an official language of India. In 1977 the Indian National Congress, which had supplied all of India's prime ministers since independence, was then unable to do so. A breakaway from the Congress Party, called the Indian National Congress-Organization (or Congress-O), founded in 1969, joined in 1977 with three other parties—the Socialist Party, the Bharatiya Jana Sangh, and the Bharatiya Lok Dal—to form the Janata Party. In March 1977 the Janata Party won half of the seats in parliament; and its head, Morarji R. Desai, replaced Indira Gandhi as prime minister. The daughter of Jawaharlal Nehru, who was the first prime minister and one of the founders of modern India, Indira Gandhi had been prime minister since 1966, and her rule had become increasingly corrupt and oppressive over the years. In May 1977 the Janata Party merged with the Congress for Democracy and thus achieved a majority in the parliament. The following year, the Congress Party split again, and Indira Gandhi formed her own faction, called the Indian Congress-Indira (or Congress-I) Party. The Congress-I Party swept back into power in 1980, and Gandhi resumed office as prime minister. The Congress-I Party retained its parliamentary majority throughout the 1980s.

Indira Gandhi was assassinated by Sikh members of her own personal guard on October 31, 1984, following the armed occupation of the Golden Temple at Amritsar, the holiest shrine in the Sikh religion and the center of the Sikh autonomy movement in the Punjab. Her son, Rajiv Gandhi (1944–1991), was sworn in as prime minister, following Hindu riots in New Delhi and other cities that killed a thousand Sikhs.

Rajiv Gandhi's government was soon faced with one of the worst industrial accidents in history. On December 3, 1984, a methyl isocyanate gas leak at the Union Carbide plant in Bhopal killed over 3,330 people and caused severe illness in an additional 20,000 people. Rajiv Gandhi continued to face Sikh unrest in the Punjab. This was not the only armed movement his government faced. In 1987 his government sent Indian troops to Sri Lanka to put down a rebellion by Tamil guerrilla forces. Despite an agreement signed that July, the armed struggle with Tamil goes on.

Charges of mismanagement and corruption in his government, as well as continuing armed struggle in the Punjab and in the Kashmir region of India, caused the Congress-I Party to lose its parliamentary majority in the elections of November 1989. Vishwanath Pratap Singh (1931–), the leader of the Janata Dal Party, was then elected prime minister. A short-lived government, it fell in 1990 when a split occurred in the party.

Briefly, Changra Shekhar (1927–) was chosen as prime minister, but he stepped down in 1991. In the ensuing election, Rajiv Gandhi was assassinated by a bomb blast in May 1991; and P. V. Narasimha Rao (1921–), a former foreign minister and the new leader of the Congress-I Party, was elected prime minister that year, defeating the Janata Dal, the largest party in the National Front coalition opposed to the continuing rule of the Congress-I Party. The Bharatiya Janata Party (BJP, the Indian People's Party), a right-wing, Hindu nationalist party, briefly formed a government after the May 1996 elections, but then a United Front coalition formed their own government under H. D. Deve Gowda of Janata Dal. The current prime minister is Atal Bihari Vajpayee of BJP, who was elected in 1998. The BJP has somewhat cooled its nationalist rhetoric in order to form a coalition with other parties because it only held a plurality, not a majority of seats, in the parliament. His government conducted nuclear tests, as has rival Pakistan, and has gone to war with Pakistan in 1999.

Nepal also has a Congress Party.

The Pakistan People's Party (PPP) is a consultative party in the Socialist International. Zulfikar Ali Bhutto (1928–1979), its leader, was elected prime minister when Pakistan lost East Pakistan, which became the independent nation of Bangladesh in 1971 with the intervention of India in the civil war. Bhutto nationalized banks and industries. He was ousted by a military coup in 1977 and hanged on the charges of committing political murder in 1979. His daughter, Benazir Bhutto (1953–), led the PPP to victory in 1988. She was the first woman prime minister in an Islamic state, only to be charged with corruption and abuse of power and dismissed from office in 1990.

THE AFRICAN SOCIALIST STATES

There are numerous African states that have socialist governments. Although opposed to Marxism-Leninism and South African apartheid, these sometimes have been one-party states. Among them are Kenya under the leadership of Jomo Kenyatta (1891?–1978), Senegal under Léopold Sédar Senghor (1906–), Tanzania under Julius K. Nyerere (1922–1999), and Zimbabwe under Robert Mugabe. In Tanzania, which became independent from British colonial rule in 1961, African socialism was based on the African traditions of *ujamaa* (Swahili for "familyhood").[10] Peasant farmers were relocated to *ujamaa* villages in the 1970s. This disrupted traditional communal life. Local chiefs who had settled community conflicts were replaced by distant bureaucrats. After twenty-five years this experiment with the *ujamaa* philosophy was abandoned in Tanzania as the nation turned to a market economy. However, tremendous problems remain with land shortages, lack of fertility, and infant mortality. And old women accused of being witches are being murdered in order to get the land they own in northwestern Tanzania in the Shingyanga region, which is experiencing a boom in gold, diamond, and semiprecious stone mining.

In 1960, the Social Democratic Party's candidate and founder Philibert Tsiranana (1910–1978) was elected as president of Madagascar. One of the outstanding African Socialists was Senegal's Léopold Sédar Senghor, who became president in 1963. In Kenya, Jomo Kenyatta, elected as president in 1964, stood as a major leader of African socialists. Burkina Faso, Cameroon, Cape Verde, Equatorial Guinea, Gabon, Mali, Mauritius, and Niger also have social democratic parties. In terms of economics, the African socialist nations have put a high priority on establishing networks of agricultural cooperatives, village industries, some state ownership of national industries, joint state-private ownership in others, and state economic planning and social services.[11]

THE ARAB SOCIALIST STATES

One Arab socialist nation includes Algeria under National Liberation Front (FLN) government Ahmed Ben Bella (1919–), who was overthrown by Hourari Boumedienne (1932?–1978) and succeeded in turn by Colonel Chadli Benjedid (1929–) and Mohammed Boudiaff. Another Arab socialist nation is Libya under Colonel Muammar Gadhafi (1942–). Egypt was another example under the Arab Socialist Union and Gamal Abdel Nasser (1918–1970) and his successors Anwar al-Sadat, who was assassinated in 1981, and Hosni Mubarak ((1928–) and the National Democratic Party. Syria has been an Arab socialist nation under the Baath Arab Socialist Party founded in 1946 by Dr. Michael Alfaq and the government of General Hafiz al-Assad (1928–), who seized power in 1970 and has ruled ever since. Iraq too has been ruled by the Arab Baath Socialist Party and, since 1979, under General Saddam Hussein (1937–). The last example of an Arab socialist society is Southern Yemen, which since 1990 has been reunited with Northern Yemen. Like the African socialist nations, the Arab socialist states have often been one-party dictatorships, frequently battling conservative Islamic organizations and other internal opponents. Generally, they have mixed economies involving varying amounts of state, private capitalist, and cooperative ownership.[12]

However, perhaps the most important distinguishing characteristic of Arab socialism is a strong component of Arab nationalism—the belief that all Arabs should unite into a pan-Arab union and fight the state of Israel. Egypt formed a union with Syria in 1958 called the United Arab Republic (UAR), but it lasted only three years. The Arab states have gone to war with Israel in the 1948 War of Independence, the 1956 Suez War, the 1967 Six-Day War, and the 1973 Yom Kippur War in an attempt to destroy the Jewish state, only to be repulsed each time. Having been born in wars of liberation from Western imperialism, the Arab socialist states have continued to do battle with the West from time to time, notably in the 1956 Suez War in Egypt and in the 1990 Gulf War after Iraq invaded Kuwait and was defeated by a combined multinational force led by the United States. Israel, however, in recent years has moved to make peace with at least some of the Arab socialist and conservative states and movements, first with Sadat's Egyptian government in 1979 and then with the Palestinians in the mid-1990s.

Lebanon, Morocco, Tunisia, and Turkey all have social democratic parties.

ISRAEL

Although many Third World nations have developed forms of socialism that, while not totalitarian Communist, cannot be considered to be democratic socialist (but rather something in between), the developing nation that has gone farthest in creating a genuinely democratic socialism is the state of Israel.[13]

The Israel Labor Party began with the Mapai Party (Mifleget Poalei Eretz Yisrael, or The Workers' Party of Israel), founded in Tel Aviv at a conference held January 5 to 7, 1933. Among the participants was David Ben-Gurion (1886–1973), one of the founders of the state of Israel and its first prime minister. Mapai's ideology was a mix of Zionist nationalism and democratic socialism. It called for not only a return of worldwide Jewry to their ancestral homeland, but also a "return to the soil," as Jews had often been denied the right to own land and to be farmers in countries in which they had come to live in during the Diaspora. Three kinds of land ownership developed in Israel, two of which are socialist in nature. In the *kibbutz*, or collective settlement, farm families live in communally owned dwellings and share equally in the work and profits. In the *moshav ovidim*, or cooperative villages, farms are owned and worked individually but the produce is pooled and sold by the villages acting as marketing cooperatives. The third form is capitalistic, the *moshava*, or smallholders' settlement, in which land is privately owned and operated. The kibbutzim and moshav ovidim were established on land belonging to colonizing organizations, especially the Jewish National Fund, and then leased to the farmers.

The General Federation of Labor, or *Histradrut*, is one of the most innovative labor unions to be found anywhere in the world. Histradrut is more than a labor union to represent workers' demands with employers. It is itself one of the largest employers in the nation, owning a large number of industrial and commercial enterprises. Histradrut also established numerous consumers', producers', and marketing cooperatives and a network of schools, hospitals, and clinics.[14] Mapai's influence on Histradrut has been a guiding force, helping it to develop along socialist lines. Mapai was also very influential on the wider Zionist movement, and it is largely responsible for the decision to declare Israeli independence on May 14, 1948.

On declaring independence, Israel was plunged into war when the following day the armies of Egypt, Jordan, Lebanon, and Syria attacked. Failing to "drive the Jews into the sea" and to destroy the fledgling Jewish state, an armistice was arranged by the United Nations.

Mapai headed the Provisional State Council during the War for Independence and afterward organized Israel's first election to its parliament, or *Knesset*. The first government chosen by the Knesset was a coalition government of Mapai along with the United Religious Front and smaller, centrist parties. David Ben-Gurion, Mapai's leader, became the prime minister, and renowned Zionist leader Chaim Weizman became president.

Of course, much of the effort of the government of Israel had to focus on defense. In 1956, the Suez-Sinai War erupted when Egypt banned Israeli ships from using the Suez Canal and blockaded the Strait of Tiran, which had been Israel's access to the Red Sea. Border incidents escalated until full-scale war broke out. Britain and France joined the war effort against Egypt because the Nasser government had recently nationalized the Suez Canal. Israeli military forces captured the Gaza Strip and the Sinai Peninsula from Egypt and had reached the banks of the Suez Canal. The fighting was halted by the United Nations, which sent an emergency force to supervise a cease-fire in the canal zone and forced the Israelis, the British, and the French to withdraw.

On the domestic side, the Labor governments were faced with the interesting question of how responsibilities would be divided between government agencies and that of the Histradrut. During the 1950s, at the request of the Histradrut labor federation, the government assumed responsibility for the educational, labor exchange, and water supply systems, which had formerly been run by the Histradrut. Other services followed this turnover of Histradrut-administered programs to the government in the 1960s.

The Ben-Gurion government was attacked in the late 1950s by parties to the left of Mapai for selling weapons to West Germany. These criticisms led to his resignation in 1959. However, he agreed to stay on as head of a coalition government, which turned out to last until 1963 when again Ben-Gurion resigned.

Mapai, still the leading party, chose former finance minister Levi Eshkol (1895–1969) as the new prime minister. The following year Ben-Gurion announced that he was preparing a report on a ten-year-old scandal called the "Lavon affair." This was about alleged blunders in espionage operations involving former defense minister Pinhas Lavon (1904–1976). The attorney general agreed to the request by Ben-Gurion for a full judicial inquiry, over the objections of Eshkol. Ben-Gurion then appealed to the central committee of Mapai; but before they could act, Eshkol resigned. However, the Knesset voted to restore Eshkol to office, and his new cabinet refused to further investigate the Lavon affair.

Ben-Gurion continued to quarrel with Eshkol over the Lavon affair and also over Eshkol's "alignment" policy of fusion of Mapai with the smaller and more left-wing, socialist and doctrinaire party, Achdut Ha'Avoda. At the tenth convention of Mapai in February 1965, the issues of the Lavon affair and the alignment policy came to a head.

The Mapai convention voted to support Prime Minister Eshkol on both issues. Also, the convention refused to agree to proportional representation of the minority in the party's governing bodies. This led to a split in which Ben-Gurion formed his own rival organization called Rafi.

Later that year in the November elections, the Labor Alignment of Mapai and Achdut Ha'Avoda won a landslide victory in the parliamentary elections, capturing forty-five seats in the Knesset to Rafi Party's mere ten seats. Prime Minister Eshkol then proceeded to form a broad coalition government.

The Six-Day War in 1967 began with the massing of troops from several Arab countries on Israel's borders and with Egypt's closing of the Straits of Tiran. Furthermore, Nasser insisted that the United Nations' emergency force, which was sent to guard the cease-fire at the Suez Canal zone in the aftermath of the 1956 Suez-Sinai War, be withdrawn. Israel responded with a preemptive strike on Egypt, Jordan, and Syria on June 5, 1967, which ended six days later in total Israeli victory. The Six-Day War left Israel in possession of the Gaza Strip and the Sinai Peninsula captured from Egypt, the West Bank of the Jordan River and East Jerusalem captured from Jordan, and the Golan Heights captured from Syria.

The following year, on January 21, 1968, Mapai, Achdut Ha'Avoda, and Rafi united to form the Labor Party. The Labor government was left with the problem of what to do with the Occupied Territories, as they became known, captured in the Six-Day War. There was an upsurge in Palestinian nationalism following the war, with the formation of the Palestine Liberation Organization (PLO) and other groups that waged a terrorist campaign against the Israeli occupiers.

Nothing was settled with the Arabs. In 1973 Egypt and Syria attempted to recapture the lands lost to Israel in the Six-Day War. Striking on October 6, 1973, which was Yom Kippur, the holiest day in the Jewish calendar, the attack caught Israel by surprise. After three weeks of fighting and many casualties, Israel was able to contain the Arab armies in the Yom Kippur War. Criticism of the handling of the problem of the Occupied Territories by the Labor government of Golda Meir (1898–1978), who had succeeded Eshkol as prime minister in 1969, led to her resignation in 1974. She was succeeded by Labor's Yitzhak Rabin (1922–1995).

The Rabin government was faced with a deteriorating economy, and it was hurt by charges that Rabin and other Labor ministers had been involved in illegal financial dealings. In 1977, the Labor Alignment of Labor and allied parties was defeated in the parliamentary election. Manechem Begin (1913–1992) of the rival, conservative Likud Party and its bloc won the election, and Begin became the new prime minister.

Begin's conservative economic policies were no better at stemming inflation or economic decline, much of it due to Israel's very high defense spending. His most significant success, however, came in the field of foreign diplomacy, when Nasser's successor, Anwar Sadat, flew to Jerusalem in November 1977 to address the Knesset and call for peace talks between Egypt and Israel. On U.S. President Jimmy Carter's invitation, a peace treaty was hammered out at Camp David, Maryland; and on March 26, 1979, the Camp David Accords were signed in Washington. The peace treaty formally ended the state of war between Egypt and Israel, and the Sinai was returned to Egypt. However, on the West Bank and the Gaza Strip, the fighting between the Israeli occupiers and the Palestinians grew worse, as the Likud government encouraged Israeli settlements in the Occupied Territories. In 1982 Israel launched an invasion of Lebanon with the aim of wiping out PLO guerrillas there; and after intensive fighting in and around Beirut, the PLO forces agreed to withdraw from the city. Israel established a security zone in Southern Lebanon. It was a costly operation, further weakening the Israeli economy. Begin resigned in 1983 and was succeeded by Likud's Yitzhak Shamir (1914–), the foreign minister. An election in July 1984 proved inconclusive, and a coalition government of Labor and Likud was formed. Shimon Peres (1923–), the leader of the Labor Party, served as prime minister for two years, followed by Shamir under this arrangement.

The uprising of rock-throwing Palestinian youth, called the *intifada*, in the Occupied Territories and the harsh measures that the Israeli government used to try to suppress it brought condemnation down on Israel from the world community. It also started a shift in Israeli public opinion, which had become increasingly weary of the endless fighting. Rejecting Likud's hardline stance, the Labor-Likud coalition government collapsed in 1989. Shamir headed a caretaker government, which faced a Scud missile attack on Israel by Iraq during the Persian Gulf War. It was the PLO's support for Iraq, which had seized Kuwait in this war, that alienated their traditionally Arab allies; and disappearing financial support pushed them to make a settlement with Israel before their movement might collapse.

Peace talks between Israeli and the Palestinians began in October 1991, and Likud's loss to Labor and the formation of a government more predisposed to make peace under Rabin in June 1992 paved the way for a formal end of hostilities between Israel and the PLO. On September 10, 1993, Israel and the PLO formally recognized each other. The Israelis would grant the PLO the right to rule in Gaza and eventually in the entire West Bank. However, the question of an independent Palestinian state was put off for five years before being permanently settled. This historic agreement went into effect on March 4, 1994. PLO leader Yasir Arafat (1929–), deserves much of the credit for the peace agreement, along with Rabin and Peres.

There are many obstacles yet to be overcome, not the least of which is opposition to the peace process by both Islamic fundamentalist movements, such as Hamas, and right-wing Israelis. The Islamic fundamentalists kept up a terrorist campaign of suicide bombings designed to derail the peace process, while a right-wing Jewish law student, Yigal Amir, assassinated prime minister Yitzhak Rabin just after speaking at a peace rally in Tel Aviv on November 4, 1995. His successor Shimon Peres attempted to carry out the peace process under these most difficult circumstances, but he was defeated in a reelection bid under a new system of direct election of the prime minister in the election of May 29, 1996, by the conservative Likud Party's Benjamin Netanyahu (1949–). The center-right Likud Party is a coalition of the Likud proper with Raful Eitan's secular nationalist party Tsomet and David Levy's recently created party, Gesher, which calls itself a "Social-National Movement." Labor was in an electoral alliance in this election with the left-secular Meretz Party, which includes the radical democratic socialist Mapam (Mifleget Poalim Me'ehedet, or the United Workers' Party), Ratz, and Shinui parties, to the left of the Labor Party. Among other left-wing parties are the United Arab List, which includes the Democratic Arab Party, Israeli's Islamic Movement, and the Arab Islamic List, and the communist Hadash (Hebrew for "New," or the Democratic Front for Peace and Equality). There are numerous other smaller secular and religious parties that exist largely due to Israel's system of proportional representation in parliamentary elections. On May 17, 1999, Ehud Barak of the One Israel Party won election as prime minister of Israel. The Fatah in the Occupied Territories is a consultative member of the Socialist International.

The Jewish Labor Bund and the World Labor Zionist Movement are among the associated organizations of the London-based Socialist International with seventy-six full-member parties. There are also associated organizations among Asian and Pacific socialists, Western and Eastern European Socialists, the Socialist press, religious Socialists, Socialist educators, and those involved in sports. The Socialist International's fraternal organizations are the Socialist Educational International, International Union of Socialist Youth, and the Socialist International Women. The Socialist International also has numerous consultative and observer parties, not all of whom are social democratic. Together they have given global democratic socialism a bright future.

NOTES

1. Harry W. Laidler, *History of Socialism* (New York: Apollo, 1968), pp. 833–842.
2. Ibid., pp. 841–842.
3. Lucian W. Pye, *China—an Introduction*, 3d ed. (Boston: Little, Brown, 1984), pp. 142–144.
4. James R. Townsend, *Politics in China* (Boston: Little, Brown, 1974), pp. 101–102.
5. Chang Kuo-t'ao, *The Rise of the Chinese Communist Party—1921–1927* (Lawrence, KS: The University Press of Kansas, 1971), p. 43.
6. A. Doak Barnett, *China on the Eve of Communist Takeover* (New York: Praeger, 1963), p. 89.
7. Laidler, *History of Socialism*, p. 842.
8. Ibid., pp. 838–841.
9. Ibid., pp. 836–838.
10. Julius K. Nyerere, *Uhuru na Ujamaa—Freedom and Socialism* (Oxford: Oxford University Press, 1968), pp. 2–3; *Philadelphia Inquirer*, August 15, 1999, p. A7.
11. Fenner Brockway, *African Socialism* (London: Bodley Head, 1963); Laidler, *History of Socialism*, pp. 847–854.
12. James D. Forman, *Socialism —Its Theoretical Roots and Present-day Development* (New York: Dell, 1972), pp. 58–61.
13. Laidler, *History of Socialism*, pp. 842–847.
14. Forman, *Socialism*, pp. 57–58.

Bibliography

Adelson, Alan. *SDS—A Profile*. New York: Scribner, 1972.

Ader, Emile B. *Socialism*. Woodbury, NY: Barron's Educational Series, 1966.

"Aims and tasks of democratic socialism" (often called the Frankfurt Declaration). In, *Modern Socialism*, ed. Massimo Salvadori. New York: Harper Torchbooks, 1968.

Armstrong, Robert, and Janet Shenk. *El Salvador—The Face of Revolution*. Boston: South End Press, 1982.

Avineri, Shlomo. *The Social and Political Thought of Karl Marx*. Cambridge: Cambridge University Press, 1968.

Baradat, Leon P. *Political Ideologies—Their Origin and Impact,* 2d ed. Englewood Cliffs, NJ: Prentice-Hall, 1984.

Barnett, A. Doak. *China on the Eve of Communist Takeover*. New York: Praeger, 1963.

Bedarida, Francois. *A Social History of England 1851–1975*. London: Metheun, 1979.

Beer, M. *A History of British Socialism*. 2 vols. New York: Harcourt, Brace and Howe, 1921.

Berki, R. N. *Socialism*. New York: St. Martin's, 1975.

Bermann, Karl. *Under the Big Stick—Nicaragua and the United States since 1848*. Boston: South End Press, 1986.

Bernstein, Eduard. *Evolutionary Socialism*. New York: Schocken, 1961.

Blatchford, Robert. *Merrie England*. New York: Monthly Review Press, 1966.

Bose, Atindranath. *A History of Anarchism*. Calcutta: The World Press Private Ltd., 1967.

Brand, Carl F. *The British Labour Party—A Short History.* Stanford, CA: Stanford University Press, 1964.

Brockway, Fenner. *African Socialism.* London: Bodley Head, 1963.

Brown, Kenneth D. *The First Labour Party 1905–1914.* London: Croom Helm, 1985.

Buber, Martin. *Paths in Utopia.* London: Routledge, 1949.

Campbell, Alastair. *Mondragon 1980.* Los Angeles: CRSP, 1982.

Cantor, Milton. *The Divided Left—American Radicalism, 1900–1975.* New York: Hill and Wang, 1978.

Capra, Fritjof, and Charlene Spretnak. *Green Politics—The Global Promise.* New York: Dutton, 1984.

Chang, Kuo-t'ao. *The Rise of the Chinese Communist Party—1921–1927.* Lawrence, KS: The University Press of Kansas, 1971.

Cole, G. D. H. *A History of Socialist Thought.* 5 vols. New York: St. Martin's, 1953–1958.

Commons, John R., and Associates. *History of Labor in the United States.* 2 vols. New York: Macmillan, 1918.

Connolly, James. *Socialism Made Easy.* Dublin: The Labour Party, 1972.

Cook, Chris, and Ian Taylor, eds. *The Labour Party—An Introduction to Its History, Structure, and Politics.* London: Longman, 1980.

Cowden, Morton H. "Early Marxist Views on British Labor, 1837–1917," *The Western Political Science Quarterly* 11 (1963): 34–52.

Curl, John. *History of Work Cooperation in America.* Berkeley, CA: Homeward Press, 1980.

Democratic Federation. *Socialism Made Plain.* London: W. Reeves, 1883.

Douglas, T. C. *Canadians Find Security.* New York: League for Industrial Democracy, 1949.

Dowse, Robert E. *The Left in the Centre, the Independent Labour Party 1893–1940.* Evanston, IL: Northwestern University Press, 1960.

Durbin, Elizabeth. *New Jerusalem, The Labour Party and the Economics of Democratic Socialism.* London: Routledge and Kegan Paul, 1985.

Duverger, Maurice. *Political Parties.* New York: Wiley, 1955.

Edwards, David V. *The American Political Experience—An Introduction to Government.* 4th ed. Englewood Cliffs, NJ: Prentice Hall, 1988.

Ellis, Harry B. *Ideals and Ideologies—Communism, Socialism, and Capitalism.* New York: Mentor, 1972.

Engels, Friedrich. *On Britain.* Moscow: Foreign Languages Publishing House, 1953.

Engels, Friedrich. *The Condition of the Working Class in England in 1844.* London: Allen and Unwin, 1892.

Fabian Tracts. Nendeln, Liechtenstein: Kraus-Thomson, 1969.

Flexer, Joe. "Canadians' Unions Face Political Crisis—Labor-Backed NDP Nearly Wiped Out in Federal Elections." *Labor Notes* (December 1983).

Foote, Geoffrey. *The Labour Party's Political Thought—A History.* London: Croom Helm, 1985.

Forman, James D. *Socialism—Its Theoretical Roots and Present-day Development.* New York: Dell, 1972.

Fremantle, Anne. *This Little Band of Prophets: The British Fabians.* New York: Mentor, 1960.

Fried, Albert, and Ronald Sanders, eds. *Socialist Thought—A Documentary History.* Garden City, NY: Doubleday, Anchor Books, 1964.

Gay, Peter. *The Dilemma of Democratic Socialism—Eduard Bernstein's Challenge to Marx.* New York: Collier, 1962.

Ginger, Ray. *Eugene V. Debs: A Biography.* New York: Collier Books, 1962. Originally published as *The Bending Cross, a Biography of Eugene Victor Debs.* New Brunswick, NJ: Rutgers University Press, 1949.

Gould, Frederick J. *Hyndman—Prophet of Socialism, 1842–1921.* London: George Allen and Unwin, 1928.

Greaves, Richard L., Robert Zaller, and Jennifer Tolbert Roberts. *Civilizations of the West—the Human Adventure.* New York: HarperCollins, 1992.

Greene, Felix. *The Enemy—What Every American Should Know about Imperialism.* New York: Vintage, 1971.

Hale, Vincent E., and Sharon Skowronski, eds. *The Greenwood Historical Encyclopedia of the World's Political Parties—Political Parties of Europe.* Westport, CT: Greenwood Press, 1983.

Halperin, Morton H., Jerry J. Berman, Robert L. Borosage, and Christine M. Marwick. *The Lawless State, the Crimes of the U.S. Intelligence Agencies.* New York: Penguin, 1976.

Hardie, James Keir. *From Serfdom to Socialism.* ed. Robert E. Dowse. Rutherford, NJ: Fairleigh Dickinson University Press, 1974.

Harrington, Michael. *Socialism.* New York: Bantam, 1973.

Hobsbawn, E. J. *Labouring Men, Studies in the History of Labour.* London: Weidenfeld Nicolson, 1964.

Hughes, Emrys. *Keir Hardie's Speeches and Writings—from 1888–1915.* Glasgow: Forward, 1928.

Hunnius, Gerry, G. David Garson, and John Case, eds. *Workers' Control—a Reader on Labor and Social Change*. New York: Vintage, 1973.

Hyndman, Henry Mayers, and William Morris. *A Summary of the Principles of Socialism*. 1884. Reprint, London: Modern Press, 1984.

Hyndman, Henry Mayers. *England for All: The Text-Book of Democracy*. London: Gilbert and Rivington, 1881.

Hyndman, Henry Mayers. *Further Reminiscences*. London: Macmillan, 1912.

Hyndman, Henry Mayers. *The Historical Basis of Socialism in England*. London: K. Paul, Trench & Co. 1883. Reprint, New York: Garland, 1984.

Hyndman, Henry Mayers. *The Record of an Adventurous Life*. New York: Macmillan, 1911. Reprint, New York: Garland, 1984.

Jaurès, Jean. "Idealism in History." In *Socialist Thought—A Documentary History*, Albert Fried and Ronald Sanders, eds. Garden City, NY: Doubleday, Anchor Books, 1964.

Kallscheuer, Otto. "Philosophy and Politics in the SPD," *Telos* 53 (Fall 1982): 83.

Key, V. O. *Politics, Parties, and Pressure Groups*. 5th ed. New York: Crowell, 1964.

Knox, William. *Lives of the Left—James Maxton*. Manchester, UK: Manchester University Press, 1987.

Kolakowski, Leszek. *Main Currents of Marxism*. 3 vols. Trans. P. S. Falla. Oxford: Oxford University Press, 1978.

Labor Party Advocate. (Washington, DC) 2, no. 8 (December 1995): 1.

Laidler, Harry W. *History of Socialism*. New York: Apollo, 1968.

Lens, Sidney. *Radicalism in America*. Rev. ed. Cambridge, MA: Schenkman, 1982.

Lerner, Warren. *A History of Socialism and Communism in Modern Times: Theorists, Activists, and Humanists*. Englewood Cliffs, NJ: Prentice-Hall, 1982.

LeRossignol, James Edward. *Backgrounds to Communist Thought—from Marx to Stalin*. New York: Crowell, 1968.

Lewis, Gordon R. "Fabian Socialism; Some Aspects of Theory and Practice." *The Journal of Politics* 14 (August 1950): 442-470.

Linton, Martin. "The Swedish Road to Socialism." In *Fabian Tracts*, No. 503. London: Fabian Society, 1985.

Luxemburg, Rosa. *Leninism or Marxism?* Trans. Ken Eaton. Leeds, UK: I.L.P. Square One Publications, 1971. Originally titled "Organizational Questions of Russian Social Democracy," *Die Neue Zeit* 22(2) (Stuttgart 1904): 484–492, 529–535.

MacKenzie, Norman, and Jeanne MacKenzie. *The First Fabians*. London: Weidenfeld and Nicolson, 1977.

Madison, James. "Federalist Paper No. 10." In *The Federalist Papers*, ed. Clinton Rossiter. New York: Mentor, 1961.

Magid, Henry H. "John Stuart Mill." In *History of Political Philosophy*, 2d ed., Leo Strauss and Joseph Cropsey, eds. Chicago: University of Chicago Press, 1981.

Marx, Karl, and Friedrich Engels. *Marx-Engels Werke*. Berlin: Dietz Verlag, 1957–1967.

McBriar, A. M. *Fabian Socialism and English Politics 1884–1918*. Cambridge: Cambridge University Press, 1966.

McLellan, David. *Karl Marx: Selected Writings*. Oxford: Oxford University Press, 1977.

Milburn, Josephine Fishel. "The Fabian Society and the British Labour Party," *The Western Political Quarterly* 11 (1958): 319–339.

Mill, John Stuart. *Principles of Political Economy*. 1848. Reprinted in *Collected Works of John Stuart Mill*, 2 vols. Toronto: University of Toronto Press, 1965.

Moore, Roger. *The Emergence of the Labour Party, 1880–1924*. London: Hodder and Stoughton, 1978.

Nairn, Allan. "Behind the Death Squads." *The Progressive* 48 (May 1984): 20–29.

Nyerere, Julius K. *Uhuru na Ujamaa—Freedom and Socialism*. Oxford: Oxford University Press, 1968.

Parenti, Michael. *Democracy for the Few*. 5th ed. New York: St. Martin's, 1988.

Pateman, Carole. *Participation and Democratic Theory*. Cambridge: Cambridge University Press, 1970.

Pease, Edward R. *The History of the Fabian Society*. London: Allen and Unwin, 1925.

Pelling, Henry. *The Origins of the Labour Party 1880–1924*. London: Macmillan, 1954.

Petersen, Arnold. *Bourgeois Socialism: Its Rise and Collapse in America*. New York: New York Labor News Co., 1963.

Pierson, Stanley. *British Socialism—The Journey from Fantasy to Politics*. Cambridge, MA: Harvard University Press, 1979.

Poirier, Philip. *The Advent of the British Labour Party*. New York: Columbia University Press, 1978.

Porritt, Jonathon. *Seeing Green—the Politics of Ecology Explained*. New York: Basil Blackwell, 1985.

Pye, Lucian W. *China—an Introduction*. 3d ed. Boston: Little, Brown, 1984.

Rappoport, Angelo S. *Dictionary of Socialism*. London: Adelphi Terrace, 1924.

Reid, Fred. *Keir Hardie—the Making of a Socialist*. London: Croom Helm, 1978.

Reid, J. H. Steward. *The Origins of the British Labour Party*. Minneapolis: University of Minnesota Press, 1955.

Rothman, Stanley, Howard Scarrow, and Martin Schain. *European Society and Politics: Britain, France, and Germany*. St. Paul, MN: West Publishing, 1976.

Sale, Kirkpatrick. *SDS*. New York: Vintage, 1974.

Schlesinger, Arthur M. Jr. *The Cycles of American History*. Boston: Houghton Mifflin, 1986.

Shaw, George Bernard. *Bernard Shaw and Karl Marx: A Symposium*. New York: Random House, 1930.

Shaw, George Bernard, ed. *Fabian Essays*. London: Allen and Unwin, 1948.

Shaw, George Bernard. *The Intelligent Woman's Guide to Socialism and Capitalism*. 2 vols. London: Pelican, 1937.

Simkhovich, V. G. *Marxism vs. Socialism*. New York: Henry Holt, 1913.

Socialist Industrial Unionism—The Workers' Power. New York: New York Labor News, 1974.

Sombart, Werner. *Socialism and the Social Movement*. London: J. M. Dent, 1909.

Sombart, Werner. *Warum gibt es in den Vereinigten Staaten keiner Sozialismus?* Tubingen: Mohr, 1906.

Sorge, Friedrich Albert, et al. *Briefe und Auszuge as Briefen von Joh. Phil. Becker, Jos. Dietzgen, Friedrich Engels, Karl Marx*. Ed. F. A. Sorge. Stuttgart: J. H. W. Dietz, 1906.

Stewart, William. *J. Keir Hardie—a Biography*. London: Independent Labour Party, 1921.

Swomley, John M., Jr. *The American Empire—the Political Ethics of Twentieth-Century Conquest*. New York: Macmillan, 1970.

Tokar, Brian. *The Green Alternative—Creating an Ecological Future*. San Pedro, CA: R. & E. Miles, 1987.

Townsend, James R. *Politics in China*. Boston: Little, Brown, 1974.

Tsuzuki, Chushichi. *H. M. Hyndman and British Socialism*. Oxford: Oxford University Press, 1961.

Tucker, R. W. *Rise and Decline among the Reds*. Philadelphia: Privately published by the author R. W. Tucker, limited edition, 1991.

Tucker, R. W. *The Debs Caucus: A Party within a Party.* Milwaukee: Socialist Party of Wisconsin, 1970. Reprint, *The Socialist Party—Bibliography and History.* New York: Socialist Party, USA, 1988.

Voorhis, Jerry. *Cooperative Enterprise: The Little People's Chance in a World of Bigness.* Danville, IL: Interstate Printers and Publishers, 1975.

Webb, Beatrice. *Our Partnership.* London: Longmans, Green, 1948.

Webb, Sidney. *Socialism in England.* London: Swann Sonnenschein, 1890.

Webb, Sidney, and Beatrice Webb. *A Constitution for the Socialist Commonwealth of Great Britain.* London: Longmans, Green, 1920.

Weinstein, James. *The Decline of American Socialism.* New York: Monthly Review Press, 1967.

Wells, H. G. *The New Machiavelli.* London: John Lane, The Bodley House, 1911.

Williams, Francis. "The Program of the British Labour Party—an Historical Survey." *The Journal of Politics* 12 (1950): 189–210.

Zeidler, Frank P. *Ninety Years of Democratic Socialism: A Brief History of the Socialist Party, USA.* New York: Socialist Party, USA, 1991.

Index

Achdut Ha'Avoda, 211
Adler, Friedrich, 52
Adler, Victor, 52
African Socialist States, 207–8
Alfaq, Michael, 208
Algeria, 208
Algerian National Liberation Front, 208
Allende Gossens, Salvador, 195–7
American Labor Party, 162
American Popular Revolutionary Alliance, 194
Anarchism, collectivist, 5; communist, 5, 105; Fabian views of, 93–94; philosophical 6; social, 4–5; syndicalist, 5, 63; terroristic, 6
Andrés Pérez, Carlos, 192
Anti-Socialist Laws, 18
Appeal to Reason, 155
Arab Socialist States, 208–9
Arab Socialist Union, 208
Arbenz Guzman, Jacobo, 179–180
Arévalo, Juan José, 179
Argentina, 197–8
Aristide, Jean-Bertrand, 190
Asian Socialist Conference, 203
Assad, Hafiz al-, 208
Attlee, Clement Richard, 123
Australia, 204
Australian Labour Party, 204
Austria, 51–55

Austrian Social Democratic Party, 51–55
Autogestion, 33
Aveling, Edward, 110

Baath Arab Socialist Party, 208
Bad Godesberg Conference, 23–24
Bakunin, Mikhail, 5
Baldvinsson, Jón, 71
Barak, Ehud, 213
Bax, Ernest Belfort, 84
Bebel, August, 17
Begin, Manechem, 212
Belgian Labor Party, 46–48
Belgium, 46–48
Bella, Ahmed Ben, 208
Bellamy, Edward, 154
Ben-Gurion, David, 209–211
Benn, Anthony Wedgwood, 127
Benson, Allan L., 156
Bérégovoy, Pierre, 33
Berger, Victor, 154–5, 159, 161
Berlinguer, Enrico, 60
Berlin Shop Stewards, 20
Bernstein, Eduard, 18–19, 92. Work: *Evolutionary Socialism,* 19
Besant, Annie, 94, 98
Betancourt, Rómulo, 191
Bevan, Aneurin, 124
Bhutto, Benazir, 207
Bhutto, Zulfikar Ali, 207

Bishop, Maurice, 191
Blair, Tony, 128
Blanc, Louis, 105
Bland, Hubert, 94
Blanqui, Louis Auguste, 26
Blatchford, Robert, 110, 116–7, 119–20, 154. Work: *Merrie England*, 117
Blum, Léon, 28
Bolivia, 193
Bolivian National Revolutionary Movement, 193
Bosch, Juan, 190–1
Boudin, Louis B., 156
Bourgeois, Léon-Victor-Auguste, 26
Brandt, Willy, 24
Branting, Hjalmar, 35
Bratteli, Trygve, 43
Brazil, 193
Bremen Left-Radicals, 20
Brisben, J. Quinn, 165
British Labour Party, 86–87, 100–101, 107, 114, 119, 121–128; adopts socialist program, 121
British Social and Liberal Democratic Party, 126–7
British Socialist Party, 87
Broadbent, Ed, 147
Brousse, Paul, 26
Brown Shirts, 22
Brundtland, Gro Harlem, 43
Buhl, Vilhelm, 40
Burma, 203–4
Burma Socialist Party, 203
Burmese Socialist Program Party, 203
Burns, John, 84, 86

Cahan, Abraham, 162
Camacho, Manuel Ávila, 173
Canada, 143–147
Canadian Labor Congress, 145
Canadian Labor Party, 144
Canadian New Democratic Party, 145–7
Cárdenas, Lázaro, 172–4
Cárdenas Solorzano, Cuauhetmoc, 174, 176
Carlsson, Ingvar, 38
Carpenter, Edward, 116

Central American Socialist Party, 181
Cerro Rico, 193
Chamberlain, (Arthur) Neville, 122–3
Chavez, Hugo, 192
Chiefley, Joseph B., 204
Chile, 195–7
Chilean Socialist Labor Party, 195
China, 202–3
China Democratic Socialist Party, 203
Chinese Communist Party, 203
Chinese Socialist Party, 203
Churchill, Winston, 122–4
Claflin, Tennessee, 153
Claramount, Ernesto, 184
Clarke, William J., 85
Coalition Caucus, 164–5
Co-determination, 24
Coldwell, M. J., 145
Cole, George Douglas Howard, 100
Communism, 6–7, 20, 115; Bolshevik, 13; Eurocommunism, 7, 60–61; Menshevik, 13
Communist Labor Party, 159
Communist Party of America, 158
Conference for Progressive Political Action, 159-0
Conference on the Future of Democratic Socialism in America, 164
Congress Socialist Party, 205
Connolly, James, 130
Cooperative Commonwealth Federation, 144–5
Cooperatives, 11, 100–106, 175–6
Córdova Alvarez, Enrique, 186
Costa Rica, 189–190
Cowen, Joseph, 79
Craxi, Bettino, 61
Cresson, Edith, 33
Curtin, John, 204

Danish Social Democratic Party, 39–41
Davidson, Thomas, 87
Davies, Emil, 96
Debs Caucus, 118, 163–4
Debs, Eugene Victor, 153, 155, 157, 160
De Leon, Daniel, 11, 87, 143, 150–2, 154
De Man, Henri, 47

Index 225

Democracy, economic, 10–11; international, 12–13; political, 8–9; social, 8–10
Democratic Action, 191–2
Democratic Labor Party of Brazil, 193
Democratic Left of Ecuador, 194
Democratic Revolutionary Front, 186
Democratic Revolutionary Party, 174–6
Democratic Socialist Federation, 163
Democratic Socialist Organizing Committee, 118, 165
Democratic Socialist Party of Japan, 201
Democratic Socialists of America, 118, 165
Dominican Republic, 190–1
Denmark, 39–41
Desai, Morarji, 205
Dobama Assi-a-yong, or Thakin, Party, 203
Douglas, T. C., 145
Drees, Willem, 50
Dutch Labor Party, 49–50
Dutch Social Democratic Labor Party, 48–49

Ebert, Friedrich, 20–21
Ecuador, 193–4
Egypt, 208
Eisenachers, 17
Eisner, Karl, 20
Ejidos, 173
El Salvador, 181–7
Engels, Friedrich, 3, 98, 112
Environmentalism, 14
Erfurt Program, 18
Erlander, Tage, 36
Eshkol, Levi, 210–1
Espionage and Sedition Acts, 156–7
Evans, George Henry, 148

Fabian Basis, 97
Fabian Parliamentary League, 94, 98
Fabian Society, 86–107, 109, 111–3, 118–20; origin of name, 88–89; permeate Liberal Party, 97–98. Work: *To Your Tents, O Israel!*, 98
Farabundo Martí, Agustín 181
Farabundo Martí National Liberation Front, 186–7

Farmer-Labor Party, 159
Fascism, 57–59
Feminism, 13–14
Fenwick Weavers, 75
Feuerbach, Ludwig, 3
Finland, 43–46
First International, 27, 149–150, 152
France, 25–35
Fraina, Louis C., 158
French Democratic Confederation of Labor, 33
French Section of the Workers' International, 27–30
French Socialist Party, 30–35
French Workers Party, 26

Gadhafi, Muammar, 208
Gaitskell, Hugh, 124
Gallegos Freire, Rómulo, 191
Gandhi, Indira, 205–6
Gandhi, Mohandas K., 205
Gandhi, Rajiv, 206
García Pérez, Alan, 194
General Confederation of Labor, 33
General German Workingmen's Association, 17
General German Workingmen's Union, 149, 151
General Strike of 1926, 122
George, Henry, 85, 88, 150
Gerhardsen, Einar, 42
Germany, 17–25
Gitlow, Benjamin, 157
Glasion, John Bruce, 116
González Márquez, Felipe, 65
Gotha Program, 17
Great Britain, 75–129
Greece, 67–71
Greenland, 143
Green Politics, 6
Grenada, 191
Gronlund, Laurence, 154
Grütli Union, 50
Guatemala, 179–180
Guatemalan National Revolutionary Unity, 180
Guesde, Jules, 26–27
Gurion, David Ben, 209–11
Guyana, 192

Guzmán Renoso, Abimael, 195
Gysi, Gregor, 25

Hadash, 213
Haiti, 190
Hansen, H. C., 40
Hansson, Per Albin, 36
Hardie, James Keir, 91, 107–16
Harrington, Michael, 118, 163–5
Hawke, Bob, 204
Haya de la Torre, Victor Raúl, 194
Haywood, William D. "Big Bill," 155
Headlam, Stewart D., 77
Hedtoft, Hans Christian, 40
Hegel, Georg Wilhelm Friedrich, 3
Hess, Moses, 3
Hillquit, Morris, 154, 156, 158–9, 161
Histradrut, 209–10
Hitler, Adolf, 21–23, 122–3
Hoan, Daniel W., 155, 161
Hornsrud, Christian, 41
Hughes, Thomas, 77
Hughes, William M., 204
Hunter, Robert, 156
Hussein, Saddam, 208
Huysmans, Camille, 47
Hyndman, Henry Mayers, 78–87, 92, 119–20, 129. Works: *A Summary of the Principles of Socialism,* 83; *England for All: The Text-book of Democracy,* 81; *The Historical Basis of Socialism in England,* 83

Iceland, 71–72
Iglesias, Pablo, 62
Independent Labor Party, 86–87, 91, 98, 100, 107–21; founding, 109
Independent Socialist Party of Germany, 19
India, 204–7
Indian National Congress, 205–6
Industrial Workers of the World, 144, 155–6
Institutional Revolutionary Party, 173–4
Intercollegiate Socialist Society, 155
International, First, 27, 149–50, 152; Second, 8, 13, 27; Socialist, 8, 189, 213
Iraq, 208

Ireland, 129–30; Northern, 130–131
Irish Labour Party, 130
Irish Republican Army, 129–131
Irish Social Democratic and Labour Party, 131
Israel, 209–13
Israel Labor Party, 209–13
Italian Democratic Socialist Party, 62
Italian Socialist Party 56–62
Italy, 56–62

Jagan, Cheddi, 192
Jamaica, 189–90
Janata Party, 205–6
Japan, 201–2
Japan Socialist Party, 201
Jaurès, Jean Léon, 26–27
Jenkins, Roy, 126
Jewish Daily Forward, 162
Jewish Labor Bund, 213
Jones, Jim, 192
Jørgensen, Anker, 40–41
Jospin, Lionel, 34–35

Kampmann, Viggo, 40
Kangaroos, 154–5
Kautsky, Karl, 154
Keating, Paul, 204
Kenya, 207
Kenyatta, Jomo, 207
Kibbutz, 209
King, William, 75
Kingsley, Charles, 76–77
Kinnock, Neil, 128
Kirk, Norman Eric, 204
Kirkpatrick, George R., 156
Kisan Mazdoor Praja Party, 205
Koerner, Theodor, 55
Ko-operative Forbundet, 38
Krag, Jens Otto, 40
Kreisky, Bruno, 55
Kropotkin, Peter, 5
Kuomintang, 202–3

Labour Emancipation League, 85
Labour Representation Committee, 86, 113, 118, 121
Lagos, Ricardo, 197
Lange, David, 204

Index

Largo Cabellero, Francisco, 63
Larkin, James, 130
Lassalle, Ferdinand, 17–18, 32–33, 105
League for Industrial Democracy, 155
Lee, Algernon, 162
Lenin, Vladimir I., 6, 19
Leoni, Raul, 191
Lib-Labs, 109
Libya, 208
Liebknecht, Karl, 20, 27
Liebknecht, Wilhelm, 17
Lloyd, Woodrow, 145
Lohia, Rammanohar, 205
Ludlow, John M., 76
Luxembourg, 48
Luxemburg, Rosa, 13, 19–20. Work: *Marxism or Leninism,* 19

MacDonald, James Ramsey, 121–2
Madagascar, 207
Majano, Adolfo, 185–6
Malta, 71
Maltese Labor Party, 71
Manley, Michael N., 189–90
Mapai Party, 209–11
Mapam, 213
Marx, Karl, 3, 27, 79–80, 83, 88, 112
Marxism, 3–4
Masses, The, 157
Maurice, Frederick Denison, 76–77
Maxton, James, 121
McLaughlin, Audrey, 147
McLevy, Jasper, 162
McReynolds, David, 165
Meidner Plan, 36–37
Meir, Golda, 211
Mexican Communist Party, 173–4
Mexican Labor Party, 172
Mexican Socialist Party, 174
Mexico, 171–176
Mill, John Stuart, 78, 88
Millerand, Alexandre, 26–27
Mintoff, Dominic, 71
Mitterrand, François, 10, 30–34
Mollet, Guy, 29
Monetarism, 126
Moore, Michael, 204
Morris, William, 83–85, 94
Moshav ovidim, 209

Movement Toward Socialism, 192
Murayama, Tomiichi, 201
Mussolini, Benito, 56–59
Mutualism, 5

Nasser, Gamal Abdel, 208
National Health Service, 123–4
Nationalist Clubs, 150–1
National Labor Union, 152
National Opposition Union, 183–4
National Revolutionary Movement, 182–3, 184
National Revolutionary Party, 172
National Socialist German Workers' Party, 21
Nehru, Jawaharlal, 205
Nenni, Pietro, 59–60
Netherlands, 48–50
New American Movement, 118, 165
New Jewel Movement, 191
New Leader, The, 163
New Left, 5–6, 60
New Socialist Party of Japan, 201
New Unionism, 107–8, 114, 151
New Zealand, 204
New Zealand Labour Party, 204
Nicaragua, 187–9
Nieuwenhuis, Romela, 48
Northern Ireland, 130–1
Norway, 41–43
Norwegian Labor Party, 41–43
Noseworthy, Joseph, 144
Nyerere, Julius K., 207
Nygarrdsvold, Johan, 42

O'Hare, Kate Richards, 158
Ortega Saavedra, Daniel, 188–9
Owen, David, 126
Owen, Robert, 75
Owen, Robert Dale, 148

Pakistan, 207
Pakistan People's Party, 207
Palme, Olaf, 36–38
Palmer, Geoffrey, 204
Panhellenic Socialist Movement, 70
Papandreou, Andreas, 70
Party of Democratic Socialism, 25
Party of the Mexican Revolution, 173

Passio, Raphael, 46
Patriotic Pole, 192
Paz Estenssoro, Victor, 193
Pekkala, Mauno, 46
Pelloutier, Fernand, 5
People's National Party, 189–90
People's Progressive Party, 192
People's Revolutionary Army, 184
People's Revolutionary Bloc, 185
Peres, Shimon, 212–3
Perón, Eva, 197
Perón, Juan, 197–8
Persson, Goeran, 38–39
Peru, 194–5
Podmore, Frank, 88
Popular Front, 28
Popular Liberation Forces, 184
Popular Socialist Party, 174
Popular Socialist Party of Brazil, 193
Popular Unity, 195
Portugal, 65–67
Portuguese Socialist Party, 66–67
Possibilists, 26–27
Praja Socialist Party, 205
Proudhon, Pierre-Joseph, 5

Rabin, Yitzhak, 211–3
Radek, Karl, 19
Rae, Rob, 147
Rafi Party, 211
Rand School of Social Science, 155, 162–3
Realignment Caucus, 163–4
Reed, John, 158
Renner, Karl, 53, 55
Revolutionary Age, 158
Revolutionary Socialist Labor Party, 152
Rocard, Michel, 32–33
Rochdale Society of Pioneers, 75–76
Rowling, Wallace Edward, 204
Russell, Charles Edward, 156
Ruthenberg, Charles E., 158

Sahlin, Mona, 38
Samyukta Socialist Party, 205
Sandinista National Liberation Front, 188–9
Sandino, Augusto César, 187

Sandler, Richard J., 35–36
Sanial, Lucien, 151
San Min Chu I, 202–3
Savage, Michael Joseph, 204
Schachtman, Max ,118, 163
Schenck, Charles T., 157
Schermerhorn, Willem, 49
Scheu, Andreas, 85
Schmidt, Helmut, 24
Schroeder, Gerhard, 25
Scotland, 129
Scottish Labour Party, 109–10
Scottish Land and Labour League, 85
Scottish Socialist Party, 129
Scullin, James H., 204
Second International, 8, 13, 27
Seidel, Emil, 155
Seitz, Karl, 53
Senegal, 207
Senghor, Léopold Sédar, 207
Shaw, George Bernard, 88–90, 95, 110. Work: *The Intelligent Woman's Guide to Socialism and Capitalism*, 95
Shining Path, 194–5
Sideris, A., 67
Sinowatz, Bruno, 55
Siumut Party, 143
Skidmore, Thomas, 148
Slesser, Henry H., 98
Smith, John, 128
Soares, Mario, 66–67
Social Democracy of America, 154
Social Democratic Federation, 78–87, 94, 100, 105, 108–9, 111, 113–4, 118, 120, 129
Social Democratic Federation of America, 162
Social Democratic League of America, 156
Social Democratic Party of America, 155
Social Democratic Party of Brazil, 193
Social Democratic Party of Canada, 144
Social Democratic Party of Finland, 43–46
Social Democratic Party of Germany, 17–25

Social Democratic Party of Great Britain, 87
Social Democratic Party of Iceland, 71–72
Social Democratic Party of Japan, 201
Social Democratic Party of Portugal, 67
Social Democratic Workingmen's Party of North America, 150
Social Democrats, USA, 118, 164
Socialism, Christian, 76–78, 114–5; common elements, 2; difficulties in defining, 1–2; democratic, 7–14; Ethical, 91, 107, 113–7, 120; forms, 2–4; Guild, 5, 100, 105–6; lack of in the United States, 165–170; National, 7, 20–23; New, 107–9, 112–4; utopian, 2–3
Socialist International, 8, 189, 213
Socialist Labor Party of America, 11, 86–7, 143–4, 150
Socialist Labor Party of Greece, 67
Socialist Labor Party of Scotland, 86–7
Socialist League, 108
Socialist Party of Argentina, 197–8
Socialist Party of Canada, 143–4
Socialist Party of Ecuador, 194
Socialist Party, USA, 13, 118, 143
Socialist Trade and Labor Alliance, 151
Socialist Tribune, 165
Socialist Workers' Party of Luxembourg, 48
Social Party of New York and Vicinity, 152
Socio-Political Labor-Union of Cincinnati, 150
Sorge, F. A., 149
South Korea, 202
Spaak, Henri-Paul, 47
Spain, 62–65
Spanish Socialist Workers' Party, 62–65
Spargo, John, 156
Spartacists, 20
Spühler, Willy, 51
Stauning, Thorvald, 39
Steffansson, Stefán Jón, 71
Stokes, J. G. Phelps, 156

Stokes, Rose Pastor, 156
Stratis, D., 67
Students for a Democratic Society, 152, 155, 163
Stuttgart Resolution, 13, 19, 27–28
Sun, Yat-sen, 202–3
Sweden, 35–39
Swedish Social Democratic Labor Party, 35–39
Swiss Social Democratic Party, 50–51
Switzerland, 50–51
Sylvis, William H., 152
Syria, 208

Tanner, Vaino, 44–45
Tanzania, 207
Thatcher, Margaret, 126, 128
Thomas, Norman, 160–3
Torp, Oscar, 42
Tory Gold Scandal, 86, 120
Trade Union Congress, 86, 97, 109, 112–3, 122, 126
Traven, B., 176. Works: *The Rebellion of the Hanged*, 176; *General from the Jungle*, 176
Troelstra, Pieter J., 48–49
Tsiranana, Philibert, 207
Tupac Amaru Revolutionary Movement, 195
Tupamaros, 195
Turati, Philipo, 56
Työmies, 43

Ujamaa, 207
Unified Socialist Party, 29
Unified Socialist Party of Mexico, 174
Union of the Left, 30–31
United People's Action Front, 185
United Socialist Party of Korea, 202
United States of America, 148–170
Universal German Workingmen's Association, 150
Uruguay, 195
Uruguayan Socialist Party, 195
Uyl, Joop den, 50

Van Acker, Achille, 47
Vandervelde, Émile, 46–47

Venezuela, 191–2
Vietnam, 203
Vietnamese Socialist Party, 203
Villa, Francisco "Pancho," 171
Vogt, Hugo, 151
Vranitzky, Franz, 55
Valdés, Miguel Alemán, 173

Wales, 129
Walling, William English, 156
Webb, Beatrice, 91, 96, 100–105
Webb, Sidney, 88–90, 92–93, 96, 99–106; arguments against producers' cooperatives and workers' control, 100–106. Work with Beatrice Webb: *A Constitution for the Socialist Commonwealth of Great Britain,* 96, 100
Wells, H. G., 98, 106–7. Work: *The New Machiavelli,* 107
Welsh Socialist Alliance, 129

Weydemeyer, Joseph, 149
Whitlam, Gough, 204
Wilson, Charlotte, M., 90, 94]
Wilson, Harold, 125, 126
Woodhull, Victoria Claflin, 153
Woodsworth, J. S., 144
Workers' Party of Brazil, 193
Workers' self-management, 12
Workies, 148–9
World Labor Zionist Movement, 213
Wright, Fanny, 148–9

Young People's Socialist League, 155

Zamora Rivas, Ruben, 187
Zapata, Emiliano, 171, 175
Zapatista National Liberation Army, 175
Zeidler, Frank, 118, 155, 163, 165
Zimmerwald Conference, 19–20, 41
Zinoviev Letter, 121–2

ABOUT THE AUTHOR

DONALD F. BUSKY has been Local Chairperson of the Socialist Party of Greater Philadelphia since 1978, and State Chairperson of the Socialist Party of Pennsylvania since 1988, as well as editor of its newsletter, *The Red Penn*. He has been a member of the National Committee of the Socialist Party, USA, and has been a frequent contributor to its publication, *The Socialist*. Dr. Busky has 19 years teaching experience and is currently at Camden County College.